THE REMINISCENCES OF
Vice Admiral John B. Colwell
U.S. Navy (Retired)

INTERVIEWED BY
John T. Mason, Jr.

U.S. Naval Institute • Annapolis, Maryland

Copyright © 1974/2002

Preface—1974

These reminiscences of Vice Admiral John Barr Colwell, U. S. Navy (Retired) were obtained in a series of eight interviews that began in April 1973 and continued through February 1974. The interviews were all conducted by John T. Mason, Jr. for the Oral History program of the U. S. Naval Institute and were held in the apartment of Admiral Colwell in Washington, D. C.

Admiral Colwell read the original transcript from the tapes and made some necessary minor corrections. The entire manuscript was then re-typed, indexed and bound and is available as an OPEN MANUSCRIPT for the benefit of accredited researchers.

Admiral Colwell's career is notable in many respects, but particularly in the Ordnance area. Chapter four is of especial interest in that it deals with the first two years of the POLARIS project. Colwell served in that time as Deputy to Admiral Raborn.

Preface—2002

The oral history transcript of Vice Admiral John Barr Colwell was among the early ones to be published by the Naval Institute. As a result, some of the refinements that have later become standard parts of the format—particularly computer word-processing of the text—were not yet incorporated. This revised transcript has been produced by computer, then annotated with footnotes to provide additional information for the benefit of the reader. The new volume has been indexed in the comprehensive format now standard for Naval Institute oral histories.

In addition to the corrections Admiral Colwell made to the original transcript, I have done some additional minor editing in the interests of clarity and smoothness. Admiral Colwell has recently given his blessing to these new changes and made a few more changes himself. The original version of the transcript is still on file at the Naval Institute.

Paul Stillwell

VICE ADMIRAL JOHN BARR COLWELL,
UNITED STATES NAVY (RETIRED)

An ordnance specialist, Vice Admiral Colwell served as assistant experimental officer at the Naval Proving Ground and had tours of duty in the Bureau of Ordnance (Research and Development), as deputy director of the Fleet Ballistic Missile (Polaris) Project, and as senior naval assistant to the Director, Defense Research and Engineering, Office of the Secretary of Defense. He is a graduate of the Naval Academy, 1931, and the Naval Postgraduate School (ordnance engineering), 1939.

As a junior officer he had duty in the battleships Maryland (BB-46), California (BB-44), and New York (BB-34), and in the destroyers Rathburne (DD-113) and Aaron Ward (DD-132). In September 1939 he joined the battleship Idaho (BB-42). As plotting room officer in that ship he participated in Atlantic patrols in 1941 and was serving in the Iceland area at the outbreak of World War II.

In November 1942 he joined the staff of Admiral William F. Halsey, Jr., Commander South Pacific Force, as assistant gunnery officer and later served as gunnery officer until January 1944. For eight months he commanded the destroyer Converse (DD-509), a unit of Destroyer Squadron 23, Pacific Fleet, known as the "Little Beavers," which won the Presidential Unit Citation. He was awarded the Bronze Star Medal and a letter of commendation, each with Combat V, for outstanding service in that command.

After shore duty at the Naval Proving Ground (1945-47), he became executive officer of the battleship Missouri (BB-63), and later (1948-51) served as fleet readiness officer on the staff of the Commander in Chief Pacific Fleet. After a tour of duty in the Bureau of Ordnance, Navy Department, he was designated aide and administrative assistant to the Deputy Secretary of Defense, Washington, D.C.

From May 1954 to October 1955 he commanded the fleet oiler Elokomin (AO-55), then served as Deputy Director of the Fleet Ballistic Missile Project, charged with development of the Polaris missile and weapon system, for which service he was awarded the Legion of Merit. In February 1958 he reported to the Philadelphia Naval Shipyard, where the Galveston (CLG-3) was in the process of conversion. He assumed command of that guided missile cruiser, first of her kind, at the commissioning ceremony on 28 May 1958. His selection to the rank of rear admiral was approved by the President on 18 July 1958, and in November of that year he reported as a member of the General Planning Group, Office of the Chief of Naval Operations, Navy Department.

In April 1959 he was assigned to the Office of the Secretary of Defense as senior naval assistant to the Director, Defense Research and Engineering. When detached in November 1960, he again joined the General Planning Group, Office of the Chief of Naval Operations. From October 1961 until September 1962 he commanded Amphibious Group Four, after which he served as Director of the Long Range Objectives Group, Office of the Chief of Naval Operations, Navy Department. On 17 January 1964 he assumed command of the Amphibious Force Pacific Fleet. In June 1965 he reported as Deputy Chief of Naval Operations (Fleet Operations and Readiness), Navy Department. On 1 August 1969 he was transferred to the retired list of the U.S. Navy.

Personal Data:

Born: Pawnee City, Nebraska, 26 November 1909
Parents: Clyde G. and Mary B. (Potts) Colwell
Wife: Grace M. Arent of Valley Stream, New York
Children: John B. Colwell, Jr.; Peter S. Colwell; James C. Colwell; Margaret D. Colwell
Education: Pawnee City High School, 1926; U.S. Naval Academy, B.S. in 1931; U.S. Naval Postgraduate School, 1939; U.S. Army Chemical Warfare School, Edgewood, Maryland, 1937

Dates of Rank:

Ensign: 4 June 1931
Lieutenant (junior grade): 4 June 1934
Lieutenant: June 1937
Lieutenant Commander: June 1942
Commander: November 1942
Captain: 1 July 1949
Rear Admiral: 1 August 1958
Vice Admiral: 18 January 1964

Decorations and Medals:

Distinguished Service Medal
Legion of Merit
Gold star in lieu of second Legion of Merit
Bronze Star Medal with combat V
Letter of commendation, ribbon, and combat V
Presidential Unit Citation (Destroyer Squadron 23)
Brazilian Order of Naval Merit
American Defense Service Medal with bronze A
American Campaign Medal
Asiatic-Pacific Campaign Medal, one silver star, two bronze stars (seven operations)
World War II Victory Medal
Navy Occupation Service Medal, Europe Clasp
National Defense Service Medal with bronze star
Vietnam Service Medal

Chronological Record of Naval Service:

July 1931-May 1933	USS Maryland (BB-46), deck and engineering junior officer
June 1933-July 1934	USS California (BB-44), staff communications, Commander Battle Force
July 1934-December 1934	USS Rathburne (DD-113), assistant gunnery, etc.
December 1934-February 1937	USS Aaron Ward (DD-132), gunnery and first lieutenant
February 1937-April 1937	USS New York (BB-34), deck division and watch officer
May 1937-June 1937	U.S. Army Chemical Center, Edgewood, Maryland, under instruction
July 1937-June 1939	U.S. Naval Postgraduate School, Annapolis, Maryland, under instruction
September 1939-September 1942	USS Idaho (BB-42), plotting room officer
November 1942-January 1944	Staff, Commander South Pacific Force, assistant gunnery officer and gunnery officer
January 1944-September 1944	USS Converse (DD-509), commanding officer
October 1944-April 1947	U.S. Naval Proving Ground, Dahlgren, Virginia, assistant experimental officer
May 1947-October 1948	USS Missouri (BB-63), executive officer
December 1948-June 1951	Staff, Commander in Chief Pacific Fleet, fleet readiness officer
July 1951-April 1953	Bureau of Ordnance, program director for the surface gun systems, research and development division
April 1953-May 1954	Aide and administrative assistant to the Deputy Secretary of Defense
May 1954-October 1955	USS Elokomin (AO-55), commanding officer

November 1955-December 1955	OpNav, head, Air Defense Branch, Operations Division
December 1955-January 1958	Bureau of Ordnance, Deputy Director, Fleet Ballistic Missile Project
February 1958-May 1958	USS Galveston (CLG-3), prospective commanding Officer
May 1958-November 1958	USS Galveston (CLG-3), commanding officer
November 1958-April 1959	OpNav, member, General Planning Group
April 1959-November 1960	Senior naval assistant to the Director, Defense Research and Engineering, Office of the Secretary of Defense
November 1960-October 1961	OpNav, member, General Planning Group
October 1961-September 1962	Commander Amphibious Group Four
September 1962-December 1963	OpNav, Director, Long Range Objectives Group
January 1964-June 1965	Commander Amphibious Force Pacific Fleet
June 1965-July 1969	OpNav, Deputy Chief of Naval Operations (Fleet Operations and Readiness)
1 August 1969	Transferred to the retired list of the U.S. Navy

DECLARATION OF TRUST

The undersigned does hereby appoint and designate as his (her) Trustee herein, the Secretary-Treasurer and Publisher of the United States Naval Institute to perform and discharge the following duties, powers, and privileges in connection with the possession and use of a certain taped interview between the undersigned and the Oral History Department of the United States Naval Institute.

1. Classification of Transcript.

    (X) a. If classified OPEN, the transcript(s) may be read or the recording(s) audited by the qualified personnel upon presentation of proper credentials, as determined by the Secretary-Treasurer of the U. S. Naval Institute.

    ( ) b. If classified PERMISSION REQUIRED TO CITE OR QUOTE, the user will be required to obtain permission in writing from the interviewee prior to quoting or citing from either the transcript(s) or the recording(s).

    ( ) c. If classified PERMISSION REQUIRED, permission must be obtained in writing from the interviewee before the transcribed interview(s) can be examined or the tape recording(s) audited.

    ( ) d. If classified CLOSED, the transcribed interview(s) and the tape recording(s) will be sealed until a time specified by the interviewee. This may be until the death of the interviewee or for any specified number of years.

2. It is expressly understood that in giving this authorization, I am in no way precluded from placing such restrictions as I may desire upon use of the interview at any time during my lifetime, nor does this authorization in any way affect my rights to the copyright of my literary expressions that may be contained in the interview.

Witness my hand and seal this 15th day of May 1974.

John B. Colwell

I hereby accept and consent to the foregoing Declaration of Trust and the powers therein conferred upon me as Trustee:

Interview Number 1 with Vice Admiral John Barr Colwell, U.S. Navy (Retired)

Place: Admiral Colwell's apartment in Washington, D.C.

Date: Thursday, 26 April 1973

Interviewer: John T. Mason, Jr.

John T. Mason, Jr.: Admiral, it's a delight to meet you. You've had a very significant naval career, and I've been looking forward to the opportunity of recording your recollections of it.

Would you begin in the proper way with a biography, by giving me the date and place of your birth and something about your family background and your very early education?

Admiral Colwell: I was born in a small town in southeast Nebraska, Pawnee City, on the 26th of November 1909. My father was a pharmacist. I grew up in a small-town environment, went to the local schools, and graduated from the Pawnee City High School.

John T. Mason, Jr.: You told me off tape that in the high school you got a fairly good acquaintance with mathematics and that sort of thing.

Admiral Colwell: The mathematics that we got in high school in those days, of course, would be considered fairly elementary today, but it was a good basis.

John T. Mason, Jr.: Did you have physics and chemistry?

Admiral Colwell: Physics, chemistry, algebra, geometry, Latin, Spanish, English, history—a fairly standard course.

John T. Mason, Jr.: You might repeat the fact that you came out number one.

Admiral Colwell: I was the valedictorian, but it was a rather small school. I think there were 30-odd in the graduating class.

John T. Mason, Jr.: Are you an only child?

Admiral Colwell: No. I have one brother and one sister, both still living and both still living in Nebraska. My brother is a state district judge.

I finished high school in 1926 and a year later went to the Naval Academy, having spent several months at a cram school in Columbia, Missouri.*

John T. Mason, Jr.: Tell me why the ambition to go to the Naval Academy.

Admiral Colwell: It's really rather difficult to recall.

John T. Mason, Jr.: Any naval tradition in the family?

Admiral Colwell: No, none, nor military tradition. I think primarily it was a desire for a good education, and, quite frankly, there was considerable appeal in a good education at minimum expense.

John T. Mason, Jr.: Understandable! Did your parents approve of this ambition?

Admiral Colwell: Oh, yes. They were quite pleased. As near as I can recall, when I entered the Naval Academy I didn't have any real ambition to make a career of the Navy, but sometime during the first year at the Naval Academy, and I don't know when this was, I came to like that life very much, and from then on I never questioned but what I was going to be a naval officer.

---

* "Cram school" was the term used for a preparatory school that covered the type of material that prospective cadets and midshipmen were likely to encounter on service school entrance examinations.

John T. Mason, Jr.: Who gave you your appointment to the Academy? How did you achieve that?

Admiral Colwell: I should be able to recall the gentleman's name. He's long since dead.

John T. Mason, Jr.: A congressman?

Admiral Colwell: He was a congressman, representative of our district in Nebraska. He was kind enough to give me a principal appointment.*

John T. Mason, Jr.: Did you get the principal appointment from him?

Admiral Colwell: Yes, I did have the principal appointment. I actually don't know just how that came about, but it did, and I was very pleased to have it.

John T. Mason, Jr.: Was it Bob Simmons, by any chance?

Admiral Colwell: No, it was not. I can't recall. He's been dead many years.

My whole period at the Naval Academy was an enjoyable experience, even plebe year!†

John T. Mason, Jr.: Well that's saying something. You liked the controlled life?

Admiral Colwell: I like discipline. I suppose that is entirely correct, yes. I probably have always liked a disciplined existence. Except for really very minor discomforts during

---

* Each congressman was able to make both principal appointments and alternates for a particular opening at the Naval Academy. Someone with an alternate appointment would get in only if the person with the principal appointment was found to be unqualified or if he decided not to accept the appointment.
† A midshipman in his or her first year is called a plebe; second year, youngster or third classman; third year, second classman; fourth year, first classman.

plebe year, I enjoyed the Naval Academy. One of my greatest problems all the time I was there was in the matter of athletics, because I am rather a non-athletic person, and there were certain physical requirements, such as in track, swimming, gymnasium, and so on, that everyone had to comply with. Some of these were quite difficult for me. However, I finally made it.

John T. Mason, Jr.: Which sport did you concentrate on?

Admiral Colwell: I tried two or three different sports, track, cross country. I even tried boxing, plebe summer, and quickly gave that up. I finally decided that active participation in sports was not really my long suit, and I became the manager of the fencing team. So, eventually, I did get my varsity letter as an athlete.

John T. Mason, Jr.: That's one way of accomplishing it! What were your favorite studies?

Admiral Colwell: I suppose mathematics, physics, and chemistry. I think they were my favorites. I studied Spanish while I was there. That was never difficult, although I never got awfully good at it. I somewhat blame that on the way the courses were given in those days. They taught languages in the classic form, rather than conversational languages, which would have been far more useful to us.

All in all, I had no difficulty.

John T. Mason, Jr.: You didn't have any problems scholastically, then, the transition from a Middle Western high school to the academy curriculum?

Admiral Colwell: None whatsoever. I made a 3.4 average to become termed a star man. I starred all four years, and graduated, I think, number six in the class.[*]

---

[*] Midshipman Colwell's standing was number six among the 441 graduates in the class of 1931.

John T. Mason, Jr.: Tell me about your summer cruises and what they contributed to your education.

Admiral Colwell: We made two summer cruises. The middle year, for the first time when my class was there, was not a cruise but was what was called aviation summer. The youngster cruise was along the East Coast in very old battleships. We went through the regular routine of being a part of the deck force and part of the engineering force, and so on. It was not an exciting cruise. We spent our time cruising up and down the East Coast at very slow speeds. We did go to Guantanamo for target practice.[*] That was always the climax of these cruises.

Aviation summer we spent in Annapolis, with some small amount of flight time in very ancient aircraft, World War I vintage. But that was exciting.

John T. Mason, Jr.: Were you intrigued with the idea of aviation?

Admiral Colwell: I enjoyed it, yes, and I suppose that's when all of us first began thinking seriously of whether we wanted to be aviators or not.

Our first class cruise was a very good one and very, very interesting. We went to Europe and had stops in Cherbourg, with leave to visit Paris, and Kiel, with leave to visit Berlin. This was in the very early days of the Hitler Youth Movement, I suppose.[†] I remember a torchlight parade in Kiel while we were there. This would have been in 1930. Those were fascinating trips, fascinating cities. We also went to Edinburgh with leave to go to London. So it was a marvelous cruise.

John T. Mason, Jr.: That was more in the tradition of the old cruises?

Admiral Colwell: Yes, and this was the kind of thing that persuaded young men that they wanted to be in the Navy.

---

[*] Guantanamo Bay, on the south coast of Cuba, near the eastern end of the island, for many years provided a fleet anchorage and training area for U.S. Navy ships.
[†] Adolf Hitler later served as Chancellor of Germany from 1933 until his death on 30 April 1945.

John T. Mason, Jr.: But you'd been persuaded before that?

Admiral Colwell: I had already made up my mind, yes. It was a very enjoyable summer.

John T. Mason, Jr.: You found them, on the whole, useful to you anyway, in that they taught you some practical aspects of what you were learning in class?

Admiral Colwell: Yes, and these were introductions to duties that one might have as a new ensign on graduation. You still had periods in the engineering force, and you stood deck watches, as a junior officer of the deck somewhat removed, actual navigation practice, and so forth. It was, I think, a good practical cruise.

John T. Mason, Jr.: In retrospect, you felt that you were truly qualified then when you were commissioned as an ensign to serve as one?

Admiral Colwell: I think we all felt that we were, and I'm quite sure that we were not! But I think all of us had a very fair share of confidence in our ability to do these jobs, in spite of finding things very, very new and very different, but we did have a basis for getting started.

    The cruises did one other thing, which I think was very important. They introduced us to the experienced petty officers in the Navy who knew how to do things, and most of them were quite patient with us and showed us how to do things. This came to be a very valuable experience. The chief, the first class petty officer, could teach a young officer a great deal.

John T. Mason, Jr.: Did you do any literary work when you were there?

Admiral Colwell: No, I didn't participate in the Trident Magazine, for example. I did work in a very minor capacity on the yearbook, Lucky Bag, as a sort of a sales representative in my company. Very minor capacity. I was really just helping out the business manager, who was a good friend of mine.

That about brings us up to graduation day, I guess.*

John T. Mason, Jr.: Which was a pretty important day and it was right at the height of the Depression?†

Admiral Colwell: Yes, it was. 1931. We were fortunate to have jobs. A lot of people didn't.

John T. Mason, Jr.: Were all the boys commissioned who wanted commissions?

Admiral Colwell: Yes. The partial-class commissioning didn't go on until later. All of our class who were physically qualified were commissioned either as Navy ensigns or Marine second lieutenants. There were a few who failed of commission for physical defects, eyes primarily. There were a couple who had found that they suffered from chronic seasickness and were not commissioned. If I remember the numbers correctly, I think we graduated about 410, which was about two-thirds of the starting group, and I believe that there were commissioned about 385, something like that—so almost everybody.

John T. Mason, Jr.: That's normal attrition, too, isn't it?

Admiral Colwell: I don't know what the figures are today, but I would guess that it's probably about normal. I'm almost certain that we had fewer voluntary resignations during the course than they have now, and this may be a matter of economics. I think part of it probably is also due to the general change in the way of life. Now people take less kindly to a disciplined existence than we did.

---

* The members of the class graduated and received their commissions on 4 June 1931.
† Following the crash of the New York Stock Exchange in late October 1929, the United States plunged into the Great Depression, from which it did not recover until the nation geared up for World War II at the beginning of the 1940s. The Depression was marked by high unemployment and many business failures.

John T. Mason, Jr.: Principally, don't you think, because they haven't had much of it from the beginning?

Admiral Colwell: That could well be. Schools, of course, were entirely different. When I went to school, permissiveness was something, a term, no one ever heard of. You did exactly what you were told—or else. I don't intend to be philosophical about that. I don't know whether it's good or bad.

John T. Mason, Jr.: But at least it does have some bearing on attrition.

Admiral Colwell: I think it does, yes.

John T. Mason, Jr.: Did you state a preference for your first assignment? Or were you given that opportunity?

Admiral Colwell: Yes, we were all allowed to state preferences. I've forgotten whether it was three or five. And people who were qualified and requested it were first sent to what they called—oh, what was the term?—it was qualification for training in piloting aircraft.

John T. Mason, Jr.: Sent to Norfolk?

Admiral Colwell: Some went to Norfolk and some went to San Diego. I had applied—

John T. Mason, Jr.: You'd gone that far in deciding what you wanted to do!

Admiral Colwell: Yes, along with a very large number of people in the class, I applied for flight training. "Preliminary flight training" was the term. I was turned down because I didn't weigh enough. You had to weigh 128 pounds, and I think I graduated at 119. I was just a little guy.

I did go to preliminary flight training about a year later, having gained enough weight so that I could qualify. I took preliminary flight training in San Diego. I never went on to Pensacola because—well, I might as well cover that now.

John T. Mason, Jr.: Yes, why not?

Admiral Colwell: There was a period of about a year after I finished preliminary flight training satisfactorily when there were no budding aviators sent to Pensacola for training. This was a matter of lack of money. In the meantime, I was in an old destroyer, one of the old four-stackers, and by the end of that year the sight in one eye had failed so that I could no longer pass the flight physical. When it opened up again, I took a flight physical, did not pass it, and that was the end of my very modest flying career.

John T. Mason, Jr.: What about your reaction to that?

Admiral Colwell: I was not greatly distressed. In fact, I don't remember that I was distressed at all. I liked what I was doing. Destroyer duty in those days, long before World War II, was very good duty for junior officers.

John T. Mason, Jr.: Pretty ideal duty, wasn't it?

Admiral Colwell: It was about as good as you could get.

John T. Mason, Jr.: Did you start out on destroyers when you graduated?

Admiral Colwell: No. I first went to the Maryland and, as I recall, I was able to get my first choice.[*] I think that's what I asked for. A number of people I knew well went there.

---

[*] The battleship Maryland (BB-46) was commissioned 21 July 1921. She had a standard displacement of 32,600 tons, was 624 feet long and 98 feet in the beam. Her top speed was 21.2 knots. She was armed with eight 16-inch guns and 12 5-inch broadside guns. She remained in active service until decommissioned on 3 April 1947, following World War II.

J.B. Colwell, Interview #1 (4/26/73) – Page 10

There were, I think, a little over 20 of us in the class who went to the Maryland. They had lots of junior officers in those days.

I stayed there for about two years, in gunnery part of the time and engineering part of the time.

John T. Mason, Jr.: Were you fortunate in having a good group of officers?

Admiral Colwell: Yes.

John T. Mason, Jr.: Who was the skipper?

Admiral Colwell: The skipper when I first went there was a Captain Morris.[*] I didn't see him very much, except when I was standing bridge watches. Ensigns stood pretty much in awe of captains in those days.

After about two years in the Maryland I went to the California.[†] As a communications watch officer for Commander Battle Force, who was a very highly regarded gentleman named Reeves.[‡]

John T. Mason, Jr.: Joseph Mason Reeves!

Admiral Colwell: Yes, and a superb gentleman he was. That was a normal one-year tour, which I did, and went from there to my first four-stack destroyer, having just made jaygee in three years.[§]

John T. Mason, Jr.: Did you have any interesting experiences under the tutelage of Reeves?

---

[*] Captain Robert Morris, USN, commanded the battleship Maryland (BB-46) from 3 February 1931 to 21 December 1932.
[†] The battleship California (BB-44) was commissioned 10 August 1921. She had a standard displacement of 32,000 tons, was 624 feet long and 97 feet in the beam. Her top speed was 21 knots. She was armed with 12 14-inch guns, 14 5-inch guns, and two 21-inch torpedo tubes.
[‡] Admiral Joseph M. Reeves, USN, served as Commander Battle Force in 1933-34, then as Commander in Chief U.S. Fleet, 1934-36.
[§] Jaygee—lieutenant (junior grade).

Admiral Colwell: No.

John T. Mason, Jr.: He was interested particularly in aviation, wasn't he?

Admiral Colwell: Oh, yes. He was an aviator himself. Incidentally, I'm sure you know he is the man, who in the first year wore a football helmet, when he was at the Naval Academy.[*]

John T. Mason, Jr.: I didn't know that.

Admiral Colwell: I believe this is a fact.

No, I didn't have any unusual experiences when I was on his staff. We had a very happy little group of communicators who all worked together, and the senior one of us was Admiral Horacio Rivero, who has been one of my close friends almost since the day we entered the Naval Academy together.[†]

At any rate, I then went to a four-stack destroyer. I was in that one and another one.

John T. Mason, Jr.: One of them was the Aaron Ward, wasn't it?

Admiral Colwell: That was the second one. The first one was the Rathburne.[‡] Both of them were very good ships, and I enjoyed my—

John T. Mason, Jr.: What duty did you have on the Rathburne?

---

[*] Reeves graduated from the Naval Academy in the class of 1894.
[†] Midshipman Horacio Rivero, Jr., USN, stood third in the class of 1931. He eventually retired as a four-star admiral. His oral history is in the Naval Institute collection.
[‡] USS Rathburne (DD-113), a Wickes-class destroyer, was commissioned 24 June 1918. Displacement was 1,060 tons, length 314 feet, beam of 31 feet, and draft of 12 feet. Top speed was 35 knots. She was armed with four 4-inch guns, two 3-inch guns, and 12 21-inch torpedo tubes. The Rathburne, which operated in both World Wars, was finally decommissioned on 2 November 1945.

Admiral Colwell: I was sort of "George." I was everybody's assistant.*

John T. Mason, Jr.: There weren't many officers on board, were there?

Admiral Colwell: No. I think there were six or seven. In Aaron Ward, at one time, through detachments and people off at mandatory schools and so forth, we wound up one summer ready to make the summer cruise to Puget Sound with only three officers, the captain, the exec, and me. The exec, who, of course, was the navigator, took the morning watch and the evening watch, the captain took the midwatch, and I had all the rest of them. But it worked out all right, and we had a pretty good summer.

John T. Mason, Jr.: You get to know more about the Navy, don't you, faster on a destroyer than anywhere else?

Admiral Colwell: That's right. Right from the very beginning I was thrown into the gunnery game, which always fascinated me, and I enjoyed it thoroughly. I was in the plotting room of the Maryland as range-keeper operator. I became the gunnery officer in the Aaron Ward, and it was from there that I applied for ordnance postgraduate training.

John T. Mason, Jr.: Obviously you had an aptitude for ordnance from the beginning, then?

Admiral Colwell: I don't know whether it's aptitude or interest. Perhaps interest is better. I was always fascinated with gunnery. Later on, as I got introduced to it through education with the ordnance side.

John T. Mason, Jr.: What was the initial fascination with gunnery? The challenge?

Admiral Colwell: The challenge of hitting the target. Well there's an initial fascination in running a range-keeper. Of course, it was an early computer used in attempting to

---

* "George" is the traditional nickname given to the most junior ensign serving in a ship.

solve the problem of target course and speed with very meager and inaccurate information, since we had no radar.

John T. Mason, Jr.: You did have planes on the battleships, though, didn't you?

Admiral Colwell: Yes.

John T. Mason, Jr.: For spotting?

Admiral Colwell: That's right. Sometimes that got to be a challenge, too, getting the spot back and getting it decoded properly.

After I had gone to postgraduate school, where most of the ordnance work was pretty theoretical, I think this was when my interest in it became more oriented towards ordnance, rather than gunnery, although I've always been fascinated with actual gunnery at sea. I became greatly interested in the ordnance side. How do these weapons work and when do they work, what are the design features that must be built?

John T. Mason, Jr.: That was the broader aspect.

Admiral Colwell: The broader aspect. Safety features, particularly.

At the end of two years at postgraduate school, the ordnance people all went on what was called the "Cook's tour" for a year, where you went to various ordnance stations.* Fortunately for me I spent the summer at the Naval Proving Ground at Dahlgren, Virginia, where my fascination was really triggered, because at the end of that summer the emergency started, and we never finished the Cook's tour. We went back to sea.

---

* A Cook's tour is one in which the tourists visit a variety of sites in cursory fashion. The name comes from a British travel agency, Thomas Cook & Son.

John T. Mason, Jr.: Well, we'll go back to the PG school and hopefully talk about it in greater detail, but let's go back to the destroyers now. You were with the Aaron Ward as the second one, and your tour of duty there was for two years.*

Admiral Colwell: Yes, about that. It was while I was there that I applied for PG school and got it.

    I guess while I was in the Aaron Ward, through one device or another, I had all the jobs there were except captain and engineer officer. I was even acting exec one time, and I loved it.

John T. Mason, Jr.: And that was on the West Coast?

Admiral Colwell: That was on the West Coast, based in San Diego.

John T. Mason, Jr.: Were there any fleet exercises or war games that were of any significance?

Admiral Colwell: From where I sat, one was pretty much like another. I'm sure that the people who were in command had a lot of differences, which they inserted or which fell upon them. But, from my position, one war game or one cruise was pretty much like another. We made pretty good cruises in those days. The summer cruise north to Puget Sound and San Francisco was always a busy time at sea and a very busy time in port and very good fun.

    I got to Panama several times. We did go out to Hawaii on one cruise. This was during the unfortunate period of the Massie thing.†

---

* USS Aaron Ward (DD-132), a Wickes-class destroyer, was commissioned 21 April 1919. Displacement was 1,090 tons, length 314 feet, beam of 30 feet, and draft of 9 feet. Top speed was 35 knots. She was armed with four 4-inch guns, one 3-inch gun, and 12 21-inch torpedo tubes. On 9 September 1940 she was transferred to the Royal Navy and renamed HMS Castleton.
† In September 1931, Thalia Massie, the wife of Lieutenant (junior grade) Thomas H. Massie, USN, a submariner stationed at Pearl Harbor, reported that she was assaulted and raped by five men—Hawaiians, Chinese, and Japanese. Five men were later apprehended and arrested, and Mrs. Massie identified all but one as her assailants. Their trial resulted in a mistrial. Lieutenant Massie, his mother-in-law, and others were then involved in the subsequent killing of one of the assailants. A jury found them guilty of manslaughter, but they were allowed to leave Hawaii rather than being imprisoned.

John T. Mason, Jr.: Thalia Massie!

Admiral Colwell: Yes. We used Lahaina Roads in Maui as our anchorage and never got near Honolulu. However, we made do with some cow pasture golf and visits to the local town.

John T. Mason, Jr.: But the bright lights were barred to you!

Admiral Colwell: They were, indeed.

John T. Mason, Jr.: What was Hawaii and what was Pearl Harbor like in that time?

Admiral Colwell: Well, let's see. When was the first time I ever saw Pearl Harbor? I don't think I ever got to Pearl Harbor until shortly before World War II.

John T. Mason, Jr.: So that says something about it; it wasn't much of a naval base, was it?

Admiral Colwell: It was getting to be. I don't know just when we started moving ships out there. I can't remember how the years went. Probably about 1937. So this would pretty much account for it. I went to postgraduate school in 1937 and left in 1939. This, I guess, would account for my not having been to Pearl Harbor before.

John T. Mason, Jr.: What effect did the Depression have upon the Navy, as you were able to observe it?

Admiral Colwell; It was quite severe in restricting the numbers of ships that were in commission, particularly in restricting the manning of those ships to quite austere numbers. For example, a four-stack destroyer probably had a crew of about 85, when 115 would have been a good number. Other ships were similarly shorthanded.

When I left PG School in 1939, I went to the Idaho. She was quite shorthanded when I got there, but we immediately began receiving substantial numbers of recruits—they were all recruits—because the emergency had begun with events in Europe. So we started building up then. New ships coming in were very few, but fortunately the building program had begun, so that by the time we began to need them they were there.

John T. Mason, Jr.: What about the caliber of the men who were recruited in the Depression years?

Admiral Colwell: They were high quality because jobs were just few and far between. Even though a seaman recruit or a seaman, second class, didn't make very much, a little bit was an awful lot better than nothing, and you remember, as all of us do, people were graduating from college and not getting jobs. I remember my brother graduated with a law degree in about 1936, I guess, and some of the people in his class felt they were lucky if they could get jobs pumping gas with a law degree. This was the kind of situation. The services were able to pick and choose. It was a very bad economic period.

John T. Mason, Jr.: What about the feeling within the fleet on the individual units like the Aaron Ward, the thought of an approaching conflict with Japan?

Admiral Colwell: Very few people believed that it was ever going to happen. It just seemed so preposterous that the Japanese would attempt to try to move across the Pacific, and they viewed our going the other way as a tremendous logistic task. I don't think very many people really believed it was going to happen.

Along in 1939 and 1940 I assume that there were lots of senior officers who saw it coming. Among the younger bracket, which I belonged to, we were more concerned with day-to-day living, our jobs, and our families.

John T. Mason, Jr.: Incidentally, your family, when did you marry?

Admiral Colwell: In 1939.

John T. Mason, Jr.: Oh, so you didn't have the problem of reduced salary and all that to contend with that some of the boys did?

Admiral Colwell: Not as much. I did for a year lose 15% of my ensign's pay.

John T. Mason, Jr.: That was expendable only on you!

Admiral Colwell: Yes that's right. It didn't make an awful lot of difference. Then, for a very short period after I made jaygee, I didn't get promotion pay. I think that was for only one month, from June until the first of July.

John T. Mason, Jr.: You got the rank but not the pay?

Admiral Colwell: That's right. The people who were a year ahead of me had a whole year of that. They got promoted, but they didn't get paid for it. Many, many years later they finally succeeded in getting that restored. Many, many years later.

John T. Mason, Jr.: I hadn't realized that that was done. This was after World War II?

Admiral Colwell: Yes. I got a few dollars back.

John T. Mason, Jr.: With interest, I trust!

Admiral Colwell: No, no interest. And at the higher rate of income tax, too, not the old rate!

John T. Mason, Jr.: Well, when you left the Aaron Ward you went to PG School?

Admiral Colwell: Yes.

John T. Mason, Jr.: Do tell me about that, concentrate on that. Where did you go? First to Annapolis?

Admiral Colwell: The PG school at that time was in Annapolis, in buildings over near the baseball field. I think they're now part of the supply department. The PG school was not moved to Monterey until some years after I left it.* At that time no advanced degrees were given, except to a very small number of people who had their second and third years in civilian institutions such as MIT and Carnegie Tech, and the University of Michigan in a course in explosives.†

John T. Mason, Jr.: Penn State?

Admiral Colwell: Might have been, I don't recall. Somebody gave a course in fuzes. I don't remember who that was. But those were the only people who got advanced degrees. They would normally finish with a master's degree. The rest of us who spent all of our postgraduate time in Annapolis did not get an advanced degree. I've never found this any handicap.

John T. Mason, Jr.: I wouldn't think so.

Admiral Colwell: If I had wished to get out of the Navy and teach school, for example, I'm sure it would have been a great help, but I didn't propose to do that.

I think we got good instruction in the postgraduate school. A number of the professors were certainly very good. I don't know whether you ever knew Dr. Bramble or not, but I had him for almost all of my mathematics courses.‡ He was not only a splendid gentleman but a very fine teacher. We had almost entirely engineering courses of one kind and another. I had Dr. Wheeler for most of my courses in electricity. We got

---

* Originally established at Annapolis, Maryland, on 9 June 1909, the Naval Postgraduate School was later moved to the grounds of the former Hotel Del Monte in Monterey, California, in June 1951.
† MIT—Massachusetts Institute of Technology.
‡ Dr. Charles C. Bramble had been with the Naval Postgraduate School since 1919, eventually becoming senior professor of mathematics and mechanics. In 1942 he began spending part of his time at the Naval Proving Ground, Dahlgren, Virginia, as head of the exterior ballistics section.

practically nothing in electronics in those days. It was a little too early for that, and, of course, nothing in computers.

John T. Mason, Jr.: Just a couple of years too early, weren't you?

Admiral Colwell: Just a bit, yes. Radar came along very soon after that. There were several courses in steam engineering, electrical engineering, and hydraulic engineering, some communications, a little bit in tactics. By and large, it was an engineering education, and I think the things that were offered were for those days quite adequate. Whether my application was entirely adequate is another question! We worked hard and we had a good time.

John T. Mason, Jr.: How large a class took this?

Admiral Colwell: Fourteen, I think.

John T. Mason, Jr.: Most of them were married at that time, were they not?

Admiral Colwell: Yes. I remember one other bachelor in our group. There were several bachelors in the postgraduate school, but not in the ordnance course, which was a very small course. We had a good time on weekends.

John T. Mason, Jr.: But pretty intensive work, wasn't it?

Admiral Colwell: It was pretty solid. We went to school a good part of all of every day and we had plenty to do in the evenings to prepare for the next day.

John T. Mason, Jr.: What did you focus on as a project?

Admiral Colwell: We didn't have projects in those days at postgraduate school. We just banged the books and everybody had the same course—that is, everybody in one group had the same course. We didn't have projects.

John T. Mason, Jr.: No special paper that you had to prepare?

Admiral Colwell: No, and there was no final paper. In fact, I don't think we had any final exams. It was this sort of thing that was different from any civilian course where you would expect to get your advanced degree. There were no papers. At least, not that kind of a paper. There were short papers prepared from time to time, but everybody did them. It was a different type of instruction from what you would expect today.

John T. Mason, Jr.: Did you work right through the summer months?

Admiral Colwell: As I recall, we had a short Christmas leave, a short spring leave, and six weeks in the summer, which was ours to do with as we wished. There wasn't anything that was really very unusual about going to the PG school.

John T. Mason, Jr.: But it was something that came along after you had more determined your course within the Navy?

Admiral Colwell: Yes, if you were fortunate enough to be ordered to the course that you had requested.

John T. Mason, Jr.: This depended upon class standing and various other things, did it not?

Admiral Colwell: I never found out exactly what they used as criteria to choose the lucky people. I'm sure that class standing had something to do with it, because the ordnance course was then considered to be one of the more difficult ones, and they wanted people who showed some historical promise of being able to handle the course.

I remember there was one man in our group who was chosen as a sort of a guinea pig, because he had been down sort of in the middle of his class, rather than at the top. And, of course, it turned out he handled it fine without any problem. But they did tend to choose people from around the top of the class for the ordnance course.

John T. Mason, Jr.: Making no allowance for the late bloomer, so to speak?

Admiral Colwell: None whatsoever, no, except this one guinea pig. I don't think a great deal of attention was paid to whether you spent your formative years in the gunnery business or not. Perhaps this had something to do with it. I had had that. I got some very nice endorsements on my request for postgraduate training. I don't know what they used.

John T. Mason, Jr.: Then came the so-called Cook's tour?

Admiral Colwell: Yes. I only got three months of that, as I said, but happily I got it in Dahlgren because proving ground work I just took to like a duck to water.* I reveled in it. Fortunately, quite a bit later on, during World War II I had a two-and-a-half-year proving ground tour, which I enjoyed thoroughly.

John T. Mason, Jr.: What was going on at Dahlgren when you were there those few months?

Admiral Colwell: It was very largely proof work at that time—proof of guns and gun mounts, armor-piercing projectiles, fuzes—the real ordnance hardware that made up the equipment for gunnery at sea was all proofed at Dahlgren.

John T. Mason, Jr.: New aspects were being, in effect, tested?

---

* Dahlgren, Virginia, on the Potomac River, was the site of the Naval Proving Ground for the testing of guns and other ordnance materials. It was named for John Dahlgren, a 19th century U.S. Navy gunnery pioneer.

Admiral Colwell: Yes. Certainly all the new stuff had to go through there and be wrung out. At that time when I went there the Cook's tour—that was in 1939—there was a very modest amount of experimental work going on. You couldn't call it research, because it wasn't that, but there was a modest amount of experimental work in thin armor plate, for example.

John T. Mason, Jr.: Was the Norden bombsight being investigated?[*]

Admiral Colwell: We were running tests of Norden sights during that period, and one of the jobs that I drew as a postgraduate student on tour was assisting in the calibration of bombs dropped by Norden sights, dropped on targets in the Potomac River.

John T. Mason, Jr.: Was my friend Ballentine there then?[†]

Admiral Colwell: Not at that time, no. Captain Hedrick was the commanding officer.[‡] I get the times mixed up between that time and when I went back at the end of the war. Some of them were the same people whom I'd known before. McClaren was there. Butch Parker was there.[§]

John T. Mason, Jr.: Among your own contemporaries, was Rivero there?

Admiral Colwell: No, he went to PG school a year after I went and he took his second two years, his last two years, at MIT, taking a special fire-control course. He and Ed

---

[*] The Norden bombsight was a precision optical device developed in the early 1930s by Carl L. Norden, a civilian consultant employed by the Navy, together with Lieutenant Frederick L. Entwistle, USN. Its gyro-stabilized automatic pilot kept the bomber straight and level during bomb runs. It was used in both Navy and Army bombers in the 1930s and 1940s.

[†] Dr. Mason had previously interviewed Admiral John J. Ballentine, USN (Ret.), on behalf of Columbia University's oral history program.

[‡] Captain David I. Hedrick, USN, was ordnance inspector in charge of the Naval Proving Ground, Dahlgren, Virginia, from April 1941 to June 1946.

[§] Lieutenant Commander Edward N. Parker, USN.

Hooper and Lloyd Mustin and Corky Ward.[*] They were the four in the special fire-control course.

Let's see who was down at Dahlgren with me during that summer. Weatherwax, who's dead now.[†] Charlie Mauro, who lives down in Charleston, I think.[‡] It seems to me there was one more, but I forget who it was.

John T. Mason, Jr.: You say you took to this like a duck to water. What contributed to that?

Admiral Colwell: It was just something that I enjoyed. I just liked it. Maybe I enjoyed hearing the guns go off! I was fascinated with test results. You fire a 16-inch, armor-piercing projectile into 14-inch armor plate, and I was fascinated with the results. It's amazing how a steel shell properly made can pass through such plate and come out on the other side with maybe only just little scratches on it. That sort of work doesn't get done any more.

John T. Mason, Jr.: In my own mind I was wondering how it compares with what goes on with OpTEvFor?[§]

Admiral Colwell: Quite different, indeed. At the proving ground—it's no longer called the proving ground because they don't do very much proving any more—you were actually proving the operation of pieces of hardware, whether a gun would shoot the way it was supposed to, whether a projectile behaved as it should, whether fuzes went off when they were supposed to.[**] Sometimes they went off before they were supposed to.

---

[*] Lieutenant Edwin B. Hooper, USN; Lieutenant Lloyd M. Mustin, USN; Lieutenant Alfred G. Ward, USN. Ward and Rivero became four-star admirals; Hooper and Mustin became vice admirals. The oral histories of all four are in the Naval Institute collection.
[†] Lieutenant Hazlett P. Weatherwax, USN.
[‡] Lieutenant Charles T. Mauro, Jr., USN.
[§] OpTEvFor—Operational Test and Evaluation Force.
[**] In 1959 the name of the command was changed from Naval Proving Ground to Naval Weapons Laboratory Dahlgren. In 1974 it was renamed the Naval Surface Weapons Center (NWSC), and in 1992 it became NSWC Dahlgren Division.

In OpTEvFor they test the operation of items of equipment, or even of entire systems to see whether it performs as it should in an operational sense, rather than in a hardware or a technical sense. And, of course, they handle a much wider variety than traditional ordnance, such as communications and what not.

John T. Mason, Jr.: Well, the hardware stage is preliminary to the operational one.

Admiral Colwell: That's correct. Unless the hardware performs technically as designed, there's no use sending it to OpTEvFor and they don't. OpTEvFor won't take it because it would be a waste of their time.

John T. Mason, Jr.: Dahlgren was under the immediate control of the Bureau of Ordnance?

Admiral Colwell: The Bureau of Ordnance. That's correct.

John T. Mason, Jr.: And the bureau determined what projects would go on there?

Admiral Colwell: That's right. They furnished the funding, they assigned the projects, and the reports went back to the bureau.

John T. Mason, Jr.: What seemed to be their order of priority in projects?

Admiral Colwell: At that time, the order of priority was proof. Strictly a hardware operation. Proving guns, projectiles, powder, fuzes. That was it.

John T. Mason, Jr.: You said you had something to do with the calibration of the bombs dropped in testing the Norden bombsight. What other programs were you immediately involved in in those four months?

Admiral Colwell: We were actually assigned to various batteries. I was assigned to the armor plate battery, where they tested armor plate and armor-piercing projectiles, one against the other. We had what we hoped were certain standards. Of course, you never knew how any particular plate was going to behave until you attacked it. It might break up, or you might put a hole through it, which is what it was designed to do.

We worked with the officers in charge of our batteries, as their assistants. We aided them in writing up their reports of tests. We conducted some few tests, generally ones that were of less importance, naturally.

In addition to that, we were each assigned a project, and mine happened to be digging into all the files, which went back to the early days of establishing a proving ground at Dahlgren, and plotting the results of armor-piercing projectiles against armor plate. And the objective of this was hopefully to be able to draw a series of curves which could then be used in proving our guesstimates on the parameters which should be inserted into tests of plate and of AP projectiles. By "parameters," I mean the striking velocity, because we fired only a very short distance, and we could vary the striking velocity and get it very accurate by changing the powder charge. We would vary that, and we would vary the angle of obliquity at which the projectile hit the plate.

We had a set of curves to make these guesstimates, but we wanted better ones, and this is what my project was. It was only modestly successful because of the great variation in the quality of the plates and projectiles on which we had records. There wasn't any way to say that this particular projectile behaved exactly like that projectile, because there wasn't any way to say that the plate was exactly the same.

We did get some curves, and I was just getting up towards the end of this when the emergency started and we were all detached. I got my orders by telephone and left the next day. So I assume that those curves may have been of some use later. But it was an attempt just to improve our way of doing things.

John T. Mason, Jr.: Did you have any observers down there when you were there? I mean, were there any, say from the Royal Navy, or anybody like that?

Admiral Colwell: We didn't have any foreign observers while I was there. Of course, there were commercial observers for tests of their own products.

John T. Mason, Jr.: From industry?

Admiral Colwell: Oh, yes. Every time they had a lot that was being tested they were there, and if you said that a lot of projectiles failed, you had an argument on your hands. This was real money. Even worse, a set of plate from a lot of armor plate represented a tremendous amount of money. So you had to be very careful that the conditions which were established for a test were the very best choice that you could make. These people looked right over your shoulder and made doggone sure that they were satisfied too.

John T. Mason, Jr.: That probably resulted in a better test?

Admiral Colwell: That's right. It was as good as we knew how to make it.

John T. Mason, Jr.: Was BuShips there also?[*]

Admiral Colwell: For some tests we did. For example, I recall one test that I assisted in was a test of a built-up steel structure, and this was a BuShips test. We banged it with some projectiles. The object was to see whether the structure would hold together, whether the welds would break, and whatnot. We did that sort of thing for BuShips.

John T. Mason, Jr.: And BuAer?[†]

Admiral Colwell: Yes. We had our own aviation ordnance division down there and our own small airfield and a small complement of aircraft. They worked on bombsights, dropped bombs, they tried out new shapes in bombs, new shapes in bomb tails, dropped bomb fuzes, tested aircraft machine guns. They did a lot of work on machine guns, in

---

[*] BuShips—Bureau of Ships.
[†] BuAer—Bureau of Aeronautics.

improving their reliability in particular. One rather lengthy project had to do with trying to find a type of lubricant for aircraft machine guns that would work when they got upstairs where it was real cold. This went on for quite some time.

John T. Mason, Jr.: Would subjects like paint be investigated down there?

Admiral Colwell: A particular kind of paint that we investigated—and I think this was in my regular tour down there along towards the end of World War II—was a paint that would change color with temperature in a predictable fashion.

John T. Mason, Jr.: A color flash or something?

Admiral Colwell: No, this was for use in the ordnance business. One application of it would be in cook-off tests, for example, of a bomb, and these things would change color in predictable fashion so that if it turned purple, for example, you knew what the range of temperature was that caused it to turn purple, or if it turned pink or sky blue or whatever. That was a specialized kind of paint for testing and something that Dahlgren was geared to do. BuShips paints, no.

    A very interesting test that I ran in my regular tour down there, when I was the assistant experimental officer for two and a half years, was radar spotting of projectile splashes. By that time we had rather an extensive stable of radars.

John T. Mason, Jr.: And perfected?

Admiral Colwell: They were good ones. So we got one which was the type used on cruisers' and battleships' fire control, put it on a tower, aimed it down river, and we ran splash tests, single-shot splashes of various sizes from 5 inches up to 16 inches, to see how far these splashes would appear on the scope so that we could spot them. As it turned out, you could see all of them as far as you could shoot them.

John T. Mason, Jr.: That must have been a surprise, wasn't it?

Admiral Colwell: It was a pleasant surprise. We really didn't know how far we'd be able to see them, although we'd been doing radar spotting in the fleet. I remember we fired a 16-inch as far as we could shoot, which was pretty close to 40,000 yards. You could spot any size from 5-inch on. That was kind of a fun test to run.

We also did the testing down there on the VT fuzes.[*] We fired them over water and took pictures of where they triggered, and actually made some angular measurements to see how close to the surface they were going off, whether they were performing as the designer said they would. And we actually put out an instruction pamphlet which included pictures of various kinds of triggers, normal height, low height, surface burst, and no burst, just a splash. We put out pictures of these in an instruction to all the fleet ships, because we were requiring rather extensive reports back from all the people who used these, in order to build up a reservoir of information about VT fuzes, because they didn't always perform as advertised.

John T. Mason, Jr.: You wanted to be sure all the controls were right?

Admiral Colwell: We were trying to get all the information we could. Although we shot a lot of them in the tests, we wanted additional information and, in particular, we wanted fleet information because they were firing under different sea conditions. The river was always flat, but at sea they'd be firing when there were waves. So we were asking for a lot of information.

This job of assistant experimental officer was really quite a fascinating one, because we had just a huge array of projects of all different kinds. We got the first models, for example, of the 8-inch automatic rapid-firing assembly turret and ran it through tests.[†] That was a very interesting tour.

---

[*] Dr. Merle A. Tuve was instrumental in the development of the proximity fuze for 5-inch antiaircraft projectiles. It was also known as the VT, or variable time fuze. For a detailed account, see Buford Bowland and William R. Boyd, U.S. Navy Bureau of Ordnance in World War II (Washington, D.C.: U.S. Government Printing Office, 1953), pages 271-290.

[†] These rapid-firing 8-inch turrets were installed in the Des Moines (CA-134)-class heavy cruisers, the first of which was commissioned in 1948.

John T. Mason, Jr.: What percentage of tests of that sort fail and have to go back to the manufacturer?

Admiral Colwell: I'd say that almost all of them had faults in the beginning, because they were given very severe testing, and faults turned up in almost 100%, things that had to be repaired.

John T. Mason, Jr.: They'd been tested in the plant, hadn't they?

Admiral Colwell: Yes, but not under these severe firing conditions. For instance, let's take this 8-inch automatic rapid-fire turret. You're handling quite heavy bits of ordnance, the projectiles and the cases. You see, these are 8-inch brass cases, where the old 8-inch guns were bag guns. There's a lot of power there. You just shove these things in the bottom of the turret, press a switch, and away it goes. So you're handling heavy equipment. You're handling it at fairly high speeds, and you're handling it in a very precise sequence. There are many interlocks involved, and any one of these can fail. You have to build in a lot of safety factors.

Another thing that is very important in this kind of a test that you cannot do in the factory, is the heat that is associated with firing. At high rates of fire, these guns get very, very hot. A high rate of fire for an 8-inch gun is, say, eight rounds a minute. A high rate of fire for a 5-inch gun might be 40 rounds a minute, and for a 20-millimeter it might be 1,200 rounds a minute. Whatever it is, they get awfully hot, so you get rather extensive sizing changes to heat, and your design must take these things into account, or sometimes you find when you actually put them to the test that the designer didn't quite hit it. This is why you can't do it in the plant.

John T. Mason, Jr.: Is the designer very often present for these tests?

Admiral Colwell: Yes, quite often.

John T. Mason, Jr.: In the case of some of these things, the Navy was merely considering the purchasing, ordering, of these?

Admiral Colwell: No.

John T. Mason, Jr.: They had been commissioned?

Admiral Colwell: This design was scheduled to be installed in ships that were already at least in the planning stage. We were confident enough that the design would be successful to go ahead and plan on it, and actually it was a very successful design. This was built by the old gun factory here in Washington, which had a superb gun-design group.[*]

John T. Mason, Jr.: Very precipitately you were summoned to leave Dahlgren, after only being there four months, and the balance of the Cook's tour was canceled?

Admiral Colwell: That's correct.

John T. Mason, Jr.: What else had been projected?

Admiral Colwell: The Cook's tour would have included some time at the gun factory. There was one week at the powder factory at Indian Head.[†] I got that. That was the first place.

John T. Mason, Jr.: Tell me about that.

Admiral Colwell: That was simply a short period. We were really just walked through the various production lines.

---

[*] The Naval Gun Factory, on M Street in southeast Washington, D.C., for many years manufactured guns for the U.S. Navy. The site has since been renamed the Washington Navy Yard. It contains the offices of a number of commands, as well residences of several active-duty flag officers.
[†] Indian Head, Maryland, was the site of a naval powder factory.

John T. Mason, Jr.: Just to see what the facilities were?

Admiral Colwell: Just to observe how they made powder, that was all. We didn't perform any functions down there, except as student observers. I think we were only there four days. I've forgotten where else we were supposed to go on that tour. It seems to me there was a short period at Rochester with Bausch and Lomb. Oh, yes, there was a period at the Ford Instrument Company on Long Island, which is now part of Sperry Rand. I can't remember where else we were supposed to go. At any rate, the entire group, wherever we were spread out, we were all sent to sea in September.

I got my orders by telephone and left the next day, drove to New York, and I was married the day after that.

John T. Mason, Jr.: This precipitate action involved that too.

Admiral Colwell: Yes, and we left immediately for the West Coast, where I joined the Idaho at Long Beach.*

John T. Mason, Jr.: All of this was because of the imminence of hostilities?

Admiral Colwell: Yes, and the buildup in ships and people was beginning. New ships were beginning to come off the line.

I became the plotting room officer in the Idaho, which enjoyed. I was in the gunnery business.

John T. Mason, Jr.: Who was skipper of the Idaho?

---

* USS Idaho (BB-42), a New Mexico-class battleship, was commissioned 24 March 1919. She was modernized at the Norfolk Navy Yard from 1931 to 1934. Among the most noticeable changes was the replacement of her cage masts with a tower bridge. As modernized, her standard displacement was 35,000 tons. She was 624 feet long and 106 feet in the beam, and maximum draft of 31 feet. Her top speed was 22 knots. She was armed with 12 14-inch guns, 12 5-inch broadside guns, and 8 5-inch antiaircraft guns. She was eventually decommissioned in 1946,

Admiral Colwell: We had two while I was there. One was Captain McKinney and the other one was Captain Raguet.[*]

John T. Mason, Jr.: Still, you were a junior officer and not in immediate –

Admiral Colwell: I was sort of intermediate then. I was a lieutenant. We did all the usual training functions that you do. That's when I went to Pearl Harbor.[†] We went out there to stay and Gracie came out with the baby, our first child, and we lived there about six months, when we went to sea one Monday morning and we didn't come back! We went to the East Coast—our battleship division and some destroyers and cruisers.[‡]

John T. Mason, Jr.: But before that you had gone out to Hawaii?

Admiral Colwell: We were based in Pearl Harbor for about eight months, I suppose. We were ordered to the East Coast because things were heating up in Europe. There was speculation that maybe we were headed for Dakar, and it might have been considered at one time, I don't know.

John T. Mason, Jr.: In order to engage the Richelieu?[§]

Admiral Colwell: I don't know. Anyway, we didn't go there. The first time I was able to mail a letter was from Guantanamo to tell my family to come on home, I wasn't coming back. They were already convinced of that.

John T. Mason, Jr.: They knew quite well that you hadn't been lost at sea?

---

[*] Captain Stephen B. McKinney, USN; Captain Edward C. Raguet, USN.
[†] Fleet Problem XXI took place in the Hawaiian area in the spring of 1940. When it was completed, President Franklin D. Roosevelt directed that the fleet remain at Pearl Harbor rather than return to its bases on the West Coast. The idea was that leaving the fleet in Hawaii would serve as a deterrent to Japanese aggression in the Far East.
[‡] Battleship Division Three, comprised of the New Mexico (BB-40), Mississippi (BB-41), and the Idaho, was transferred to the Atlantic Fleet in June 1941 because of the growing concern about the German forces in the Atlantic.
[§] Richelieu was a French battleship.

Admiral Colwell: Yes.

John T. Mason, Jr.: What was the state of Pearl Harbor when you were there those eight months?

Admiral Colwell: We were on partial alert.

John T. Mason, Jr.: This was in the day of Richardson, wasn't it?[*]

Admiral Colwell: Yes. It was primarily just a darned good training ground because the weather was good. We went to sea regularly and trained regularly, and usually came in on weekends. We led a pretty normal existence. When we left there it was in July of 1941, still five months before the Japanese entered the picture.

We were sent east in order to beef up the Atlantic Fleet, because the only battleships we had in the Atlantic at that time were ancient. The Idaho, Mississippi, and New Mexico were fairly ancient, too, but they'd been modernized and we had 14-inch guns. A pretty good ship.

We hung around the East Coast for the summer, and then I suppose it was about in September we escorted a convoy of troops to Iceland and we stayed there until the seventh of December. We made sorties from time to time from Iceland. The most miserable weather I ever hope to see, absolutely awful. Presumably we were there in order to keep the Tirpitz from causing any harm.[†] Fortunately we never met the Tirpitz, as she would probably have killed us.

As soon as the debacle at Pearl Harbor was known, we left the next day for Norfolk, where we got about a month's quick overhaul and some small antiaircraft guns, and then out to the West Coast.

---

[*] Admiral James O. Richardson, USN, served as Commander in Chief U.S. Fleet from 6 January 1940 to 1 February 1941.

[†] The Tirpitz was a modern German battleship that was holed up in Norway. Her sister ship, the Bismarck, had been sunk by the British in May 1941.

J.B. Colwell, Interview #1 (4/26/73) – Page 34

John T. Mason, Jr.: Tell me about the convoy duties and the dangers of convoying in the North Atlantic.

Admiral Colwell: There were German submarines in the North Atlantic at that time. Of course, we were not belligerents.

John T. Mason, Jr.: This was a Neutrality Patrol, was it?[*]

Admiral Colwell: It was a sort of Neutrality Patrol, that's right. When we were at sea we steamed with lights on and a spotlight on the American flag, and we were not molested in any way.

John T. Mason, Jr.: But you were escorting troops?

Admiral Colwell: Yes.

John T. Mason, Jr.: U.S. troops?

Admiral Colwell: U.S. troops, but to Iceland not to Europe.

John T. Mason, Jr.: Had the fact that we were sending troops to Iceland been announced publicly?

Admiral Colwell: I don't think so. This was sort of in the Never-Never Land of whether we were in the war or weren't. We had obviously stretched the rules of neutrality by giving the British the old destroyers in what was called a trade for bases.[†] I don't think it

---

[*] In the period from 1939 to 1941—when the United States was not yet an active combatant in World War II—the American republics maintained what was called a Neutrality Patrol of a zone in the western Atlantic. Ostensibly neutral, it in fact aided Britain in its war against Germany.

[†] In September 1940 President Franklin D. Roosevelt concluded a deal with Prime Minister Winston Churchill of Great Britain whereby the United States transferred 50 destroyers to the Royal Navy for use against German submarines. In return the United States received 99-year leases to British bases in the West Indies, Bermuda, and Newfoundland.

was any such thing.

John T. Mason, Jr.: We did get bases!

Admiral Colwell: We got bases, that's right.

We lost a destroyer during this period.[*] That was probably a mistake on the part of the submarine that sank it. At any rate, there we were. We saw no hostile forces.

John T. Mason, Jr.: You had shore leave at Reykjavik?

Admiral Colwell: Such as it was. Our anchorage was quite a long way from Reykjavik.

John T. Mason, Jr.: Was it in the fjord up above?

Admiral Colwell: In the fjord, that's right. Hvalfjordur, I think is the name of it. We finally managed to scrounge a Quonset hut from somewhere, and set up a little club over on the beach, and if you didn't have the duty you could go over there from four to six, assuming the wind wasn't blowing, which frequently happened.[†]

John T. Mason, Jr.: And if the hut was still standing!

Admiral Colwell: If the hut was still standing. The winds are very peculiar up there. They suddenly go from zero to 50 knots.

At any rate, I went to Reyjkavik once because I had the shore patrol and had to go. It wasn't worth the trip.

John T. Mason, Jr.: How were you received by the Icelanders?

---

[*] On 31 October 1941, the German submarine U-552 torpedoed and sank the four-stack destroyer Reuben James (DD-245) with the loss of 115 lives. She was escorting a convoy from Halifax, Nova Scotia, to the British Isles and was lost about 600 miles west of Ireland. She was the first U.S. warship lost to enemy action in World War II.

[†] A Quonset hut is a semi-cylindrical metal building that can be shipped to an advance base area and erected quickly.

Admiral Colwell: They pretended we weren't there. You walked down the street, and they would pass you by and never look at you.

John T. Mason, Jr.: This meant they didn't really want you there?

Admiral Colwell: They didn't want us there at all. This was a government-to-government agreement, of course, but the people pretended we weren't there. It didn't really make any difference. It rained all the time anyway, so there wasn't any point in going to Reykjavik. There wasn't anything to do after you got there, except walk up and down in the rain. And you could do that on board ship!

John T. Mason, Jr.: They didn't have any clubs or anything for amusement?

Admiral Colwell: Not a thing. You can buy a bottle of beer. I was on shore patrol and wasn't allowed to have a beer, anyway!

John T. Mason, Jr.: This must have contributed to a morale factor, did it not?

Admiral Colwell: Strangely enough, it didn't seem to make an awful lot of difference. We kept busy with training. Of course, the only place we had to show movies was on deck, but we rigged windscreens. It got dark about 3:00 o'clock in the afternoon, so we started movies at 4:00. It didn't seem to bother people very much. Just keeping dry and warm was enough of a chore to keep your mind off of other things, but going to sea up there was just a miserable experience, because the wind would blow and it was cold, waves were running high. Of course, we stood condition watches on the guns all the time we were at sea, not knowing what might happen.

John T. Mason, Jr.: Well, how was it explained? I mean, we were neutrals, and yet we were there in the thought that the Tirpitz might come out and if she did what was to be our action?

Admiral Colwell: None of us really knew. Maybe the captain did. We were all expecting that this thing would finally blow sooner or later, and our being up there was an obvious admission that everybody else expected it to blow. We didn't have any doubt but what if we met the enemy we would fight.

John T. Mason, Jr.: As you say, it would have been a somewhat unequal fight, wouldn't it?

Admiral Colwell: It would have been bad news for us because she had us out-gunned, out-ranged, out-speeded, and out-every-thing. A superb ship.

John T. Mason, Jr.: Was there any open liaison with the Royal Navy while you were in Iceland?

Admiral Colwell: Yes. They had ships in the same anchorage and we visited back and forth quite frequently, socially.

John T. Mason, Jr.: And their purpose was the same? Did they have a battleship there?

Admiral Colwell: The King George V was there. They were there for the same purpose.

The only thing that was really interesting about that period—this is probably not a very good way to put it, but a certain fascination was the Northern Lights. I had seen them very slightly before when I was just a boy growing up on the plains of Nebraska. But up there they were just a marvelous, beautiful picture that helped pass the time when you were standing a night watch and your feet were freezing.

John T. Mason, Jr.: But, of course, they were visible only when it wasn't raining?

Admiral Colwell: Yes!

John T. Mason, Jr.: You were just telling me, off tape, about the rigors of attempting to sail in Icelandic waters. Would you give me a picture of what happened on the Idaho when you went out on a mission?

Admiral Colwell: On one of these training trips, which I suppose was six, eight, or ten days, or whatever it was, the wind blew just continuously at about 60 or 70 knots, and huge seas running, so that the ship actually worked in the seaway and quantities of water got inside the ship around the turret barbettes, and we actually had to establish regular watches to bail the water out down below.

One of the more amusing things that happened on that little jaunt was that the observation aircraft blew away, even though they were tied down. In the Idaho, in the process of taking flight from the quarterdeck catapult, this strain resulted in the breaking of the steel restraining straps, and also the shaft of the restraining pinion. That left the catapult free to swing, and it went round and round and round like a carousel until we got back in and could corral it and tie it down. In our sister ship, the Mississippi, her planes blew away also, but as I remember, when the quarterdeck plane blew away it pulled the catapult out by the roots and left a large hole in the overhead of the wardroom, which gave them a little patching problem.

John T. Mason, Jr.: I would think it would be particularly difficult for destroyers to function under those circumstances?

Admiral Colwell: It was extremely difficult. It wasn't unusual at all for a destroyer to find it impossible to get people to move about on deck, so that the fireroom watch couldn't be relieved. I remember hearing of one where the fireroom watch had to stay on for 18 hours because nobody could get below to relieve them.

Interview Number 2 with Vice Admiral John Barr Colwell, U.S. Navy (Retired)

Place: Admiral Colwell's apartment in Washington, D.C.

Date: Tuesday, 22 May 1973

Interviewer: John T. Mason, Jr.

John T. Mason, Jr.: Well, sir, it's good to see you this morning. Last time, we broke off while you were still on duty in Iceland, and I note from the record that you were on duty in Iceland when the Japanese struck at Pearl Harbor. How did this change your life? Your tour of duty?

Admiral Colwell: The primary change was one of locale, I guess. I was already fairly well broken into the business of being away from home a great deal. As I recall, our battleship division, which by then constituted almost all the battleships that we had afloat, sailed the next day and went to Norfolk, where we had about a month of overhaul, the fitting of our first radar and of some 1.1 small-caliber antiaircraft up until that time.

John T. Mason, Jr.: Did you bring on board some ordnance people to help indoctrinate, especially with the radar?

Admiral Colwell: We got some training while we were there in the Norfolk Navy Yard, and our technicians were taught how to maintain it. These radars were pretty elementary jobs at that time.

John T. Mason, Jr.: Had you had any prior knowledge of radar?

Admiral Colwell: None; I didn't even know it existed.

John T. Mason, Jr.: And the utmost secrecy was still maintained, wasn't it, as to the installation and so on?

Admiral Colwell: Yes, that's true. It was regarded as a very-high-quality secret. As a result, in retrospect, it stayed secret from our own people rather than from anyone else, I suppose.

John T. Mason, Jr.: What is your observation on that kind of a policy?

Admiral Colwell: I think it's shortsighted. I think it's easy to understand why it happened that way. Nothing as new, as revolutionary as radar, which was certainly one of the great discoveries in the art of warfare—it's quite easy to understand why people fear to let it become very well known. I think that fear tends to obscure what is usually a fact, and that is that the enemy already knows as much about it as you do. He may even have a better one. The principles of radar were not unknown in many countries of the world. As I say, I think it's easy to understand, but it's a mistake.

John T. Mason, Jr.: There's something quite interesting about the idea that in the fullness of time new ideas are universal.

Admiral Colwell: It's a very interesting thing and, from what I've read, it occurs in many, many disciplines. For instance, even in medicine. Almost the same discovery will be made in two different parts of the world with no intercommunication, so I've heard.

Radar, for example—the British were at just about the same point that we were. I don't know how much interplay there had been between the two countries, probably some.*

John T. Mason, Jr.: Very little, I believe. Everybody thought it was a secret.

Admiral Colwell: I don't know where the Germans were at that time, but I'd be surprised if they weren't about in the same spot. The Japanese, I don't know, but from the way they

---

* For more on this topic, see James R. Leutze, "Technology and Bargaining in Anglo-American Naval Relations: 1938-1946," U.S. Naval Institute Proceedings, June 1977, pages 50-61.

handled their night actions early in the war in the Pacific, I would think they must have had some radar, either that or superb vision!

John T. Mason, Jr.: You say the 1.1 guns were installed, and, as we know, they later showed up some inadequacies. Were these soon apparent to you?

Admiral Colwell: Yes. It was very difficult to keep the mounts in operation, which was not due to one defect, but several. Later on they began to work better. I think it was due to the ministrations of Admiral Mustin, who worked them over.[*] But they never had very wide application in the U.S. Navy, because we soon began to get in large quantities the Swedish Bofors 40-millimeter and the Swiss Oerlikon 20-millimeter, which behaved much better. So the 1.1 was just phased out of existence. The 40-millimeter Bofors and the Oerlikon 20-millimeter became our standards.

John T. Mason, Jr.: Did you have prior knowledge of the Bofors and the Oerlikons through the British?

Admiral Colwell: No.

John T. Mason, Jr.: They were in use on their ships.

Admiral Colwell: I didn't have prior knowledge of the Oerlikon, and my knowledge of the Bofors was in a completely different configuration. The British had one they called a pom-pom. It was sometimes called a Chicago piano.

John T. Mason, Jr.: I never heard that name!

---

[*] Lieutenant Lloyd M. Mustin, USN. See the Naval Institute oral history of Mustin, who retired as a vice admiral.

Admiral Colwell: I imagine that's an American term that was applied to it. As I remember, it was a multiple-barrel, belt-fed 40-millimeter, and it had fairly short barrels. By contrast, the U.S. version was a rather long barrel, about 60 calibers, I think, and it was clip-fed, and the mount configuration was entirely different, as it naturally would be when you go from belt feed to clip feed.*

That was my only knowledge of the Bofors before they began to be installed in the U.S. fleet, and then, of course, I had—

John T. Mason, Jr.: And then, of course, they were manufactured—

Admiral Colwell: In this country, that's correct, as was the Oerlikon. As I recall, there was long litigation after the war about manufacturing rights and how much we owed the foreign companies.

John T. Mason, Jr.: Especially the Swiss, I think.

Admiral Colwell: I think it was both. I didn't have anything to do with that.

John T. Mason, Jr.: That must have been an exciting period and especially for you, an ordnance-oriented person, to get all those new bits of ordnance on board.

Admiral Colwell: It was exciting, and it was a very, very busy time obviously. Among other things, I learned to become in a sort of an elementary way a radar operator. And after we left Norfolk to go around to the West Coast, of course, we practiced with it almost continuously, trying to find out just exactly what it would do and what it would tell us when we couldn't see, at night and so forth.

As I recall, the operation of that first radar that we had—and I can't remember its designation, but it doesn't matter—

---

* In this case caliber is used to indicate the length of the barrel; by multiplying the diameter times the caliber, one gets the barrel length.

John T. Mason, Jr.: It was rather a large installation, wasn't it?

Admiral Colwell: Yes.

John T. Mason, Jr.: A bed-spring type of thing?

Admiral Colwell: No, we didn't get one of those very long-range bed-spring types. We got a very early model of a fire-control radar, and, as I recall, it was mounted on top of one of the main battery directors. It was not very useful for search because you had to train the director in order to search, which was fairly slow. So it didn't work out very well for that. But we worked with it and finally got so that we could get some very useful information out of it. This was before the days of the round PPI that gives you a real radar picture.* All you got was a series of spikes across a horizontal line, but at least you knew when there was a target and you knew how far away it was, and the bearing.

After we had finished up in Norfolk, as I mentioned, we went around to the West Coast and based in San Francisco. Pearl Harbor, of course, was still a shambles. We operated out of San Francisco from time to time, made a couple of long cruises, one out toward the Aleutians and one down toward the southwest.

John T. Mason, Jr.: You were a unit of what fleet at that point?

Admiral Colwell: Good question! I would just have to say Pacific Fleet. I'm sure that we had another task force designation, but I've no idea what it was.

Our time in San Francisco we maintained an alert watch. There had been one or two instances of Japanese submarines surfacing off the West Coast and firing an odd shell here and there which didn't do any damage. But, of course, the city was blacked out, and we maintained a very alert watch against saboteurs.

---

* PPI—plan position indicator, a type of radar that presents essentially a geographical picture with one's own ship in the center of the scope and surrounding ships, planes, and land areas shown in their respective positions in terms of range and bearing.

John T. Mason, Jr.: The Nisei were very suspect, were they not?*

Admiral Colwell: Yes, improperly so. They'd all been moved out by then. One of the more unfortunate chapters in U.S. history, I believe. As far as I know, we never had any even bare indication of sabotage, but a ship tied up to a pier in a large harbor was a fairly obvious and not too difficult target, so we did maintain a good watch against sabotage, both inside and outside the ship.

John T. Mason, Jr.: What was your specific purpose in going to the Aleutians and the other—?

Admiral Colwell: My memory on dates isn't too good, but I believe the trip up toward the Aleutians must have been at the time of our occupation of Attu. And the lengthy cruise down toward the southwest, I think, must certainly have been at the time of the Battle of the Coral Sea. Besides that, I don't remember anything specific about the period in San Francisco, and eventually we were moved out to Honolulu.† This, I would guess, would have been probably in August of 1942.

John T. Mason, Jr.: Were things beginning to shape up in Pearl at that time?

Admiral Colwell: Yes, they were. The ships that could be raised had been raised, battleship row was cleaned out, and the ones that could be brought back into service—which was most of them—had gone back to the West Coast for repairs. Of course, the Arizona was a complete loss, and the Utah and Oklahoma were still there, lying on their sides. The harbor clean-up of black oil was still going on. Some very bright fellow had

---

* The Nisei were sons and daughters of Japanese immigrants. They were American citizens by virtue of being born in the United States, and in many instances their parents had become naturalized. Shortly after the attack on Pearl Harbor, the U.S. Government evacuated many of these Japanese-Americans in inland internment camps because of a fear that these individuals would cause sabotage.
† The Battle of the Coral Sea was in early May of 1942.

invented a small self-propelled barge that sort of lapped up the black oil from the surface of the water. I think it was called a Juicey Lucy. The cleanup was in quite good shape.

We were beginning to have the nucleus, once again, of a fairly powerful fleet. The aircraft carrier force, of course, was still very small and they had been engaged in almost continual battle here and there. The Saratoga had taken a torpedo, the Enterprise had suffered damage. When was Midway? Was that 1943?

John T. Mason, Jr.: That was in 1942 also.*

Admiral Colwell: In 1942. Well, we'd lost the Yorktown at Midway. The carriers were the true workhorses all through the war, of course, and they were in such short supply that they were just really running ragged. But by that time we were beginning to have once again the nucleus of a powerful fleet.

Things were about to begin in the South Pacific and the long road back. I believe that the landing in Guadalcanal was in August of 1942.† Does that sound right?

John T. Mason, Jr.: Yes.

Admiral Colwell: In September I was detached from the Idaho and ordered as gunnery officer to a ship called Copahee, which was a tanker converted into a small aircraft carrier.‡

John T. Mason, Jr.: She was one of the first, then, of the jeep types?

---

* From 4 to 6 June 1942, U.S. and Japanese naval forces fought a battle northwest of Midway Island in the Pacific. After Japanese bombers had struck the island, carrier-based U.S. dive-bombers attacked and sank the Japanese carriers Hiryu, Soryu, Kaga, and Akagi and the cruiser Mikuma. U.S. ships lost were the carrier Yorktown (CV-5) and the destroyer Hammann (DD-412). The battle was both a tactical and strategic victory for U.S. forces.
† On 7 August 1942, U.S. Marines invaded the islands of Guadalcanal and Tulagi in the Solomons chain as part of the first U.S. counteroffensive in the Pacific War. The primary purpose was to gain control of an airstrip on Guadalcanal and thus to prevent the Japanese from achieving control of the surrounding air and sea regions.
‡ The Copahee, a Bogue-class escort aircraft carrier, was commissioned 15 June 1942 with the designation AVG-12. She was reclassified as ACV-12 on 12 August 1942 and as CVE-12 on 15 July 1943. She had a standard displacement of 7,800 tons, was 496 feet long, 70 feet in the beam, and had an extreme width of 112 feet. Her top speed was 17 knots. The ship was originally armed with two 5-inch guns and could accommodate approximately 30 aircraft. After her war service she was decommissioned on 5 July 1946.

Admiral Colwell: Yes, that's right, and some of her sisters functioned throughout the war as small carriers, primarily for aircraft transport. Of course, they still had their enormous oil capacity, so they were sort of in a double role.

Copahee was supposed to be somewhere in the South Pacific, so after some delay waiting for transportation, I set sail for the South Pacific in a small, very elderly transport called the William Ward Burrows. Eventually, after a stop in Fiji and another stop in Espiritu Santo and several engine breakdowns, it arrived in Noumea, which was the headquarters of the South Pacific Force by that time.

John T. Mason, Jr.: And Admiral Halsey was there?

Admiral Colwell: Admiral Halsey was there, having very recently arrived and taken command of the South Pacific Force.[*] I naturally checked in with his staff, Copahee being nowhere in evidence at all. Nobody down there knew where Copahee was, some guessing that she had gone to the East Coast. This really didn't break my heart at all because I didn't feel that I was getting much of a promotion in position by going as gunnery officer of the Copahee, which had a few 40-millimeters, and I've always liked to think that maybe those orders were a mistake.

At any rate, no Copahee, and there I was. Admiral Halsey had a very small staff and was building a staff. One of my good friends and classmates was his flag secretary.

John T. Mason, Jr.: He being?

Admiral Colwell: Doug Moulton, who was an aviator.[†] He had resigned before the war, came back in when the war started, and stayed with Admiral Halsey throughout the war, eventually again leaving the service as a rear admiral. Doug said, "You might just as well

---

[*] Vice Admiral/Admiral William F. Halsey Jr., USN, served as Commander South Pacific Area from 18 October 1942 to 15 June 1944. He was promoted to four-star rank in November 1942.
[†] Lieutenant Horace Douglass Moulton, USNR.

become attached to Admiral Halsey's staff. We need somebody with ordnance and, so, if you're interested, I'll suggest that you be attached to the staff as assistant gunnery officer."

I said, "Fine, I'm your boy."

And that's the way it happened, and this was for me a very interesting and busy period.

John T. Mason, Jr.: Tell me what kind of installations we had in Noumea.

Admiral Colwell: At first, the staff was quartered in the Argonne, which was a pretty old ship with the Service Force and had at one time been the flagship of the Service Force, or whatever they called it in those days. Probably the train—the sea train. We were quartered in the Argonne, which was entirely too small, and besides it was rather a wasteful use of the ship which had extensive repair capability. So we obtained a building ashore, requisitioned it, which became the headquarters, and we then commuted back and forth for a time, living in the Argonne and using the headquarters building ashore.

In the meantime, a Quonset village was being built in the town of Noumea.

John T. Mason, Jr.: The Seabees were active, were they?[*]

Admiral Colwell: Yes. I think there were two Seabee units already in Noumea. They were building the Tantuta Airfield, which was up the island a way, and another smaller airfield which was quite close to headquarters.

They built a Quonset village to house the staff. The admiral and a few senior members of his staff were housed in a requisitioned house, which I believe had belonged to the Japanese consul. So that was a nice touch. Later on some other houses were requisitioned, as the staff grew.

John T. Mason, Jr.: Was Carney with him at that point?[†]

---

[*] Seabees is the nickname applied to members of the Navy's mobile construction battalions (CBs).
[†] Rear Admiral Robert B. Carney, USN, served as chief of staff to Admiral Halsey from July 1943 until shortly after the conclusion of World War II.

Admiral Colwell: Not at that point.

After a fairly brief period in this first building, we quickly outgrew that also and moved into another much larger building, which then became the permanent headquarters. It was such that proper security could be maintained. There was room enough for the staff to work, and so on. We continued then to live, most of us, and mess at the Quonset village. It was quite satisfactory.

John T. Mason, Jr.: Was Noumea within reach of Japanese planes?

Admiral Colwell: No, it was not. As I recall, it was about 800 miles, air miles, from Noumea to Guadalcanal. We had two intermediate bases. One at Espiritu Santo, which actually became a very large one.

John T. Mason, Jr.: A repair base?

Admiral Colwell: A repair base, supply base, and a very large airfield—one runway, but a great long one—the longest one I'd ever seen.

We had another good anchorage and smaller naval base on the island of Efate at Vila.

During my time on Admiral Halsey's staff—and my assignment throughout that period was assistant gunnery officer—I traveled throughout the area quite extensively and got to know a lot of the people and got to know the anchorage areas and so forth quite well.

John T. Mason, Jr.: And this was all done by plane?

Admiral Colwell: Yes, I think I only went to sea twice during that period for any extensive time. I went out with Saratoga one time on what was primarily a training cruise out from Efate, and we came back to the same anchorage. The other one was a trip by destroyer down to Sydney, when I was fortunate enough to get ten days' leave.

J. B. Colwell, Interview #2 (5/22/73) – Page 49

John T. Mason, Jr.: That was a great place for leave, wasn't it?

Admiral Colwell: That was R&R of very high quality.*

John T. Mason, Jr.: Why?

Admiral Colwell: The people were so friendly, it was a big city. There were things to do. There were racetracks and night clubs. It was a great deal different from the daily grind.

I had one rather unusual pleasure. I was invited to have lunch with the Wine and Food Society of New South Wales.

John T. Mason, Jr.: That was curious. How did it happen?

Admiral Colwell: Well, I had a room in a private home. A number of the citizens of Sydney had listed their homes as available for paying guests. I was very fortunate to get one of these. The gentleman who was my host was a member of the Wine and Food Society, and he took me to lunch one day, and it was fun.

John T. Mason, Jr.: It was a big banquet?

Admiral Colwell: Not very large because they were on pretty tight rations, and finding things to make an unusual lunch was pretty difficult. But they pursued their usual form where, after the luncheon, various people were called upon to present the part of the luncheon which they had been responsible for. One man had the wines, another had the entree, and so on. Then other people got up and criticized the meal, just as they'd been doing it for years, I suppose.

John T. Mason, Jr.: Gourmets!

---

* R&R—rest and recreation.

Admiral Colwell: Gourmets, yes, and it was fun. As a guest and particularly a foreigner I was asked if I'd care to say a few words. So naturally I was expansive in my praise of the Wine and Food Society, and I disagreed with all the members who'd been protesting the quality. It was all a very pleasant affair.

John T. Mason, Jr.: The Australians, I take it, were quite in contrast with the Icelanders?

Admiral Colwell: Oh, very much so, yes. The Australians were very friendly. Of course, we were allies, and they'd already taken a pretty bad beating in North Africa. I suppose there was hardly a family that hadn't suffered a casualty.

Well, to get back, my travel throughout the area was by necessity almost entirely by air.

John T. Mason, Jr.: Did this entail some hairy experiences?

Admiral Colwell: Not really. There was one that had some potential. I was flying into Guadalcanal one day in a DC-3, which was, of course, the workhorse of the area of the world as far as that goes. It still is in some places. At any rate, I'd gone up to Tan Son Nhut to catch a ride to Guadalcanal.[*]

I checked in with the office up there—oh, our local airline was SCAT, South Pacific Combat Air Transport—so I'd gone to check with SCAT, and they said, "Sure, we've got one going in just a few minutes. It's got a load of belly tanks, and if you can squeeze yourself in you can go." So I said fine. And, sure enough, that was the load, belly tanks and me, and no place to sit down. An eight-hour flight, and cold.

Anyway, we got almost to Guadalcanal and we started to circle, so I finally managed to attract the attention of one of the crew members and asked him what was going on. It developed that they were having a massive air raid on Guadalcanal. That was the day that

---

[*] Tan Son Nhut was an airstrip in New Caledonia, near Noumea, that the South Pacific Force staff used for all its air traffic while based nearby.

the Aaron Ward was sunk and another ship.* So there we were circling around south of Guadalcanal, just hoping that none of the Japs chose to take that route home. Fortunately, they didn't. They were probably all low on gas anyway.

John T. Mason, Jr.: So were you, I take it?

Admiral Colwell: We had enough to get in. Eventually the "all clear" was sounded at Henderson Field, and we straightened ourselves out and went on in.†

We went through some enormous growing pains in the area and, of course, without the Seabees we'd still be there struggling. We built a very large ammunition dump on Noumea, using the prefabricated sectional magazines, which we then covered with earth. They made very good magazines. We built an equally large one, or maybe larger, on Espiritu Santo and that became the major unloading point for ammunition. We built smaller ammunition stowages in other places. In the harbor of Tulagi we obtained some concrete barges and filled those with destroyer ammunition.

We built an antiaircraft training school on the island of Noumea and trained, I suppose, literally thousands of people in the arts of attempting to shoot down aircraft. We had all sizes of antiaircraft weapons there. Fuel storages we built, floating storage and tank storage.

In the meantime, of course, the ships were working all the time.

You asked about Admiral Carney. He was commanding officer of a cruiser, I believe the Denver, and then when he was promoted to flag rank he came to the staff as chief of staff. I couldn't tell you what the date was.

John T. Mason, Jr.: But he came to Noumea?

Admiral Colwell: To Noumea, that's correct.

---

* On 7 April 1943, while covering the LST-449 off Togoma Point, Guadalcanal, the destroyer Aaron Ward (DD-483) was attacked by Japanese aircraft and sunk.
† Henderson Field was the U.S. Navy-Marine Corps airstrip on Guadalcanal. It was named in honor of Major Lofton R. Henderson, USMC, who was lost in action during the Battle of Midway.

John T. Mason, Jr.: What were your specific duties as assistant gunnery officer on the staff?

Admiral Colwell: One of my primary duties was in the ammunition supply area, in conjunction with the gunnery officer on the Service Force, South Pacific, also headquartered in Noumea. We determined what the ammunition requisitions should be for the Navy, and these, of course, were primarily guesses. We estimated how much we were going to use in combat, how much we were going to use in training.

John T. Mason, Jr.: Not having had too much experience in combat, it was hard to tell?

Admiral Colwell: It was very hard to tell, that's right. And, of course, at this time the fighting was still going on full bore in Europe, and Europe had—or at least we all felt that they had—sort of a priority call on any type of supplies, including ammunition.

John T. Mason, Jr.: Indeed, that was an agreement at the very top, wasn't it?

Admiral Colwell: I think that that's true. At various times we were a little bit short in terms of ammunition, but this was primarily a matter of distribution. We had ammunition stored in a lot of different places, and you can't move it from Noumea to Guadalcanal, for example, or to Tulagi for a bunch of destroyers; you can't do that just overnight by snapping your fingers. We were never out of ammunition, but we were low in some places because of distribution. This was eventually cured as we got additional stowage. This was also a problem.

John T. Mason, Jr.: In that climate!

Admiral Colwell: To begin with, we had ammunition stowed in the open, and this was not only bombs which would pretty much take care of themselves, but it included cans with cartridge cases and depth charges, even dynamite. In the middle of the night, down in

Noumea, one night we were all awakened by a tremendous explosion. Nobody knew exactly what this was, but we soon found out that it was one of our bomb dumps which was in sort of a bowl in the hills out at the ammunition depot, which was maybe five, six, or seven miles from the city. Bombs were being unloaded from a ship into dump trucks, and the men driving the dump trucks didn't have very much respect for high explosives, so they were backed up to the edge of this sort of bowl, opened the tail gate and raised the dump truck body and just let the bombs roll down the hill till they came to rest among other bombs.

Well, eventually, the inevitable happened. Two bombs decided that they didn't care much for each other, and they went off. Then the whole place was going off.

In another area of the ammunition depot, we had a very large pile of 5-inch cartridge cases in their aluminum cans and not too far away was a rather large stack of dynamite in boxes. Well, fragments from the exploding bombs landed among the cartridge cases and set some of those afire. Of course, they didn't explode, they burned. That had the makings of a pretty good conflagration. Then another fragment landed in the dynamite, and it went off and blew the fire out.

We never found the man who had been running the dump truck. We found a couple of fragments of his bones.

John T. Mason, Jr.: Why hadn't the supply people kept closer security on these things?

Admiral Colwell: Well, you just have to remember that this is the way things go sometimes when you're out in a forward area. There are always too few people to supervise. And they'd been doing it this way for a while and nothing had ever gone off, so it got to be routine, I suppose.

John T. Mason, Jr.: This inevitably caused a tightening up, losing so many—

Admiral Colwell: Oh, yes. They didn't roll them down the hill any more after that.

We had one other explosion, in the harbor, at Noumea. A ship that was handling ammunition had sort of a minor explosion, not bad. We also lost one entire ammunition ship. I believe the name of it was Mount Hood.*

John T. Mason, Jr.: Yes, she was at—

Admiral Colwell: Manus?

John T. Mason, Jr.: Or was it Espiritu?

Admiral Colwell: I think Manus. Of course, this was much later. She disappeared in one flash.

John T. Mason, Jr.: She was right in the midst of a big number of ships.

Admiral Colwell: Yes, that's right.

There was another ammunition dump explosion, which happened to be on the island of Guadalcanal, and it was an Army dump and 25,000 tons in it. I remember that. That threw 75-millimeter shells and odds and ends all over the place. I don't recall whether anybody was killed in that or not.

I visited Guadalcanal rather frequently in that period. It was very good business to get a firsthand look at how things were going. The first time I went up was in December of 1942, which was a month after I'd reported to the staff. Judge Eller and I went up together.† He was on CinCPacFlt staff and had come down to visit us.‡ He later became a commodore and was the Navy historian, as you recall, for quite a period.§ We went up to see how things were going. Well, actually things were going very badly indeed, because it

---

* On 10 November 1944, at Manus in the Admiralty Islands, the ammunition ship Mount Hood (AE-11) exploded. All on board were killed.
† Commander Ernest M. Eller, USN. The oral history of Eller, who retired as a rear admiral, is in the Naval Institute collection.
‡ CinCPacFlt—Commander in Chief Pacific Fleet.
§ As a retired rear admiral, Eller served as Director of Naval History from October 1956 to January 1970.

was such a miserable place to try to work. It rained almost incessantly and the mud was about hip deep. You could not move without a four-wheel-drive vehicle. People were living in tents. If you were lucky, you might have had some boards for a part of the tent floor so that when you got out of your cot you didn't sink into the mud. That's if you were very lucky.

The mosquitoes were frightful, the malaria rate was high. There wasn't anyplace where you could store anything without having it sink into the mud. The Japs were only a few hundred yards away in practically any direction. Air raids were daily. It was a pretty miserable place, but the fighting was going on and it was turning in our favor, and eventually we cleared them out.

John T. Mason, Jr.: Your purpose of going there was in the interests of ammunition distribution, was it?

Admiral Colwell: Yes, and also to get a firsthand look at what conditions were. For example, the fighters operating from Henderson Field had to be supplied with belted .50-caliber ammunition. We had the ammunition, but the belting was a very slow process because, to start out with, we had only hand-cranked belting machines. Eventually, we got some electric-powered ones, and they did have electric power from portable generators. They even had ice from a Japanese ice machine.

John T. Mason, Jr.: Yes, I heard of it being used.

Admiral Colwell: Yes, it was from time to time. We eventually got some electric-powered belters, and they worked them so hard that the motors would burn out. Then they would be back to the old system until we could get new motors flown down from the West Coast.

It was just a very difficult existence, and you can't do anything but admire all the people who were there, the way they overcame these horrible disadvantages and fought at the same time. The morale was high. The Japs used to send a lone bomber down every night and he was known as Washing Machine Charlie. He came down every night, everybody knew he was coming, so you didn't bother to go to bed until Charlie showed up and dropped a couple of bombs, usually out in the ocean and far away, then went home again. Then everybody would come out of his slit trench and turn in. The slit trenches were usually full of water and surrounded by mosquitoes.

Eventually, the ingenuity of the American man and the enormous supplies that were placed at his disposal enabled us to build four-lane coral roads which were hard as cement pavement, three or four feet above the surrounding terrain so that they were always almost dry and as passable as any paved street. Adequate housing in the form of Quonset huts was brought in, the people policed up their living areas, made gravel walks so that you could walk around in the mud, the messes were all screened. Medical units came in and eradicated the mosquito from areas where people worked and lived and turned them back into the jungle to the point where the mosquito didn't bother you unless you went into the jungle.

By that time the Japs were well on the move westward and, eventually as expected and as planned, Guadalcanal became a backwater. In between were numerous battles, skirmishes, landings on other islands. I later participated in some of these, after I left the staff.

John T. Mason, Jr.: While you were still on the staff, perhaps you'd talk some more about your duties in addition to ammunition. What about spare parts and things of that sort?

Admiral Colwell: This was primarily a matter which was handled by the Service Force. They had the repair ships and the shore-sited repair facilities. They handled that end of it.

I got into the ammunition requisitioning because it was so intimately connected with operations. You could say that this should have been left to the Service Force, and maybe it should. I worked with them, and it was an amicable arrangement. My boss and I both felt it was something that was so vital to operations that we had to keep an eye on it. Of course, we had a much better day-to-day feel for where ships were going to be operating, where ammunition would be required, and we therefore inserted ourselves into the business of moving ammunition and of positioning ammunition when it first arrived.

John T. Mason, Jr.: Yes, you were really at a vantage point!

Admiral Colwell: That's right. I don't feel that we encroached on the Service Force because of that. Spare parts, repairs, this was really their fundamental business and they did it.

John T. Mason, Jr.: Did you set up the AA training school on Noumea?*

Admiral Colwell: Only to the extent that anyone in my staff position would have. We rounded up a young man who looked as though he could go out and scrounge whatever was necessary, and we said, "Okay, you are now in charge, go and build it." We found him a place to build it, and he went to work. When he had trouble requisitioning equipment, why, he'd come and see us and we'd help him. But he built it and he was a good one.

John T. Mason, Jr.: Who was he?

Admiral Colwell: I can't remember his name. He was a young reserve officer. Most of our officers were reserve.

John T. Mason, Jr.: There must have been plenty of room on Noumea. What about the native population?

Admiral Colwell: It's not large. We actually didn't bother them much. The island didn't have a large population. There were large areas in the interior that didn't have any people on them at all, so we could requisition and lease those particular parts that were needed. I didn't get into that part of it. It was a legal affair.

John T. Mason, Jr.: Did it have the same kind of climate and daily rains and all that?

---

* AA—antiaircraft.

Admiral Colwell: No, it was really quite a nice climate. It gets rather chilly in the wintertime. Sitting outdoors at the movies in the wintertime, we'd wear sweaters and overcoats and still be pretty cold. It was pretty warm in the summer. Really not a bad climate at all. The island, before the war, had two primary exports, as I recall. One of them was chrome ore, and the other one was deerskins. They used to export about 75,000 deerskins a year. When we arrived the deer were still there in the hills and sometimes rather close in to the city. I recall one of the camps quite near Noumea finally had to publish a regulation that M-1s will not be used to hunt deer within the confines of the camp.* These high-velocity slugs were traveling through people's tents, and they got a little touchy.

I never went hunting there, but I know a lot of people did, back up in the hills, and I had some very good venison at times.

The people there were very friendly. I had very little to do with them, but they seemed like nice people.

John T. Mason, Jr.: You traveled a great deal. Did the other members of Halsey's staff also travel constantly?

Admiral Colwell: Many members traveled a great deal. The admiral himself traveled some. The operations officer stayed pretty close to the store. He was the key, really, the moving force on the staff. We had quite a large intelligence section, and they all traveled all the time. The Service Force people, traveled a lot, just to make sure that things were happening the way they should.

John T. Mason, Jr.: How did the admiral himself function?

Admiral Colwell: I don't know too much about that. My contacts with Admiral Halsey were very few. The gunnery department was a section of the operations department, so my

---

* The M-1 Garand was a standard rifle used by U.S. infantrymen during World War II and beyond.

boss and I had daily dealings with the operations officer and his assistant. We worked very closely with them. I saw the chief of staff on occasion, but primarily our working relationship was with the operations officer and his staff.

John T. Mason, Jr.: In those early operations, the coast watchers stationed on the islands were terribly important. Do you want to talk about them?

Admiral Colwell: They were terribly important. I met a few of them. They would come out occasionally for a few days' rest, or perhaps go down to New Zealand or Australia or go home for a few days, and then back again.

John T. Mason, Jr.: How did they come out?

Admiral Colwell: They'd be brought by boat, say, to Guadalcanal and then flown out.

I never knew very much about the details of that operation because that was understandably held pretty closely. I used to see regularly dispatches that we got from them because they would contain useful information on Japanese movements or what they had heard from natives and so on. I met a few of these men in Noumea. They were a remarkably non-flamboyant group.

John T. Mason, Jr.: What was their background, largely?

Admiral Colwell: As far as I know, they were planters and traders in the area, so that I would assume that they all had some knowledge of the local language or languages. Of course, pidgin English was sort of the universal language in the area. Everybody in the islands understood pidgin English. They had to know the locale that they were working from, the terrain. They obviously had to be accepted by the natives because they were strictly in their hands—their heads were in their hands.

John T. Mason, Jr.: So they may well have operated plantations on the islands where they served as coast watchers?

Admiral Colwell: I would suspect that almost without exception they were probably planters and traders. I can't verify that.

John T. Mason, Jr.: The ones you met?

Admiral Colwell: I didn't get to talk to them very much. They didn't talk about what they were doing. Their actual mode of operation, I guess everyone knows as much as I do about it. They remained hidden and they moved a lot. They had radios. They relied on the natives. Some were caught and killed.

John T. Mason, Jr.: Were the Japs fully aware of this system?

Admiral Colwell: Oh, I think so. I would be greatly surprised if they weren't trying very hard to use radio direction finders on them.

In fact, I guess it was on the island of Bougainville, I remember the Japs brought dogs to try and track down a particular coast watcher, and he was really on the run. An air strike went in there and by the greatest good fortune, he said, managed to hit the dog pen. He thanked us very much!

John T. Mason, Jr.: You say, Admiral, that you saw the dispatches that were sent in by the coast watchers. What was the gist of the information that they imparted?

Admiral Colwell: Well, of course, these were primarily of an operational intelligence nature. They might include such immediate information as ship movements—something is coming down the slot, and he might give information on what it was.

John T. Mason, Jr.: Were they good at ship identification?

Admiral Colwell: Oh, yes, if they could get a good look at it. Of course, so many of the movements were at night, especially after we began to build our own air power down there. They couldn't move very well in daylight, very close to us. But they might get some immediate information of that type. More likely, you would get some accumulated information, such as barge routes. At one time when the Japs were being very hard pressed, they were using barges, coming down from, I suppose, Bougainville and Rabaul to reinforce the Jap army on the upper end of Guadalcanal. And naturally it was very important to us to get those barges while they still had people in them, rather than on the way home, although we were happy to have them either way.

A coast watcher might send information on barge groups. Where do they hole up during daylight, how many of them are there, how big are they, are they well armed, are they escorted? This sort of information might be supplied by coast watchers, and was. Information on forces in place on a particular island. How many Jap forces are there, how well equipped, what do they have in the way of support, do they have large artillery or only small artillery? Tremendously useful operational intelligence.

John T. Mason, Jr.: Was there conversation with them by radio? Were questions put to them by radio?

Admiral Colwell: It was not a simultaneous back-and-forth conversation, as I recall. Specific questions might be asked. He probably wouldn't know the answer to that at any one time. He would simply receipt for the question, and then he'd get an answer back. I'm imagining some of this because, as I said, I didn't know too much about it except I saw the product.

Admiral Carney, I would guess, would have total recall on a lot of this. As chief of staff, he was privy to all of the intelligence details, which I was not, and I didn't need to be. We were operating under the proper form of need-to-know.

John T. Mason, Jr.: Something in the nature of a footnote. You spoke about pidgin English being used extensively and understood by all these natives, I take it, then, there was a uniformity to pidgin English?

Admiral Colwell: Yes. I understand that that's true. Here again, as far as I was concerned, this was all hearsay because I had no direct connection with it. I think it was widely understood, yes. What I'm saying is that pidgin English was very widely understood between the whites and the natives a sort of a universal language, like Swahili in some sections of Africa.

I had another rather interesting experience on the island of Espiritu Santo one time. I was there visiting, and down through the camp came a group of perhaps 10 or 12 young native boys, or young men, all clad in bright red loincloths. When I inquired what this was all about, it developed that these young men had come down from one of the villages up in the hills and were being shown around the camp. It was probably a local clergyman or someone who could speak to them—I don't know how this was worked out, but we used these bright red target sleeves for antiaircraft and aircraft practice, towed by aircraft. Well, they were absolutely fascinated with this bright red cloth, so they got a couple of old sleeves and they cut it up and gave each one of them a chunk of it, so they promptly put it on! The thing that fascinated them completely was flush toilets. They spent about half a day just flushing the toilet and watching the water come in and run out, flushing it again. They never had seen anything like that before.

We actually had rather minor contact with the natives on these islands, except that the mature men worked on the docks as stevedores. In Guadalcanal, when the Japs first went in there, they pretty much went back into the hills, went into hiding and all the women were taken away. They hid the women back in the mountains. As you went farther south and got down towards Noumea, for example, why, then, of course, they just continued their normal life. Many of the men worked on the docks as stevedores.

John T. Mason, Jr.: This was voluntary on their part?

Admiral Colwell: Oh, yes, and they were well paid. There's an interesting thing about that.

When we first went into Guadalcanal and wanted to hire the local men who had always worked in the plantations there—the coconut plantations—we had to send a rush order down to Australia for silver shillings, because that was the only way they would take pay. They knew what a silver shilling was. They didn't know what dollars were, at least not then, and you paid them in silver shillings or they didn't work. Well, they very rapidly found out what a dollar bill was and the price of things began to go up. I thought that was an interesting point when they first went in.

One of the Seabee items that became just indispensable down there was the 6 by 6 by 6 steel plate pontoon. We finally set up a factory near Noumea so that they could be shipped down in flat plate and we'd weld them into pontoon sections down at Noumea so that they didn't take up much room. But they were used for everything under the sun. We made floating docks of them, bridges over streams, particularly we made barges. These barges were really quite large and we put one, two, three, four of these great big outboard motors on them so that they were self-propelled. Then we'd take small ones, maybe about the size of this room, and put a couple of outboard motors on that and that would be a tug. You could either pull or push with it.

They became water stowage cisterns—everything under the sun, absolutely indispensable. Of course, they're still being used by the amphibious forces. This is what the causeways are made of that they use from the LSTs.[*]

John T. Mason, Jr.: Well, as things progressed and Guadalcanal became secure and so forth, and you began to pursue the Japs farther away, Noumea then became somewhat too far distant?

Admiral Colwell: Yes, and it became strictly a headquarters town. Of course, everything was done by radio anyway, so another few hundred miles didn't make any difference, and

---

[*] LST—tank landing ship, an amphibious warfare ship capable of putting her bow directly onto a beach, opening bow doors, and lowering a bow ramp to permit vehicles to exit.

the facilities were there—large communication facilities, large intelligence facilities, and adequate space for the operators and planners and logistics people to work.

A lot of people, I think, didn't like to believe that that was a sensible thing to do because it appeared that all of these high-level staff people were resting very comfortably a long way from the shooting. But it is very sensible because this is the way you run a war today, when you are widespread, communications are almost instantaneous; it is sensible.

John T. Mason, Jr.: Not only sensible, but wise, isn't it?

Admiral Colwell: Yes.

John T. Mason, Jr.: The mastermind in a war has to be safe from destruction!

Admiral Colwell: It actually becomes almost essential.

After the war moved farther west, then Halsey's staff was shaken down to an operational staff and it did go aboard ship, and he and Spruance alternated in the operational mode.* This, again, was forced. It became a matter of necessity, because they were then so far away that there wasn't any reasonable home base for them to work from. So that they did go aboard ship, and they had the Third Fleet and the Fifth Fleet. The fighters were the same, but the staffs were different.

During this period in the South Pacific it was quite sensible to keep the staff there in Noumea.

John T. Mason, Jr.: What contact did your people have with MacArthur and the staff he was building?†

Admiral Colwell: That was primarily pretty high level. This was admiral stuff. I had no

---

* Admiral Raymond A. Spruance, USN, served as Commander Fifth Fleet during the Central Pacific campaign in 1944-45. See Thomas B. Buell, The Quiet Warrior: A Biography of Admiral Raymond A. Spruance (Boston: Little, Brown, 1974).
† General Douglas MacArthur, USA, Commander Southwest Pacific Area and Force.

contact with him whatsoever. Operations had some contact when there was a need to coordinate operations, for instance. On the island of New Britain there was some coordination required there, just so we didn't bump into each other. For instance, if we wanted to send some ships up and do a little hammering around, we didn't want MacArthur's air force to start hammering our ships by mistake. That was about the size of it. We were pretty well separated by geography.

John T. Mason, Jr.: Was there any immediate relationship with our Anzac allies?[*]

Admiral Colwell: Yes. The New Zealanders had three or four small frigates or corvettes, or whatever you want to call them, which were attached to Halsey's forces and they operated in the south as antisubmarine units. One of them was actually named the Kiwi, as I recall.

John T. Mason, Jr.: That's right. She was.

Admiral Colwell: And she got a submarine, incidentally. She caught one on the surface, damaged it, and rammed it, and sank it. I got to know that little group. The captain must have weighed 300 pounds! A great ferocious beard. His executive officer was a little taller and not quite as big around, but a huge man. Then there was another man on board—he must have been the chief engineer—he was also huge, and then there was a little skinny guy, who was "George." He had all the odd jobs. They were a very tough group. When they went out on the town, stand back!

We also had on the staff a New Zealand liaison officer; of course, this is understandable because we had New Zealand forces. I don't recall that we had any Australians on the staff.

John T. Mason, Jr.: They were MacArthur-oriented?

---

[*] During World War II the Anzac area comprised the land and water areas of eastern Australia, New Zealand, British New Guinea, the Solomons, Loyalties, and Fijis.

Admiral Colwell: Yes. We had an Australian cruiser for a while, the Hobart. I think she got banged up in one of the battles.

John T. Mason, Jr.: I think you had a New Zealand cruiser, the Leander, also?

Admiral Colwell: That's right, we did. I forget. Maybe both of them got banged up.

We got supplies from our allies. In fact, we used to get New Zealand beef, and it was marvelous, very good indeed.

John T. Mason, Jr.: Food and things of that sort, not ammunition?

Admiral Colwell: No. All of our ammunition came from the States. One of the difficulties with integrating the Australian and New Zealand forces into our forces was the matter of ammunition supplies.

John T. Mason, Jr.: Different caliber guns?

Admiral Colwell: Different calibers, completely different. We used to stock some small amounts so that they could replenish. We pretty much left that up to them. Whatever they wanted to store, we'd store it.

Well, I've about run out of anecdotes, I guess.

John T. Mason, Jr.: Well, after a considerable period on Admiral Halsey's staff, you were given a destroyer of your own.

Admiral Colwell: Yes. I was very fortunate.

John T. Mason, Jr.: Was this something you sought?

J. B. Colwell, Interview #2 (5/22/73) – Page 67

Admiral Colwell: Actively. I was very fortunate to get command of the Converse.* Her skipper was taken ill and detached, so that the ship was temporarily under command of her executive officer. I'm not quite sure just how this happened. Undoubtedly, it had to be a recommendation by some of my superiors in the staff, up to the chief of staff, who was then Admiral Carney.

John T. Mason, Jr.: I take it you'd been making overtures for a command?

Admiral Colwell: Oh, yes, not officially but whenever I got a good opportunity, why, I'd put in a bid. I was doubly fortunate on this because at that time a destroyer command was considered to be something rather special, and people who were not well versed in destroyers, and recently so, had very little chance of getting a command. This changed later on when we got more of them. My last experience in destroyers had been quite some years before in old four-stackers, so I really was very fortunate to get this command.

The Converse was a member of Destroyer Squadron 23, which was Arleigh Burke's squadron of Little Beavers.† So I very proudly became a member of the Little Beavers. The Little Beaver Squadron was known throughout the South Pacific very favorably, and with a man like Burke in the driver's seat, you knew that you were going to get a lot of things to do, and we did.

John T. Mason, Jr.: For instance?

Admiral Colwell: Well, shortly after I'd taken command—I think I went up to Espiritu and went aboard the ship and took command.

John T. Mason, Jr.: On 7 January 1944.

---

* USS Converse (DD-509), a Fletcher-class destroyer, was commissioned 20 November 1942. She had a standard displacement of 2,050 tons, was 376 feet long, and 40 feet in the beam. Her top speed was 36 knots. She was armed with five 5-inch guns, ten 40-millimeter and seven 20-millimeter guns, and ten 21-inch torpedo tubes. She served during World War II and was decommissioned 23 April 1946.
† Captain Arleigh A. Burke, USN, was Commander Destroyer Squadron 23 in the Solomons during fighting there in 1943-44. He later served as Chief of Naval Operations from 1955 to 1961.

Admiral Colwell: That's correct. And after some brief training exercises in the Espiritu area, we went back to the Solomons, to an anchorage in Tulagi, and then immediately began a rather continuous series of operations from Tulagi up towards the Japanese positions.

While I had the ship we didn't develop any more sea battles of the type that had already taken place, for instance, up around Bougainville. We had a number of contacts with individual aircraft during that period in the Solomons. While I had command of <u>Converse</u> we never had any multiple raids—sort of catch-as-catch-can single aircraft contacts, and unfortunately we never succeeded in knocking any of those down. Fortunately they didn't succeed in hitting us, either.

We made two forays which were rather extensive. In one of these we went well up towards Truk. This was almost immediately after the very large U.S. raid on the island of Truk, which had pretty well decimated their forces. We ran up that way, and the objective there was to intercept any reinforcements that might be on their way up from Rabaul. We actually did intercept one ship, which we sank, and got back some survivors.

John T. Mason, Jr.: A transport ship?

Admiral Colwell: A small transport, I would guess. This was later identified by intelligence people as a tug. It wasn't a tug. I got a good enough look at it before it sank, and it wasn't a tug. I'd say a small transport was right, and it had aboard quite a number of aviation personnel who were on their way to Truk. On the way back, we bombarded Kavieng for about an hour and gave it a pretty good pounding.

We then went back into Tulagi, refueled, re-ammunitioned, because we were almost empty, and went back and gave Kavieng another going-over about four days later, as I recall. In the meantime, they'd been practicing.

John T. Mason, Jr.: You mean the Japs had been practicing?

Admiral Colwell: They'd been practicing, and it wasn't quite as much fun that time, but we were not hit. It was after that that I got my first medal.

John T. Mason, Jr.: Had you known Burke before you joined up with this task force?

Admiral Colwell: No.

John T. Mason, Jr.: How did he operate with his skippers?

Admiral Colwell: Oh, very closely indeed. He always explained exactly what he planned to do, wanted to know whether there were any suggestions, usually making it clear that the fewer the better.

John T. Mason, Jr.: The fewer suggestions?

Admiral Colwell: The fewer suggestions, and he didn't want to hear any objections, either. He thought these things out very carefully and way beyond. This first run, for example, up towards Truk and back, unsupported, he had five destroyers. On the face of it, it looked as though it might be a pretty tough mission, but it turned out it wasn't.

John T. Mason, Jr.: Truk was supposed to be a Jap bastion.

Admiral Colwell: He knew that Truk had just taken a pasting and that they weren't going to be so powerful. He knew that. He was a great guy to work for. We'd come in from a run and take our turns at the fueling piers or barges to get filled up.

John T. Mason, Jr.: This was at Tulagi?

Admiral Colwell: This was Tulagi. While this was going on, he'd send a message over: "There is coffee in the flagship." And we'd go over and tell him anything that had been occurring that he didn't already know, which usually was nothing.

John T. Mason, Jr.: A kind of post mortem!

Admiral Colwell: We'd have a little post mortem and, as likely as not, he'd tell us what the next operation was going to be and how soon we were going—and it probably was going to be that night.

John T. Mason, Jr.: Burke explained things well, you say?

Admiral Colwell: Yes. After he got to be CNO, a number of people used to complain that he was not very articulate. He tended to rush his words and sentences so that they didn't come out in beautiful grammar at all, and sometimes they were rather hard to figure out. This was true even of his congressional testimony, because I used to have to correct some of it. But during the war, in that destroyer squadron, there was never any doubt about what he wanted you to do. He explained things very carefully, and you were expected to get it the first time.

He commanded loyalty to an extreme. I would say everybody in his ships felt it. One young man I heard express himself by saying he felt that Commodore Burke was responsible for keeping us all alive. He was a great guy to go to sea with.

John T. Mason, Jr.: His natural ability as a leader!

Admiral Colwell: Yes.

John T. Mason, Jr.: And his daring, I suppose.

Admiral Colwell: Oh, I should say! Daring is right.

John T. Mason, Jr.: I've noticed in him another quality and that's almost a transparent honesty and integrity, which is a compelling factor too.

Admiral Colwell: I think that's true.

After that first run up to Truk and Kavieng, we came in and, of course, everybody was exhausted.

John T. Mason, Jr.: Were we thinking in those days of taking the island of Truk?

Admiral Colwell: I don't think so. I don't think anybody felt it was necessary.

We got in from that and were refueling and taking on ammunition, and Burke sent for all of us to meet him up at a little officers' club over on the beach—he sent for us to meet him up there, where the press was waiting. This was the first time I had ever been interviewed by the press and I was properly impressed. We just talked to these people and it was a very pleasant social occasion.

I remember one of them was asking us where we were from, all of the various skippers. One of them said he was from Pipestone, Montana, and then my turn came and I said I was from Pawnee, Nebraska. The fellow said, "My God, no wonder they call you the Little Beavers. You're all Indians!"

John T. Mason, Jr.: This title was because of your intense activity?

Admiral Colwell: Yes, and the cartoonist who drew the strip with Little Beaver in it—did you ever know this cartoon strip?[*] Well, Little Beaver was a little Indian boy about that high, and he was sort of an undersized aide to Red Ryder. So that's the Little Beaver, and he drew for Admiral Burke a big color sketch of Little Beaver and sent it to him. That's how come they came to be named the Little Beavers after he got that. I believe that it was

---

[*] Fred Harman (1902-1982) was one of the country's foremost painters of the American West. He was also the creator of the cartoon strip, "Red Ryder and Little Beaver."

the receipt of this thing that brought on the name, rather than vice versa.

John T. Mason, Jr.: I see.

Admiral Colwell: But this happened before I ever got to the squadron, so I'm not sure about that. You might ask Burke.

And then we had this picture of Little Beaver copied and painted on all of our bridge structures. Every squadron had an insignia. I guess they still do.

John T. Mason, Jr.: I suppose Tokyo Rose used this in some way too?[*]

Admiral Colwell: Probably. I don't know.

The time that I had in Converse was a most enjoyable period.

John T. Mason, Jr.: It was a period of eight months.

Admiral Colwell: Only eight months, that's right.

John T. Mason, Jr.: Was there any R&R in those eight months?

Admiral Colwell: No.

John T. Mason, Jr.: It was constant operations?

Admiral Colwell: Constant operations. We quickly moved from the Solomons out to the west. We went first to Majuro, and then to Eniwetok. We then went on to Saipan, Iwo Jima, Guam, parts of all of those operations.

---

[*] "Tokyo Rose" was the nickname of an English-speaking Japanese woman who made radio broadcasts during World War II. Full of Japanese war propaganda, they were aimed at U.S. servicemen in an attempt to demoralize them. For the most part, she was entertaining rather than effective.

J. B. Colwell, Interview #2 (5/22/73) – Page 73

John T. Mason, Jr.: When did you lose Burke from this command?

Admiral Colwell: As I remember, we lost Burke just about the time we left Solomons. He may have taken us as far as Majuro, but I rather doubt it. I think he was transferred to his new job at sea and made a commodore.

John T. Mason, Jr.: He was transferred at sea with Mitscher.*

Admiral Colwell: Yes, and we got a new squadron commander.

John T. Mason, Jr.: During the time you were with the Converse and the Little Beavers did you lose any of your units?

Admiral Colwell: No. In fact, we never had one hit. Some ships in the squadron had been hit before I joined the squadron. In fact, there was one of them that never did come back to us, I think. For some time we operated with five ships because one of them was having serious boiler trouble or something. Converse was never hit. She hadn't been hit before I got there, although she had a couple of bent plates from a near miss by a bomb. All the time I had her until I left her she never had a man hurt from any enemy action.

John T. Mason, Jr.: Did you serve as escorts or a task force? I mean escort of convoys?

Admiral Colwell: After we left the Solomons where we operated just as a group of destroyers primarily—

John T. Mason, Jr.: Marauders!

---

* In March 1944 Burke became chief of staff to Vice Admiral Marc A. Mitscher, USN, who was Commander Task Force 58, the Fast Carrier Task Force.

Admiral Colwell: Yes, that's right. Occasionally we went out with our papas, who were a division of cruisers and they sort of took care of us when they came in. Admiral Merrill had the division.* We went out with them occasionally, but usually it was just the destroyers.

After we left the Solomons and started west, then we became an integral part of the Fast Carrier Task Force and worked with various groups. One time, as I recall, we went out of Majuro and headed back up towards Pearl to reinforce the screen of a new group coming down—some new carriers and new destroyers. We went out to reinforce the screen. I almost got rammed one night.

After we left Majuro and went out to Eniwetok—and, of course, this was the preparatory period for the assault in the Western Pacific, beginning with Saipan.† We were with the Fast Carrier Task Forces throughout this passage and the initial assault up there. We made one run up to the Bonins for air strikes on the Bonins.‡ We were part of the escort, then came back to Saipan. We made one individual attack on Guam, a bombardment attack by destroyers and cruisers. This was the first attack on Guam.

John T. Mason, Jr.: Was that well fortified by the Japs?

Admiral Colwell: Not particularly. In fact, we were coasting around well within range of some of their antiaircraft guns. They were up on a cliff. We could see them, and they never tried to shoot us. They kept them pointed up all the time. Maybe they wouldn't depress that far, I don't know. We did some damage there, in the harbor of Guam. Of course, that wasn't laid on originally because I guess we hoped to get it intact, but there wasn't a great deal there—a little oil storage, an airfield.

Then we were with one of the elements of Task Force 58 for the Battle of the Philippine Sea—the first day, which was the big day of action.§ The second day was the pursuit and, by that time, our entire group was low on fuel, so we were sent over to the eastern side to fuel, and we did not participate the second day. We didn't see very many

---

* Rear Admiral Aaron S. Merrill, USN, Commander Cruiser Division 12.
† The preparatory attack on Saipan was on 12 June 1944.
‡ The strike on the Bonins was on 15 June 1944.
§ This battle, in the vicinity of the Marianas Islands, was on 19-20 June 1944.

Jap planes that first day. The aircraft took care of them so magnificently that we saw very few.

One came through the screen on our group, alone, a single plane, and from a distance—he was low—he looked like one of our fighters, and it appeared as though he was coming in to land for fuel, ammunition, and whatever. He made a long landing approach on the carrier, and as soon as he got close enough we could see he was a Jap, so everybody started shooting at him as much as they could. We were pretty well restricted because you'd shoot a little bit, and then would be one of your own ships in the way and you'd have to wait. Nobody hit him. He came right up to the fantail of this carrier, and everybody was just waiting for him to lay an egg in the middle of the flight deck. He got up to the fantail, cut out to the side, flew up alongside, dropped his bomb in the water, did no damage, and then started flying away. The aircraft caught him out on the edge of the screen and shot him down.

Why he decided to do that, having already committed himself to an attacking run—he gave it up at the last moment and dropped his bomb in the water.

John T. Mason, Jr.: Was he possibly a kamikaze type who changed his mind?

Admiral Colwell: I don't know. He may have been.

John T. Mason, Jr.: But he lost his life, anyway!

Admiral Colwell: Yes, he was shot down.

John T. Mason, Jr.: Did the Converse have more modern radar equipment than what you first knew when you went out to the South Pacific?

Admiral Colwell: Oh, yes. We had good radar. We had three. We had an air-search radar which, incidentally, went out of action about the time we left Eniwetok. The gears bound on it so that it wouldn't turn, but there were so many other air-search radars in the task force that it didn't really make any difference. At least that's what I told the admiral when he asked me if I wanted to stay there or go back and join somebody else. I said, "No, I'll stay, thank you." Then, we had a good fire-control radar for the 5-inch battery, and we had a good surface-search radar. We were pretty well outfitted for those tasks. In fact, they don't do an awful lot better today.

After we'd been out in this area for a time our relief showed up. By this time Converse and her sisters had been out of the States for something over two years of almost continuous running, and they were all due for overhaul. I had only one ship service generator running, so whenever we went to general quarters, which was most of the time, I'd put one half of the ship on the generator that was left and put the other half on diesel. Our search radar was out. We were all—

John T. Mason, Jr.: Limping!

Admiral Colwell: Limping We were badly in need of overhaul.

John T. Mason, Jr.: What about the problem of barnacles?

Admiral Colwell: We were slowed down; we were dirty. The engines needed overhaul. We had steam leaks all over everywhere and so on. We needed new guns. They'd been doing shore bombardment so much that the guns were getting close to the limit.

So we were relieved and started for home. We stopped off in Eniwetok and left off almost all of our ammunition because we weren't going to need it, and picked up a small convoy of transports. I suppose they were probably carrying wounded, I don't know. But we picked up this small convoy of transports, took them back to Pearl and stayed for a couple of days, and then went on to San Francisco.

John T. Mason, Jr.: During that period in Pearl, did the commander-in-chief come on board?

Admiral Colwell: No, he did not. I guess we really only stayed there one afternoon. I remember we were parked way over in one of the back areas that was just an absolute fright to get into. It took us about an hour to get turned around and back into this awful spot.

John T. Mason, Jr.: Did you feel battle weary?

Admiral Colwell: I did when I got through with that. I thought they could have found us a better place since we were only going to stay one afternoon anyway.

John T. Mason, Jr.: What was the state of the men on board, after that long tour of duty?

Admiral Colwell: I don't know, I guess maybe "gung ho" is about as good an expression as any. They were always ready for whatever was coming up.

Just before we got back into Pearl I issued an order that there would be no beards going ashore.

John T. Mason, Jr.: There had been beards on board?

Admiral Colwell: Oh, yes, and some of them quite luxuriant. Two or three of them were a little unhappy about that, I heard. They just wanted to show them to their wives probably!

John T. Mason, Jr.: What was your reason? It was not covered in the Navy Regs, was it?

Admiral Colwell: No, I just thought that they ought to go ashore looking as sharp as we could make them, not like they'd been living out in the boondocks. It may have been a mistake. Maybe it was my own youth!

John T. Mason, Jr.: Anyway, they obeyed?

Admiral Colwell: They didn't have any beards going ashore. They all looked sharp.

I remember we had an anchor pool coming in to San Francisco. Everybody put in so much, and this was a pretty good one.[*] It was a $500.00 pool. One of the chiefs won it, and he was on his way home to be married. So I figured that that was poetic justice, or something—some kind of justice.

At any rate, I took Converse into the Navy yard in San Francisco, went home on leave, and while I was at home I was informed that I was to be relieved and go to shore duty.

John T. Mason, Jr.: Well, this was what you expected?

Admiral Colwell: Yes, it was. I'd been at sea since 1939 and this was almost five years. So I trotted myself back out to San Francisco just long enough to read my orders and hand over the keys to my relief, then came back to Washington.

That was a very happy time out in the Western Pacific. We had a fine cruise. A great bunch of people.

John T. Mason, Jr.: I suppose there's always one command that is the favorite one. Was this it?

Admiral Colwell: This was my first one, so I suppose maybe that was it. Yes! My first command, a destroyer in wartime! Nothing could beat it, and nobody got hurt. That makes it even better. I had a great bunch of people. Admiral Ray Peet was my gunnery officer, now a vice admiral—very smart, very sharp.[†] I had an excellent executive officer. My communications officer and general quarters officer of the deck was a Philadelphia lawyer and he was unbelievably good.

---

[*] An anchor pool is an arrangement in which crew members bet on the expected time that the ship will anchor or moor. The individual whose bet is closest to the actual time wins the pool.
[†] The oral history of Vice Admiral Raymond E. Peet, USN (Ret.), is in the Naval Institute collection and contains his own recollections of service in the Converse.

John T. Mason, Jr.: Reserve?

Admiral Colwell: Yes.

John T. Mason, Jr.: What percentage of your men were reserve?

Admiral Colwell: All, but three. The exec and Peet and I were the three, and the rest were all reserves, and we had about 20, I guess.

John T. Mason, Jr.: Sorry I interrupted you. You were about to tell me about the Philadelphia lawyer.

Admiral Colwell: It's just that he was so good. He was tremendous. I'd like to run into him again, a wonderful Irishman. He loved to tell what he thought were dialect stories, and he was a terrible storyteller.

Another officer I had was Barney Levin, who is a lawyer in Norfolk, and I understand that he is largely responsible for getting the Virginia law changed so that you can buy liquor by the drink in Virginia.

That was a good outfit.

John T. Mason, Jr.: And I assume they all got shoreside billets, or most of them.

Admiral Colwell: I guess I was the only one that left at that time. I think so, and they all went back to the war. Ray Peet went to another assignment. He'd been the exec in the Converse.

We were getting some changes then because more and more new ships were coming off the line all the time, and they were draining off people who had some experience in order to leaven new crews. As far as I know, they all lived through it.

John T. Mason, Jr.: Well, you came back to Washington and then to the Naval Proving Ground?

Admiral Colwell: Yes. I was assigned to the Bureau of Ordnance, being an ordnance postgraduate. I was detailed there but stayed only a very short time because a man at the proving ground had a chance to go to London. There was a third man involved in this, who wanted the job that I had here in Washington, and I wanted the job that the other gent had already in Dahlgren, so we made the three-way exchange musical of chairs. So I was only here as little as two or three weeks, I've forgotten.

John T. Mason, Jr.: What was your job intended to be here?

Admiral Colwell: It was somewhere in the production end in fire control, sort of a medium-grade position. I wasn't very enchanted with the idea, whereas Dahlgren really appealed to me, where you could get into the business of why things did what they did, because the job was assistant experimental officer. This just appealed to me.

John T. Mason, Jr.: This was for new stuff?

Admiral Colwell: It was a very happy change for me because I loved my tour at Dahlgren. I was there two and a half years, and it was just a great time. Again, something never dull, something different every day.

John T. Mason, Jr.: I would think considerably enriched because of your background with the fleet?

Admiral Colwell: Oh, yes. Of course, this was true of all of your ordnance PGs. Almost without exception, we would be in ordnance and gunnery in the fleet, and then you would come back ashore with that experience to work with. This is the way the thing is designed, and they expected that you would get not less than two tours—ordnance tours—ashore.

This sometimes worked to people's disadvantage, if they got more than two, because they would get so slotted in that when selection time came around this would turn out to be a disadvantage, no matter how good a job you'd done or how good a job you would have.

John T. Mason, Jr.: Then you'd become a victim of the system!

Admiral Colwell: You became a victim of the system, that's right. I was able to escape the system, but I thoroughly enjoyed my tour in Dahlgren. There was something to seize your interest every day, particularly in the experimental department where I was.

One of the things that we worked on down there, and I didn't even know what it was, had to do with the fuzing, for the first atomic bomb. We were dropping these pieces of equipment into the river and taking measurements on how much travel they had, where they went off, and all this sort of thing. I didn't know what was going on. They were labeled as the Michigan fuzes then, or something.

John T. Mason, Jr.: But what they were to be attached to?

Admiral Colwell: I just assumed that they were something for a bomb! But that was something I didn't need to know and nobody ever bothered to tell me, and I didn't ask Most of this stuff was not that exotic.

John T. Mason, Jr.: What were some of the things that you tested?

Admiral Colwell: We had one installation down there called the Armor and Projectile Laboratory, and it was a laboratory where experimental work was done on various types of armoring substances, not necessarily steel. They were able to put all sorts of physical tests on steel plate, aluminum plate, ceramics, bullet-proof glass, mattresses, you name it. We had our own enclosed firing range where we could bang this stuff with smaller-caliber stuff.

We did experiments on very-high-velocity pellets. We could shoot a ball-bearing pellet 4,000 or 5,000 feet per second. We ran, oh, just practically a continuing series of experiments on bomb shapes, controlled fragmentation cases. The same thing for projectiles.

We ran the shelf-life tests on VT fuzes, and for the early ones it was very short. One of the prime difficulties in the South Pacific was the VT fuzes. You'd barely get the things in the area and get them loaded aboard ship, and you'd run out of shelf life, just through travel time. These were the types of growing pains that you expected in new ordnance, and people found out how to make batteries that would live longer, and today, why, you can have all the shelf life you want.

What else did we do? All sorts of aircraft ordnance experiments. Better bomb racks, explosive devices to eject things from bomb racks so that they wouldn't hang up and they wouldn't freeze up. What kind of lubrication can you get that will permit a .50-caliber or a 20-millimeter machine gun to operate in an aircraft when it's 60 degrees below? Ordinary grease freezes up just as hard as it can be, and then it won't fire. Maybe it will fire once. This sort of thing.

John T. Mason, Jr.: I take it some of this was general research, really, general experimentation, wasn't it, without any specific project in mind?

Admiral Colwell: We had both kinds. For instance, some of the armor projectile work was in the nature of not what the scientists would call fundamental research. It was exploratory.

Then we'd get specific assignments.

John T. Mason, Jr.: Like the VT fuze?

Admiral Colwell: Yes. The same thing is true of most of your ordnance laboratories today. It's a proper division of effort.

John T. Mason, Jr.: How closely did you work with the boys in the Bureau of Ordnance?

Admiral Colwell: Very closely. We were back and forth and on the phone all the time.

John T. Mason, Jr.: Did you have latitude in that you could experiment in certain areas yourself simply because you had an idea that might develop something?

Admiral Colwell: Oh, yes. Or as much as you had time for. The assigned tasks usually kept you pretty busy. But we had some latitude.

John T. Mason, Jr.: This was in the days of George Hussey, was it not?[*]

Admiral Colwell: Yes, and Malcolm Schoeffel.[†]

John T. Mason, Jr.: Did the testing process take you to the fleet too?

Admiral Colwell: We had ordnancemen who would go out to the fleet on specific problems. For example, if we had a gun mount that malfunctioned, we would send people out, and they still do, to try and determine exactly what the problem was. But then they would come back and the proving ground then would try and develop some way to fix the problem.

A slightly different kind of thing. Suppose you had a gun explosion, which we did have and still have from time to time. The first object is to determine what caused the explosion. Was it a mount malfunction, was it a ammunition malfunction, and so forth? It could be lots of different things. Then, having determined to some degree of satisfaction what had probably caused it, you would design a whole series of tests at the proving ground and try and duplicate it precisely. This would prove, then, what caused it, and then

---

[*] Rear Admiral George F. Hussey, Jr., USN, served as Chief of the Bureau of Ordnance from December 1943 to September 1947. He was promoted to vice admiral as of December 1945.
[†] Rear Admiral Malcolm F. Schoeffel, USN, served as Assistant/Deputy Chief of the Bureau of Ordnance, 1946-48. His oral history is in the Naval Institute collection.

you could design a remedy. This sort of thing still goes on.

We had a series of gun explosions off Vietnam and they had to go through this same process until they found it.

John T. Mason, Jr.: Newport News?

Admiral Colwell: Yes. Now, that one was different. These others were 5-inch. They found what the problem was, and it was an ammunition problem, later fixed. The Newport News had a bad 8-inch gun explosion.* I haven't heard the final on that.

John T. Mason, Jr.: Lloyd Mustin wrote the report.

Admiral Colwell: Yes, and as far as I know, they think they know what caused it. I haven't been in on that particular thing. Chief Masterson and Lloyd Mustin were the expert investigators on that.†

John T. Mason, Jr.: You were there, at the Naval Proving Ground, when ComTEvFor came into being with Admiral Willis Lee, were you not?‡

Admiral Colwell: I don't think so. Let me see. I left there in the spring of 1947, and I don't think OpTEvFor was in yet. It may have been.

John T. Mason, Jr.: I'd have to check that out, but it seems to me that as you explain what you did at the Naval Proving Ground there was a certain redundancy in what this new setup was to accomplish, knowing about what you were doing at the proving ground?

---

* At 1:10 A.M. on 1 October 1972, while the heavy cruiser Newport News (CA-148) was on a firing mission off the coast of Vietnam, a faulty 8-inch projectile detonated prematurely in the center gun of turret two. The shells in the powder train leading up from the magazine burned rapidly, and consumed the air supply. All told, 20 men were killed as a result of the incident.

† Vice Admiral Kleber S. Masterson, USN (Ret.); Vice Admiral Lloyd M. Mustin, USN. The oral histories of both are in the Naval Institute collection.

‡ In the summer of 1945 Vice Admiral Willis A. Lee, Jr., USN, commanded Task Force 69, which conducted anti-kamikaze operational tests in Casco Bay, Maine. The force evolved into the Operational Development Force and was later renamed Operational Test and Evaluation Force (OpTEvFor).

Admiral Colwell: No, I would think not, because looking at the experimental side, at the Proving Ground, this had to do solely with pieces of equipment, whereas in OpTEvFor they had to do with the operation of the total equipment, or a total system, or tactics for a system, and, this sort of thing is additional to what we did at the proving ground.

John T. Mason, Jr.: More sophisticated in its approach?

Admiral Colwell: Well, it's operational, whereas what we did at the proving ground had strictly to do with hardware.

John T. Mason, Jr.: And yet you said certain of your men went out to the fleet.

Admiral Colwell: Oh, well, that would not be in terms of experiment. That would be in terms of trying to solve a specific hardware problem, a design problem.

OpTEvFor will take a complete equipment. Let's take it from the other end. Say we have a new gun mount, and it goes to the proving ground. There, they wring it out and find out if it will fire as many rounds as it is supposed to. Does it have any pieces that tend to break easily? If so, they'll work with the designer and manufacturer to try and get redesign and get it fixed. Then, after it is certified from a hardware point of view, it will go to OpTEvFor, and they will design a new series of tests which are intended to prove or disprove its utility in its assigned role—that is, will it put the bullets near an aircraft target in a shipboard environment, does it interact properly with its fire-control system, can you do shore bombardment with it?

Now, at the proving ground they find out what the pattern of a group of five shots is under proving ground conditions from a single gun. Maybe you give OpTEvFor two or three of them and mount them in a ship, and now what did you feel. It's this difference.

John T. Mason, Jr.: I thank you for the clarification.

Admiral Colwell: There was some new equipment that came down to the proving ground for initial tests while I was there. I actually had no personal part in these tests, except that being on the ground I watched these things happen.

One item, for example, was what we called a Mark 102 rocket launcher, which was an automatic launcher for 5-inch, fin-stabilized rockets. Incidentally, it had been designed and built in a very short time by the gun factory here in Washington. This thing showed up, and I took a look at it and I said, "Boy, that thing will never in this world shoot," but it shot the first time, just exactly the way it was advertised to shoot.

John T. Mason, Jr.: Even the experts can be wrong!

Admiral Colwell: Yes. The Navy went ahead and built quite a number of them, and they were installed in batteries on small ships, which were LSM hulls.[*] You remember the LSM?

John T. Mason, Jr.: Yes.

Admiral Colwell: And these were called LSMRs—LSM, rocket. They performed very nicely. The rockets had a max range of about 5,000 yards, but they would lay down a terrific barrage in an amphibious landing.

Another piece of hardware that came down and was just a magnificent design was the 8-inch automatic, rapid-fire gun which went into the turrets in the Newport News class, which is one of the finest ships we've ever built, a beautiful piece of ordnance.[†] That first one came down for a test and, although it's an extremely complex mount with lots of interlocks and so forth, it performed quite well at the very outset. It had bugs in it, yes, just as you would expect.

---

[*] LSM—medium landing ship, a type of craft used for amphibious landings, generally used to carry troops to an invasion beachhead and put them ashore on ramps at the bow of the vessel.

[†] The class comprised USS Des Moines (CA-134), USS Salem (CA-139), and USS Newport News (CA-148), all commissioned in 1948-49. The were armed with rapid-fire 8-inch guns in which the powder came in a single brass casing, rather than being in silk bags as was the case with previous 8-inch cruiser guns.

John T. Mason, Jr.: Is this the one that exploded?

Admiral Colwell: One of those, that exploded, that's right. The entire turret—you shove ammunition in at the bottom and turn the switch on "on," and it just starts shooting, and it shoots at about eight rounds a minute. A ship full of those is an extremely powerful weapon. It's a beautiful piece of machinery.

John T. Mason, Jr.: Was the proving ground doing any testing for foreign navies, allied navies?

Admiral Colwell: Not that I recall. I don't believe we did. I don't have any recollection of that.

John T. Mason, Jr.: Even though it's labeled a "naval" proving ground, the interrelationship with the other services is obvious. Were there any pertaining to aircraft, the Army Air Force, at that time, which got involved with the Naval Proving Ground?

Admiral Colwell: Only to the extent that a particular piece of ordnance might be used by both Army Air Corps and Navy aircraft. We did a lot of work with aircraft ordnance, but primarily Navy. It was only where a piece of ordnance might be used by both.

We did have a continuing exchange of information with the Aberdeen Proving Ground.

John T. Mason, Jr.: Like Good Housekeeping, you put a seal of approval on some of these things, and then were they turned over for manufacture?

Admiral Colwell: Oh, yes.

John T. Mason, Jr.: Did you have any surveillance duties in terms of manufacture?

Admiral Colwell: No, that was a matter for the Naval Inspection Service. We had no responsibility for quality control or anything of that nature. Once the proving ground said It would shoot, then it was presumably ready to manufacture.

Today, you have the OpTEvFor group inserted in the middle of that chain, so that they have to say it's ready for service use.

John T. Mason, Jr.: After the proving ground?

Admiral Colwell: After the proving ground turns it over and they say it'll shoot. And they frequently find things that have not been found before.

John T. Mason, Jr.: Under a different set of circumstances?

Admiral Colwell: Under different circumstances. Under operational conditions. You have very controlled conditions at the proving ground. In OpTEvFor, they're operational conditions and different people with different levels of competence taking care of this equipment. Maybe it doesn't work for them and some additional design changes must be made.

So it actually results in better equipment going to sea.

John T. Mason, Jr.: It seems to me that this is a step that in the civilian world isn't always attended to. I mean the product comes out and is operated by different people and it doesn't stand up the way it was intended.

Admiral Colwell: Well, take an automotive proving ground, for example. I've never been on one. I don't know how they operate, but unless they introduce into their proving ground operations this sort of man-in-the-street driving an automobile and taking care of it and so forth, they're not going to find out whether they've got a good product or not. Because their proving ground drivers and their proving ground maintenance men are real pros. I don't know whether they do that or not. You're not going to find all the bugs, but your average garden variety of automobile driver will break it if it can be broken.

Interview Number 3 with Vice Admiral John Barr Colwell, U.S. Navy (Retired)

Place: Admiral Colwell's apartment in Washington, D.C.

Date: Thursday, 14 June 1973

Interviewer: John T. Mason, Jr.

John T. Mason, Jr.: Good to see you on this fine morning, sir. I think you had an addendum to the chapter on the proving ground?

Admiral Colwell: I think possibly I might just add one thing. The people I worked with at the proving ground were highly intelligent people and extremely knowledgeable in this ordnance field. It therefore was a great opportunity for me to be taught.

John T. Mason, Jr.: They were all uniformed people, were they?

Admiral Colwell: Not entirely, and even some of those who were in uniform were in uniform only for the duration. There were such people as Dr. Bramble, who had been my mathematics instructor at the postgraduate school, and Dr. Sawyer from the University of Michigan. Such people as that, extremely bright people.

John T. Mason, Jr.: Scientists?

Admiral Colwell: Scientific types, and these people were tremendous instructors without intending to be so, perhaps, in logical thinking and attempting to view things from all sides as much as possible and thus avoid premature conclusions.

John T. Mason, Jr.: You'd already achieved that ability, had you not?

Admiral Colwell: To some extent, but I don't think that I had achieved real maturity in thinking yet. This was a great opportunity. It was not only a privilege but a great pleasure to know these people, these scientists.

That's about all I had to add.

John T. Mason, Jr.: None of these people were anti-militaristic, were they?

Admiral Colwell: Oh, heavens, no. Dr. Bramble, for example, was a captain in the Naval Reserve. Dr. Sawyer was at that time a commander and later became, I believe, a commodore. That must have been during the first atomic tests in the Pacific after the war.

John T. Mason, Jr.: Well, sir, after you left the proving ground you got an assignment as executive officer on the Navy's premier ship, did you not?

Admiral Colwell: Yes, I did, and that was a pure delight. I was executive officer of the Missouri for 18 months under two magnificent commanding officers, and I just enjoyed every minute of it.* It was a great job.

My first commanding officer in the Missouri was Robert L. Dennison.† As you know, he progressed up the line to four stars, and he and I have maintained contact to some extent over the years and have remained close friends. I value his friendship very highly. I think Admiral Dennison is certainly one of the most capable senior officers that I've ever known—a splendid mind and tremendous common sense, a very logical thinker. He, incidentally, is a Ph.D. in engineering, as you probably know.

John T. Mason, Jr.: He combines, it seems to me, all these abilities, intellectual abilities, with a very charming personality.

Admiral Colwell: I have found it so. He has, as you might expect, very little time for dull people and slow thinkers. But he has a delightful sense of humor and, well, we're good

---

* USS Missouri (BB-63) was commissioned 11 June 1944. She had a standard displacement of 45,000 tons and full-load displacement of 57,600 tons. She was 887 feet long and 108 feet in the beam. Her top speed was 33 knots. Initially she was armed with nine 16-inch guns, 20 5-inch guns, and 80 40-mm guns in quad mounts, and 49 20-mm guns in single mounts. She was best known as the site of the Japanese surrender in September 1945.
† Captain Robert L. Dennison, USN, commanded the Missouri from 2 April 1947 to 23 January 1948. His oral history is in the Naval Institute collection.

friends, and I value his friendship.

My second commanding officer in the Missouri was James Thach, who later became a vice admiral, then was stricken and has been dead now some years.* He was a brother to John Thach, who was also known as Jimmy Thach.

John T. Mason, Jr.: I know, and how confusing it is! He's a four-star admiral.

Admiral Colwell: Yes, that's right. James Thach was the older one, and possibly that's why John Thach was also called Jimmy.† I don't know. At any rate, they were both splendid commanding officers.

We got along very well. The ship, I think, got along well. We had some very interesting cruises. Assuredly, the most interesting one was the one that we made to Rio when Admiral Dennison was the commanding officer.‡ We were the host ship, the entertaining ship, during the presence of President Truman and his personal family and his official family in Rio for the signing of the Inter-American Defense Treaty.§

John T. Mason, Jr.: Tell me about some of your recollections of that visit to Rio.

Admiral Colwell: I guess the first one was on entry. We came in fairly early in the morning, and the harbor of Rio is a very large one. As we were proceeding up the harbor, I was conning the ship into the anchorage.** This was something that Admiral Dennison did; we always took turns and it happened to be my turn. I was conning the ship in, we had a pilot, and, as we worked our way up towards the anchorage, I would check the chart and he'd sort of put his finger down and say, "Well, you can put it down in there wherever

---
* Captain James H. Thach, Jr., USN, commanded the Missouri from 24 February 1948 to 5 February 1949. He died 4 July 1962.
† The explanation for the younger brother's nickname is in the Naval Institute oral history of Admiral John S. Thach, USN (Ret.).
‡ The Missouri was a Rio de Janeiro, Brazil, from 30 August through 8 September 1947.
§ Harry S. Truman served as President of the United States from 12 April 1945 to 20 January 1953. His daughter Margaret was the sponsor of the ship, which she christened at the time of launching on 29 January 1944.
** The individual with the conn—normally an officer—directs the ship's movements in course and speed.

you like." I noticed there was a ferry crossing, and there were a great many merchantmen in this general area that he kept pointing at.

I questioned him about this, "Shouldn't we choose another spot?"

There seemed to be lots of space in there, and he said, "No, you go ahead and put your ship where you want it. They'll move," and they did.

John T. Mason, Jr.: The question was would they move in time!

Admiral Colwell: Oh, yes, they didn't sit around at all. They just up-anchored and moved, just as he said they would. That was my first introduction.

We, of course, established a shore patrol, as is customary, but prior to our arrival, as we later learned, the police had rounded up 1,200 or so known thieves, pickpockets, criminals of all types, and simply put them in jail for safety while we were there. So we had no incidents of any kind. It worked well.

John T. Mason, Jr.: You had a model crew going ashore!

Admiral Colwell: Yes! There were numerous entertainments, of course while we were there—luncheons, evening entertainment, various kinds. Several of us were given Brazilian decorations at a very large formal luncheon at the Brazilian Naval Club; I believe that was the name of it. We entertained as host ship for the ambassador at a very large reception on board the Missouri. The ambassador, of course, furnished the guest list and invited all of the guests. There were many, many of them. It was a big outfit. He sent out card tables and chairs and palm trees and all sorts of things, and we prepared food.

John T. Mason, Jr.: And no spike in the punch?

Admiral Colwell: No spiked punch, that's right. The Brazilians like to eat, and they like sweets, so we had a very large buffet table and they enjoyed it. It was good.

At one time we had on board the two presidents, President Truman and the President of Brazil.* I think by actual account at that time we had 17 ambassadors on board. Of course, all of these people got salutes as they arrived. And innumerable generals and admirals of assorted varieties. It was quite a day, and it went off very well indeed.

One day, which must have been a Sunday, I suppose, a couple of us were invited to be the guests of some of the local people to drive up to Quitandiuba, which is Petropolis, a summer resort for the people of Rio, where it gets awfully hot. A huge hotel had been built up there, and the primary attraction was to have been a very large gambling room. Well, when the hotel was about 99% complete, the President passed a new law that there wouldn't be any more gambling, which sort of slowed down the activity at the hotel. It was a lovely hotel. We had lunch there on this very pleasant day.

At the climax, after the signing of the treaty, President and Mrs. Truman and Margaret Truman moved aboard. We had, of course, two flag-officer cabins. The President took the admiral's cabin. Mrs. Truman and Margaret took the chief of staff's cabin, which was also a flag cabin, somewhat larger. We had fitted it out with twin beds before we left the States. Their cabin was used as their mess room, and that left the President's cabin for his personal use.

He also had with him several of his official family: General Vaughan, Admiral Foskett, Steelman, I think.† Does that sound right?

John T. Mason, Jr.: John R. Steelman.

Admiral Colwell: John Steelman. Mat Connelly, who later came to trouble, and I think spent some time in jail.‡ And there was an older gentleman who was sort of, I suppose, an appointments secretary or something. I can't remember his name. Very nice old gentleman. At any rate, they were all very nice. We had a most pleasant trip back. We

---

* The President of Brazil was Eurico Gaspar Dutra.
† Major General Harry H. Vaughan, USAR, was the presidential military aide. Rear Admiral James H. Foskett, USN, served as presidential naval aide from July 1946 to January 1948. John R. Steelman was assistant to President Truman from 1946 to 1952.
‡ Matthew J. Connelly was Truman's appointments secretary. In May 1960 he began serving a prison sentence for income tax evasion. In November 1962 President John F. Kennedy pardoned him.

had intentionally not held the "crossing the line" ceremonies on the way down so that we could have them on the way back while the President and his crowd were aboard. That was a big day.*

We'd made proper preparations for this thing before leaving the States, including a lot of fancy costumes and so on and various dignitaries in Neptunus Rex's retinue. We had ourselves quite a time.

I'd forgotten this, but we also had with us a Life magazine photographer who took a lot of pictures and we had a write-up on the trip back in Life magazine.†

John T. Mason, Jr.: And the big event—crossing the equator, I suppose?

Admiral Colwell: Yes

John T. Mason, Jr.: Did you have a stable of reporters on board?

Admiral Colwell: Oh, heavens, yes. I think we had about 40. We also had a group of Secret Service, as you would expect, but they were so pleased with the security arrangements that we had made, using our own Marine detachment, that they expressed themselves as not having very much to do. They just let the Marines take care of it.

John T. Mason, Jr.: It must have strained even the facilities of a battleship like the Missouri.

Admiral Colwell: We were absolutely packed. As a matter of fact, those ships, as large as they are, do not have large staff facilities, so that doubling up in small rooms was just the order of the day. They have surprisingly small staff facilities for a ship as large as that and one that was built as a fleet flagship. Anyway, people doubled up, and they seemed to me very happy about it. We had good weather; it was a very good trip. We had, I guess, 18 days, or something like that.

---
* The equator-crossing initiation ceremonies were on 11 September 1947.
† "Truman and U.S. Win Friends at Rio, Life, 15 September 1947, pages 35-39.

John T. Mason, Jr.: Do you have any specific recollections of Truman or his family?

Admiral Colwell: I have one in particular. On two separate occasions I was invited to have dinner as the President's guest, which was very pleasant. All of the people—they couldn't have been nicer. Mrs. Truman, I've often said, reminded me of my mother. A very sweet woman.

To move on from that particular cruise—oh, and incidentally, it was on that cruise where President Truman got to know Admiral Dennison, so that some months later when Admiral Foskett left Mr. Truman as his naval aide, Admiral Dennison moved into that job overnight.[*] I may tell you a little bit more about that, and then we can skip back.

John T. Mason, Jr.: All right.

Admiral Colwell: We were in the Brooklyn Navy Yard under overhaul when Admiral Dennison—then a captain, of course—received a call from I believe, Admiral Fechteler saying, "You are the new naval aide to the President. How soon can you be here?"[†]

Dennison said, "Well, how soon do I have to be there?"

Fechteler replied, "Preferably, this afternoon." This was about 8:30 or 9:00 o'clock in the morning. So Denny said, "Well, I have command of a battleship, as you know, and I am required to go through certain exercises and turn it over to somebody."

So Fechteler said, "Can your executive officer take command?"

And he said: "Certainly he can."

So he said, "Fine. You turn it over to him tomorrow morning and be down here as soon thereafter as possible."

That's exactly what happened.

John T. Mason, Jr.: That came as quite a shock to you, I suppose?

---

[*] Dennison served as President Truman's naval aide from February 1948 to January 1953.
[†] Vice Admiral William M. Fechteler, USN, served as Deputy Chief of Naval Operations (Personnel) from 1947 to 1950.

Admiral Colwell: That was a shock to everybody concerned, because this was all very hush-hush, and Admiral Fechteler didn't advise anybody else in the chain of command in the Atlantic Fleet. So I relieved Admiral Dennison the next morning in the traditional fashion and then sent out the usual dispatch.*

John T. Mason, Jr.: What was your rank then?

Admiral Colwell: I was a commander. I sent out the usual dispatch to the CNO, the fleet commander, the type commander, that Commander John B. Colwell assumed command USS Missouri this date vice Captain R. L. Dennison, detached.

Well, as I heard some time later, this dispatch arrived in Norfolk at the fleet headquarters where the immediate reaction was, "What in the world has happened to Dennison, and who in the hell is Colwell?" That, of course, all got sorted out pretty rapidly as soon as Denny arrived in Washington.

I had command of the Missouri for a month, while we were in the yard. I didn't get to take her to sea, but that of course was really a tremendous thrill.

John T. Mason, Jr.: A premature command for you, wasn't it?

Admiral Colwell: Yes, and I actually got orders to command, so that on the brass plaque in the commanding officer's cabin in the Missouri—I presume it's still there—I show as commanding officer for a month, Commander Colwell, because I had orders to command her.

To go on from there, then, Jimmy Thach arrived to relieve me and took over the ship. We eventually finished our overhaul. This was during one of the numerous demobilization businesses. At one time we were down to between 800 and 900 men, I think, in the ship, of whom 17% were stewards, incidentally.

John T. Mason, Jr.: Lots of service!

---

* Commander Colwell served as commanding officer of the Missouri from 23 January 1948 to 24 February 1948.

Admiral Colwell: We had lots of stewards. At one time we were so short of boilermen that we couldn't possibly get under way. That was getting along towards the end of the overhaul, but by the time we were ready to leave, why, we could go to sea and we did. We went through the refresher training in Guantanamo and actually did pretty well, in spite of being shorthanded and a fairly green crew. I think our allowance at that time was only 1,250, and this was a number that came into play, incidentally, many years later when the New Jersey was recommissioned during the Vietnam War.[*] There was a big argument about how big a crew she needed, especially from people who didn't want her commissioned at all.

John T. Mason, Jr.: Well, 1,250 would be adequate for combat?

Admiral Colwell: That's true. It would be very slender. I've forgotten how many she finally got. It may have been 1,500.

At any rate, Jimmy Thach took over the ship and then we made a very interesting midshipmen's cruise to the Mediterranean, where we made port in Villefranche, Lisbon, Algiers. That also was a good cruise.

John T. Mason, Jr.: On a cruise like that, where you served as the exec, did you get involved with the midshipmen in any way?

Admiral Colwell: Not very much, because the Naval Academy furnishes a substantial number of officers who serve as the administrative force as well as instructors for the midshipmen. The ship's company does some instructing, yes, but we were not particularly involved with the administration. The senior officer we had with us on that one was Bub Ward, who was later a rear admiral, and he and I, of course, worked very closely together.[†]

---

[*] The battleship New Jersey (BB-62) was recommissioned on 6 April 1968 at Philadelphia for Vietnam War service, then decommissioned at Bremerton, Washington, on 17 December 1969.
[†] Commander Norvell G. Ward, USN, was then on the Naval Academy staff. The oral history of Ward, who eventually retired as a rear admiral, is in the Naval Institute collection.

John T. Mason, Jr.: Was there another battleship accompanying you? I mean, the whole contingent was not on board the Missouri?

Admiral Colwell: No. I can't recall the total number that we had, but there were destroyers, I think two. Then there was an amphibious ship with us, primarily for boating purposes, because we couldn't carry enough boats to meet the requirements.

The harbor of Villefranche—and this was the first time I had ever seen it—is a simply beautiful one. It's sort of a bottle shape, a round bottle with a narrow neck opening. You may know it. But it's also rather small, and the Missouri is a very large ship. The water there is fairly deep for anchoring, but we used up the entire harbor. It's a lovely spot.

All good things come to an end, so after about 18 months I left the Missouri, but then I went to another excellent job. I was moved out to Pearl Harbor to be the fleet readiness officer on the staff of the fleet commander.

John T. Mason, Jr.: Who was the commander then?

Admiral Colwell: The commander then was Admiral Ramsey, a splendid gentleman.[*] He was later relieved by Admiral Radford, another splendid gentleman.[†] Of course, I was able to take the family, and we lived in Navy quarters in the Makalapa area.

John T. Mason, Jr.: Which is pleasant!

Admiral Colwell: Which is pleasant indeed. I had a busy but most pleasant and most satisfying two and a half years in that job.

John T. Mason, Jr.: Tell me about the scope of your job.

---

[*] Admiral DeWitt C. Ramsey, USN, served as Commander in Chief Pacific and Commander in Chief Pacific Fleet from 12 January 1948 to 30 April 1949.
[†] Admiral Arthur W. Radford, USN, served as Commander in Chief Pacific and Commander in Chief Pacific Fleet from 30 April 1949 to 10 July 1953.

Admiral Colwell: It's a little difficult to describe. It encompassed a great many things. The job was basically in the operations department, so that I worked for the operations officer who, to begin with, was Whitey Taylor and was later Fitzhugh Lee, both of whom were to become vice admirals.*

John T. Mason, Jr.: Quite a staff to serve on!

Admiral Colwell: Yes it was. Oh, it was a splendid job, great future in it.

The job encompassed training on all types, as the word "readiness" implies. Not too long after my arrival, we become embroiled in the Korean War, and then my duties just sort of branched out.† Everybody did what had to be done, and I inherited a few things that hadn't normally been in that office, I suppose, such as working on increases in personnel allowances for the various staffs in the Japanese area. You wouldn't think that that would fall under me, but it did.

John T. Mason, Jr.: Well, I suppose through the chain of training and so on?

Admiral Colwell: Yes, and you can put almost anything into readiness, if you want to.

John T. Mason, Jr.: I was going to ask how closely did you work with BuPers?‡

Admiral Colwell: Oh, yes, very closely, and also, of course, the Service Force Pacific was right there on the same hill with us. And I worked very closely with the logistics people, particularly ammunition supply, with the Service Force people, which was sort of like going back again into the big war in the South Pacific—back in the ammunition business.

---

* Captain Edmund B. Taylor, USN; Captain Fitzhugh Lee, USN. The oral history of Lee, who retired as a vice admiral, is in the Naval Institute collection.
† The Korean War began on 25 June 1950, when six North Korean infantry division and three border constabulary brigades invaded the South Korea. The troops were supported by approximately 100 Russian-made T-34 tanks. In New York that same day the United Nations Security Council adopted a resolution condemning the invasion.
‡ BuPers—Bureau of Naval Personnel.

We immediately, of course, went on a six-and-a-half-day week. We only worked half a day on Sunday, unless you had something to do.

John T. Mason, Jr.: This was at the outbreak of the Korean War?

Admiral Colwell: Yes, that's right. It was all very interesting and I enjoyed it thoroughly.

John T. Mason, Jr.: Did you get to Korea yourself?

Admiral Colwell: Not during hostilities, no, I did not. I went to Japan several times, but not to Korea.

John T. Mason, Jr.: What were your missions in Japan?

Admiral Colwell: They were mainly "how-goes-it?" trips, largely again to do with personnel and with ammunition.

There was a rather amusing occurrence shortly after I joined the staff. I was a commander when I arrived, but within a matter of just days the captains' selection was to be published. That year the selection board had taken a very small group out of the next lower class, which happened to be mine, and I was selected for captain. There were 10 or 12 of us, I guess, in the class of 1931.

Dennison, of course, was in the White House, and as soon as the list had been approved by the President, he called me on the phone. This all came through the fleet commander's switchboard, of course. I talked to Denny, and he said, "Well congratulations, Captain." I said something ridiculous like, "You don't mean it."

And he said, "Of course, I mean it, you fool. If I didn't mean it, do you think I'd be calling you from Washington?"

John T. Mason, Jr.: Typical!

Admiral Colwell: Typical. So I thanked him and sat back in this rosy glow.

Oh, incidentally, the man I was relieving was still there, and he was also a commander. It developed that he had been selected, but he didn't know it, so for a whole day almost I was a selected captain and he wasn't! Even though he was senior to me. That irritated him a little too.

Anyway, I was sitting there, and word came up that the chief of staff wanted to see me. So I went down, walked in, and he said:

"I understand you've been talking to the White House?"

I said, "Yes, sir, I have," and told him why.

He said, "Congratulations," and I went back upstairs.

About two minutes later they said the admiral wanted to see me. "I understand you've been talking to the White House?" So I again explained what it was and he congratulated me, and of course, was the end of that.

Everybody had a lot of fun over that one!

We made several trips to Japan with the admiral or the chief of staff from time to time, several trips back to the coast to confer with type commanders, and mainly it was just a very busy time.

John T. Mason, Jr.: What about the supply of ammunition? Was it adequate?

Admiral Colwell: Yes, as I recall, we didn't have any difficulties.

John T. Mason, Jr.: Did you have anything to do with mines and the supply of them?

Admiral Colwell: Oh, yes. That was all part of the ammunition train.

John T. Mason, Jr.: That was a problem, was it not?

Admiral Colwell: Yes. In those days our mine stockpile wasn't very good. It was pretty obsolescent. It took some doing to get things going. You have to get geared up for something like that. The number of people available was small, but we eventually got it taken care of as best we could with the resources at hand.

John T. Mason, Jr.: Why hadn't we improved our mine facilities?

Admiral Colwell: That's a pretty long story. Mining, historically, in the U.S. has not received very high priority, as compared with torpedoes and this sort of thing. It just never seemed to be glamorous enough to attract the attention that it needed.

John T. Mason, Jr.: It was too static in nature?

Admiral Colwell: Yes. It just didn't have any glamour, in spite of the fact that it's a very effective weapon, and everybody knows it is. At any rate, at that time, our mine situation wasn't very good. Minesweeping also suffered during peacetime. It's not very glamorous either. It always becomes very important as soon as the shooting starts.

John T. Mason, Jr.: And there was a great need for mines in the Korean War?

Admiral Colwell: Well, minesweeping was really more important than mining, I would say, because most of the shipping used by the North Koreans was very small stuff.

John T. Mason, Jr.: Coastwise mostly?

Admiral Colwell: Coastwise, it was small stuff, and against such shipping mining is not particularly effective unless you have a very agreeable set of shallow water that you can work with. If the water is deep at all, it's very difficult to mine it effectively against small craft.

Well, the Korean thing just progressed, as history has recorded it. We kept working every day, and that's about the way it was. After two and a half years, why, I was transferred in a sort of routine transfer.

John T. Mason, Jr.: Did you, as part of that command, get involved with the United Nations aspect of the whole thing?

Admiral Colwell: I didn't, individually. The staff, of course, did. I didn't get into that part of it.

John T. Mason, Jr.: Did we not have to supply them with ammunition?

Admiral Colwell: Oh, yes, but that was a sort of a minor effort. It didn't amount to very much. That's the sort of thing the Service Force took care of as a routine logistic problem.

John T. Mason, Jr.: Explain to me how the Service Force dovetailed into the activities of the CinCPacFlt command.

Admiral Colwell: The Commander Service Force, was in fact—and he may have been in name, I've forgotten—the fleet commander's deputy for logistics, so he worked directly with the admiral. We talked back and forth, staff to staff, on any mutual problems. It was a very close relationship, even physically close. The Service Force headquarters were about a block away on the same hill.

John T. Mason, Jr.: They still are.

Admiral Colwell: They still are, that's right, and they still have that same close relationship. As a matter of fact, I was just out there last, week. That's where I got the sunburned lip. The Service Force commander now has designation as Deputy CinCPacFlt for Logistics. I think when I was out there it was that same way, so there must have been a change in between.

Admiral Low was the Service Force commander and, if he didn't have such designation, he was in fact, if not in name.*

This brings us up, I guess, to leaving the lovely Hawaiian Islands, where one of our children was born, incidentally. He's the only Kamaaina in the family.

---

* Vice Admiral Francis S. Low, USN, served as Commander Service Force Pacific Fleet from March 1947 to November 1949.

John T. Mason, Jr.: So your day in paradise came to an end, as you say!

Admiral Colwell: Yes, and we loaded up the family and flew back in one of the old Mars flying boats, which, as I recall, was 17 hours, from Honolulu to San Francisco. That's a long time, but we felt that that was better than riding a transport. Eventually we arrived in Washington

John T. Mason, Jr.: Were you happy at coming back to Washington?

Admiral Colwell: So-so, I guess.

John T. Mason, Jr.: This was to the Bureau of Ordnance?

Admiral Colwell: That was to BuOrd, that's right. That didn't really enchant me very much. It was sort of a routine job.

John T. Mason, Jr.: What was it?

Admiral Colwell: I was sort of midway up in the staff, in the Research and Development Division, as an administrative type. A pretty pedestrian kind of a job really.

John T. Mason, Jr.: Any particular projects that were interesting at that moment?

Admiral Colwell: Not really. This was more on the administration side, fooling with the budget and that sort of thing.

John T. Mason, Jr.: Who was chief of bureau?

Admiral Colwell: It must have been Schoeffel.* Anyway, I sat out that job for a while, and then when Mr. Wilson came down from Detroit into the Secretary of Defense job he brought with him as his deputy Roger Kyes.† Roger was looking for a military administrative assistant. I don't know just how this might have come about, but I was nominated as one of the candidates to serve as aide to Mr. Kyes. So I had an interview with him, in his office.

John T. Mason, Jr.: Had you met him before?

Admiral Colwell: No, never. Somewhat to my surprise, as a result of that interview, he said, "Go get yourself a set of orders and report," which I did naturally.

So I sat in the outer office, sort of watching the door for Mr. Kyes, for about 13 months, until the day he left. His relief was Mr. Robert Anderson, who brought with him his own administrative assistant.‡ Mr. Kyes went out one door, and I went out the other at the same moment.

John T. Mason, Jr.: Tell me about Mr. Kyes.

Admiral Colwell: Mr. Kyes was a very intelligent man and a very fine big-business man. He knew a great deal about production. He had an incisive mind. He was tough, and I think probably in a business that size, particularly in the automotive business, he had to be tough to survive.

John T. Mason, Jr.: He was General Motors too?

---

* Rear Admiral Malcolm F. Schoeffel, USN, served as Chief of the Bureau of Ordnance, 1950-54. His oral history is in the Naval Institute collection.
† Charles E. Wilson served as Secretary of Defense from 28 January 1953 to 8 October 1957. He was nicknamed "Engine Charlie" because he had previously been chairman of the board of General Motors. Roger M. Kyes, who had been vice president of the General Motors Corporation, served as Deputy Secretary of Defense, 1953-54.
‡ Robert B. Anderson served as Secretary of the Navy, 1953-54, as Deputy Secretary of Defense, 1954-55.

Admiral Colwell: He was General Motors. He and Mr. Wilson were inseparable. They even thought alike, and we used to believe that you could put them in separate rooms and pose the same question, and they would come out with the same answer word for word.

John T. Mason, Jr.: The indoctrination at General Motors must be pretty good!

Admiral Colwell: Yes. He was a pretty tough administrator, but there isn't anything wrong with that.

John T. Mason, Jr.: Can you cite an example of his toughness?

Admiral Colwell: No, not really, nothing in particular. He was often accused of being Wilson's hatchet man. I never saw any instances of this at all, never. I don't think it was true. He got a write-up in Life magazine, which really hurt him very deeply, because it was sort of snide in a number of ways.[*] He was a sensitive man.

John T. Mason, Jr.: Did this imply that the press didn't care too much for him?

Admiral Colwell: Well, they didn't know him. They never got a chance to know him. He wasn't in a position to hold press conferences. I think that there were a lot of mistaken ideas that got circulated around town, and people picked them up and accepted them—the hatchet-man idea. I actually enjoyed knowing Mr. Kyes, and we remained friends. After he left I used to see him here in town from time to time at such things as the NSIA meetings.

I often described my year in that job as highly instructive and not very much fun. It was most instructive, because you were really sitting in the seats with the mighty in the Pentagon, and, well, you saw all of the service secretaries, all of the assistant secretaries, all of the high-ranking officers, lots of people from Capitol Hill. Bedell Smith was a very

---

[*] Robert Coughlan, "...The Ugliest Man Since Abe Lincoln," Life, 10 August 1953, pages 86-94, 96, 98, 100.

frequent caller.* He was then, I guess, head of CIA. It was most instructive. It was a very hard-working job.

John T. Mason, Jr.: Was this why it wasn't fun?

Admiral Colwell: No, not really, except that there was never any change to it. Mr. Kyes had no hobbies. His hobby was work, so it was drive, drive, drive. We'd get there about 7:30 in the morning, and I rarely got home before 9:00 o'clock at night. That's routine in the Pentagon today, and it's a lot of foolishness. It isn't necessary.

John T. Mason, Jr.: Doesn't it drain a man of his energies, intellectual and physical?

Admiral Colwell: Sure it does. Mr. Kyes never took a day off, because he had no hobbies. I don't know what he did on Sundays. Nothing, I guess. He maintained an apartment here in town. His family stayed in Michigan, where he had children in school. Mrs. Kyes came down from time to time, and he went home on occasion. But mostly he stayed right here and worked every day.

John T. Mason, Jr.: Had he set for himself a time limit on the job?

Admiral Colwell: I believe he had. At the time he left, he said that he had agreed to come for a year. I think it was actually about 14 months. I was with him 13 months. We very frequently had dinner in the Secretary's dining room, because he didn't want to go home. He was alone; he didn't want to eat alone, so the staff would stay and we'd have dinner together.

My wife was asked one time what she thought of this job that I had, since I was gone all the time, and she said: "Well, I really liked it better when he was at sea, because then I used to get mail."

---

* General Walter Bedell Smith, USA, served as Director of Central Intelligence/Director of the Central Intelligence Agency from 7 October 1950 to 9 February 1953. In 1953 he left active military service to become Under Secretary of State in the Eisenhower Administration.

I only made one trip with Mr. Kyes, but it was really a dandy. We took the Secretary's plane and along with us we had Frank Nash, who was Assistant Secretary for International Affairs; the Secretary of the Air Force—I can't remember what his name was, but he was a nice gentleman; General Erskine; and we had two or three aides—three besides myself.[*] This was a beautiful trip.

The first stop, except for refueling at Goose Bay, was Thule. This was in September.

John T. Mason, Jr.: Did you have a specific purpose?

Admiral Colwell: Just inspection and high-level discussions with various people.

We stopped in Thule and in Iceland, and then we went into England, and we were in London two or three days. Then Bonn and Frankfurt in Germany, Salzburg, Luxembourg, where I met—who was the gentleman who put together that steel consortium in Luxembourg? He was a Frenchman, Mr. Monnet.[†] In fact, we all had dinner together one evening. Then Rome, Turin, Athens, Istanbul, Ankara.

John T. Mason, Jr.: This was the grand tour!

Admiral Colwell: It really was. Paris, Madrid, Lisbon, and finally home—30 days.

John T. Mason, Jr.: Were there defense matters that were being discussed?

Admiral Colwell: These were defense matters.

---

[*] Harold E. Talbott served as Secretary of the Air Force from 4 February 1953 to 13 August 1955. General Graves B. Erskine, USMC (Ret.), served from June 1953 to October 1961 as Assistant to the Secretary of Defense.
[†] Jean Monnet of France was president of the High Authority of the European Coal and Steel Community, which went into effect in July 1952.

John T. Mason, Jr.: As you went up to Greenland, were you concerned about the DEW Line?*

Admiral Colwell: This was more just an inspection and familiarization stop than anything else.

John T. Mason, Jr.: Was the DEW line in being then?

Admiral Colwell: I think it was. I've forgotten. We had aircraft, of course, stationed at Thule. That's a very interesting place. You could look up there, and there was a glacier staring you in the face. We arrived there early in the morning, about 7:00 o'clock, I guess, and the temperature was just about 30° or 32°, but it was so dry it wasn't cold. They told us that the humidity up there is actually less than it is in the Sahara. Just living in temperatures like that poses a lot of difficulties. How do you dispose of your waste? It was interesting.

At any rate, that was a marvelous trip. Of course, red carpet all the way.

John T. Mason, Jr.: Did you have a specific mission in Ankara?

Admiral Colwell: Discussions with the Turks, defense matters, and the same in Athens.

John T. Mason, Jr.: I imagine you had to talk with both groups on the same trip?

Admiral Colwell: Oh, yes. We hit most of Europe on that one. From Salzburg, as a side trip, we drove up to Berchtesgaden.† In September it's absolutely magnificent.

At that time we still had the Rhine River Patrol, so while we were in Frankfurt we got aboard two of the patrol boats at Frankfurt and went down river to Bonn, and that's a

---

* DEW Line—Distant Early Warning Line, a chain of radar sites built 1,200 miles from the North Pole in the early 1950s as a means of detecting Soviet bombers approaching the United States over the Arctic.
† Berchtesgaden, a town in the Bavarian Alps of Germany, was the site of a villa that was often used by German Chancellor Adolf Hitler in World War II.

beautiful trip. The weather wasn't very good, but it was still beautiful. I've recommended the trip to travelers many, many times and they're never disappointed.

John T. Mason, Jr.: How did Mr. Kyes disport himself on this trip? I mean, was he a driving type of businessman?

Admiral Colwell: Work, work, work, that's right. The other aides and I had attempted to set up a schedule which would give us weekends in attractive places. You might just as well do it that way as to stop in some stupid place. But it didn't really make very much difference, because Saturdays and Sunday turned out to be working days, anyhow, somewhat to the consternation of the people that he was working with, I might add. They didn't understand that.

I remember when we stopped at Madrid, a gentleman was hosting us for dinner, and he was taking us from place to place around the city and stopping at various spots, just killing time because he was planning to take us to dinner about 11:30, the fashionable hour in Madrid. Well, about 9:30 Mr. Kyes said, "I'm ready for dinner." The host tried to remonstrate a little bit with him and said, "Well, in Madrid there isn't any place open at 9:30 for dinner."

As I recall, Mr. Kyes said something like, "Find one. I'm ready for dinner." So we drove around for a while and finally beat on the door of a very, very fine restaurant and persuaded somebody to open it and let us in, and we had dinner. And they were upset, because they didn't have any staff on hand and dinner wasn't ready, but we were in and we had dinner before anybody else even thought about having dinner in Madrid.

He was a man of very decided tastes.

John T. Mason, Jr.: An American businessman!

Admiral Colwell: Yes.

John T. Mason, Jr.: What about the set-up of the Defense Department at the beginning of the Eisenhower regime?* Was the concept different from what it had been under Forrestal?†

Admiral Colwell: There had been a gradual growth, which I think was to be expected. Forrestal had started the thing, and his concept, of course, was a very small supervisory and executive staff. Wilfred McNeil was sort of his Assistant Secretary for all purposes for a while.‡ Mr. McNeil, whom I came to admire very much, of course, was still there when I was there, and he was then the comptroller and a sort of a senior advisor on a great many matters. He carried a tremendous amount of information in his head and knew everybody in town. But by that time there were some assistant secretaries. One of the most important was the man I mentioned, Frank Nash, who is now dead, who was the Assistant Secretary for International Security Affairs, the ISA Department.

General Erskine was a special assistant for intelligence.

Of course, the office worked directly with the three service secretaries, and on a day-to-day basis, with the Joint Chiefs. So there had been a gradual growth from the concept of Forrestal. I think that's a fairly normal thing. You can call it Parkinson's Law, if you want to.§ It kept growing and, of course, today it's heaven knows how much larger than it was in those days. This is one reason why everybody works till 9:00 o'clock every night. There are too many people. They manufacture work. If, by some miracle, you could reduce the size of that staff to one-third of what it is today, people could start going home at 6:00 o'clock, I think.

John T. Mason, Jr.: And we'd still survive!

---

* Dwight D. Eisenhower served as President of the United States from 20 January 1953 to 20 January 1961.
† James V. Forrestal served as Secretary of Defense from 17 September 1947 to 27 March 1949.
‡ Wilfred J. McNeil was a special assistant to Secretary of Defense James Forrestal in 1947. He later served as Assistant Secretary of Defense and DoD Comptroller from 1949 to 1959.
§ C. Northcote Parkinson was a British professor who conceived a number of tongue-in-cheek, albeit apropos, "laws" concerning human behavior. His best known is, "Work expands to as to fill the time available for its completion." See his book, Parkinson's Law and Other Studies in Administration (Boston: Houghton Mifflin, 1957).

Admiral Colwell: And we'd survive handsomely. Decisions would get made by people and not by mounds of paper.

At any rate, when Mr. Kyes left, I left.

John T. Mason, Jr.: Tell me about Mr. Wilson as the Secretary. You must have had the opportunity to observe him frequently.

Admiral Colwell: Yes, I did. He was a very quiet man. I didn't have very many personal dealings with him.

John T. Mason, Jr.: Did he have the same kind of drive as Kyes?

Admiral Colwell: No, he didn't appear to, but he had a will of iron, I think. He always sort of presented the appearance of a quiet little grandfatherly type who was just sort of overseeing things. I'm sure that this was not true. But I had very few personal dealings with Mr. Wilson. What few I had were always very pleasant.

John T. Mason, Jr.: What was Mr. Kyes' particular area of endeavor?

Admiral Colwell: Anything that Mr. Wilson was concerned with. In fact, Mr. Kyes had a piece of paper signed by Mr. Wilson which made him his alter ego. So he was more than a deputy. He was authorized to act for Mr. Wilson or in place of Mr. Wilson at any time on his own initiative—full authority, his alter ego.

John T. Mason, Jr.: And the Joint Chiefs understood this?

Admiral Colwell: Oh, yes. This was official. So there was no particular area of assignment to Mr. Kyes as deputy.

John T. Mason, Jr.: That sort of arrangement could only happen with men who are personal friends?

Admiral Colwell: That's true, and where they had complete confidence and thought alike, and they did.

John T. Mason, Jr.: Has it ever happened since? That kind of arrangement?

Admiral Colwell: I don't know. It could have, but I don't know whether it has or not. I think it would be very rare to find two men who had that enormous mutual trust and confidence and understanding. That I think would be most unusual, but another Secretary might set up the same arrangement just in order to get the work done. I don't know.

John T. Mason, Jr.: Why would a man like Mr. Kyes come into a job like that, with supposedly a time limitation of a year in mind? It takes a while to master a job.

Admiral Colwell: I think part of this is ego, self-confidence, arrogance, if you want to call it that. I think he felt that he was such a good production man that he could clean up the mess in a year and go on home. I don't think it ever occurred to him that he couldn't finish it.

John T. Mason, Jr.: What was this mess?

Admiral Colwell: Oh, scheduling was bad. For example—I'm not picking on the Air Force, but it's an example that comes to mind—the scheduling of airplanes versus engines on a particular model of aircraft was completely out of whack. They should have done it themselves. He found it and straightened it out.

John T. Mason, Jr.: What about ship contracts and that sort of thing?

Admiral Colwell: He was interested in anything at all that had to do with production particularly, a long line like producing aircraft or ships. But he was interested in anything that had to do with production, and he was a very good production man.

John T. Mason, Jr.: Was he also interested in R&D?*

Admiral Colwell: Yes, I would say so. He had a very wide-ranging interest, and a very quick mind, very incisive. A real good man.

John T. Mason, Jr.: Did you, in that job, make some important contacts which were useful to you as you developed your own career?

Admiral Colwell: Probably so. I really haven't any instances that I can cite, but I guess you rarely know how much good is done for you by knowing other people. You don't know who they talk to, you don't know what they say. Certainly there wouldn't be very much in the way of written matter, but I think you can expect that there's a great deal of word-of-mouth advertising, if you want to call it that, and it could be either good or bad. Of course, my fitness reports were matters of official record, and these were signed by Mr. Kyes. They were good ones but no better than I'd gotten from other people. I wouldn't expect that a selection board would have given them any particular weight just because they were signed by Mr. Kyes.

John T. Mason, Jr.: Well, the nature of the job was so much different from the sort of thing a naval officer usually does.

Admiral Colwell: Yes, that's true. It was quite similar to the job of administrative assistant to CNO or to the Secretary of the Navy. These jobs, of course, have become more important as time went on, where the time of the CNO is more taken up, so his administrative assistant has had to assume more authority. I had very little authority. In fact, I would say that I had none when I was working for Mr. Kyes. He didn't want anybody making appointments for him. He made his own.

John T. Mason, Jr.: Did he answer his own telephone?

---

* R&D—research and development.

Admiral Colwell: No, but he didn't want anybody signing him up to see anybody if he didn't know about it and if he didn't approve of it. Maybe he didn't want to see him, and he would think nothing of just not seeing him. If he didn't feel like it, he wouldn't return telephone calls. When he was living down here alone, he would even accept social engagements and then not go. He was a man unto himself.

John T. Mason, Jr.: One can understand why the press wrote articles about him that weren't too complimentary!

Admiral Colwell: He didn't make any effort to endear himself to people; that's for sure.

John T. Mason, Jr.: You said he was very sensitive, however?

Admiral Colwell: He was sensitive personally. If people said nasty things about him, it hurt. Maybe he was a little one-way that way; I don't know.

    I just thought of something that always amused me. Shortly after I got to his office, and I suppose it was the next day or something like that, I was talking to him and he said, "Now, Captain, if we're going to be together for the next year I can't just be calling you Captain. What do people call you?

    So I said, "Well, sir, I'm generally and widely known as J. B."

    He heard it as J. D. and he called me J. D. for the rest of his life! He knew perfectly well that my initials were J.B., but he wouldn't change, and, as he was leaving, at one of the closing activities, I asked him to give me one of his autographed pictures to add to my rogues' gallery. He said, "Sure," so he inscribed it to J.D. He wouldn't change!

John T. Mason, Jr.: I suppose that says something, but—

Admiral Colwell: I suppose it does, yes.

John T. Mason, Jr.: What about relationships with the Joint Chiefs in that job?

Admiral Colwell: I was not involved with the Joint Chiefs, except in a sort of peripheral way. Of course, Kyes dealt with them on a more or less continuous basis, and they were in and out of the office singly and in groups.

As near as I can remember, I was never called in to sit in on a session with them in Kyes's office. In fact, for the whole time I was sort of at arm's length as far as what went on. It was not a position of real responsibility.

John T. Mason, Jr.: Largely because of the nature of the man himself?

Admiral Colwell: Largely, yes, that's true.

John T. Mason, Jr.: In that day, the Defense Intelligence set-up had not been—had not come into being?

Admiral Colwell: No, that's right.

John T. Mason, Jr.: So you had to deal with the various service intelligence offices?

Admiral Colwell: That's right. Erskine had his own office for the intelligence business, but this was, as near as I could gather, largely the black side, the clandestine side, and he didn't talk to anybody about it.

John T. Mason, Jr.: But as for using the several services and their intelligence-gathering arms, would you comment on that? I mean, there's been so much comment on whether it's effective to have a central defense intelligence set-up superimposed on the others, or whether it was better as it was.

Admiral Colwell: I think you can make an argument both ways, so I don't think there's a fixed answer to it. As the office of the Secretary of Defense became stronger and centralization proceeded, then the Secretary of Defense certainly felt that he had to have his own intelligence office to whom he could speak and get a single answer. I think I would probably feel the same way.

So the Defense Intelligence Agency was established.* I don't think that it's all worked out as handily as was advertised, because the three services still have their own intelligence organizations, and I don't object to that either. But it's meant a proliferation of people in the intelligence business. The Defense Intelligence Agency turns out intelligence papers which may have three different views in them. Army, Navy, and Air Force views may be entirely different, and they're all presented. So where are you? You might just as well have kept the three in the beginning. I don't think there's a single answer to it, but certainly the advertised ends of the Defense Intelligence Agency don't appear to me to have been met.

John T. Mason, Jr.: And how does the International Security Affairs office tie in with intelligence?

Admiral Colwell: Well, of course, one of the strongest props that they have to support their views has to be intelligence estimates. That's one of the beginning parts. They work with the State Department. They work with the various elements of the NATO organization, SEATO and CENTO, Australians and New Zealanders, and so on.†

But one of their principal props, as I call it, certainly has to be intelligence estimates.

John T. Mason, Jr.: Well, you said when Mr. Kyes left you went out the other door?

Admiral Colwell: Yes. I went back to sea.

John T. Mason, Jr.: This was to fulfill a certain requirement?

---

* The Defense Intelligence Agency became operational on 1 October 1961 as the nation's primary producer of foreign military intelligence.
† NATO—North Atlantic Treaty Organization, which was established in 1949 as a means of coordinating defense against a potential attack from the Soviet Union. SEATO—Southeast Asia Treaty Organization. CENTO—Central Treaty Organization.

Admiral Colwell: Yes. I rejoined the Navy, and got command of an oiler with the Atlantic Service Force, the USS Elokomin.* I had her for about 15 months. I first took her to an overhaul in Boston and then, at the end of the summer, went to work as a fleet oiler, which I enjoyed. I really did.

John T. Mason, Jr.: What's entailed in that?

Admiral Colwell: There is, or at least there was at that time, a great deal of independent steaming. You were much your own boss, going from point to point and meeting ships here and there, and always delivering fuel. And we were good at it. At the time I left the ship, we counted up, if my memory serves, in the approximately 12 months of active service that's discounting three months in overhaul, I believe we fueled 425 ships from actual count, some such figure.

John T. Mason, Jr.: At sea?

Admiral Colwell: At sea.
I had a good cruise to the Mediterranean with the Sixth Fleet with the Elokomin.

John T. Mason, Jr.: That would be for six months?

Admiral Colwell: Approximately six months. Then I had another cruise supporting a midshipmen's practice squadron, where we went to northern Europe. I had two ports, in Bergen, Norway, and Stockholm. The run into Stockholm is a very interesting one. You go through some quite narrow passages through the archipelago there, and then a long, narrow entrance into the harbor of Stockholm. We were told that that was the biggest ship they'd ever had in there.

John T. Mason, Jr.: What was her tonnage?

---

* USS Elokomin (AO-55), a Cimarron-class fleet oiler, was commissioned 30 November 1943. She had a full-load displacement of 25,525 tons, was 553 feet long, 75 feet in the beam, had a maximum draft of 32 feet, and a top speed of 18.3 knots. She was armed with one 5-inch gun and four 3-inch guns.

Admiral Colwell: Loaded, we ran about 25,000 tons. Those two ports were interesting. We had a good cruise with the midshipmen.

John T. Mason, Jr.: Where did you refuel? What was the source of your supply?

Admiral Colwell: In the Mediterranean, we always went back to Naples and fueled from the commercial sources there, Mobil or whoever. They had a fuel terminal inside the harbor. So I was in and out of Naples a great deal. I spent more time there than any place else.

We had more than one oiler with the fleet, so we would meet with the fleet as they left a port, or possibly, as they were about to enter a port, and we would fuel them up and then we would do what they called "consolidate," where two oilers would steam along together. One of us would be designated to empty the other one, take everything he had. As soon as he was empty, why, then he would hightail it for Naples to load up again.

John T. Mason, Jr.: And, empty, what kind of ballast did you have?

Admiral Colwell: Water, and then you have to get rid of that well before you enter port.

John T. Mason, Jr.: You mean you put water in your tanks?

Admiral Colwell: Yes. Oh, yes, we'd ballast down. Then, if you had been the receiving ship in consolidation, you might be half full, and you'd stick around with the fleet in order to fuel anybody who needed it until this other fellow got back with a full load. By that time, you'd be empty and you'd hightail it for Naples.

On the midshipmen's cruise we took enough with us so that we never had to refill. The demand was small—a small number of ships.

John T. Mason, Jr.: Well, when the fleet is operating, say, in the Mediterranean, the Sixth Fleet or forces that were operating in some kind of an exercise, where do you stand off?

Admiral Colwell: The Service Force ships, which would include oilers, gasoline tankers, stores ships, refrigerator ships, ammunition ships, would usually join up in our own formation and go off in the North Forty and wait to be called. We'd conduct our own tactical exercises while doing this.

John T. Mason, Jr.: "North Forty" is not a naval term!

Admiral Colwell: No. We'd just go to some convenient point, knowing where we were going to be expected to be for the next replenishment. We'd go somewhere near that, and we'd hold tactical exercises.

John T. Mason, Jr.: What would your speed be in cases like that?

Admiral Colwell: My ship would make almost 19 knots. She had been built as a commercial tanker and taken over when she was brand new. She never served as a commercial tanker. But the engineering plant was designed to run at something very close to maximum speed, so when I was going anywhere that's the way I steamed. I'd ring up 18 knots, and away we'd go. Fueling speeds at that time were generally 12 to 14 knots. That's a very comfortable fueling speed. Some of the ships that we worked with could make only 14 or 15—that's other Service Force ships. So, if we were steaming in company, why, we'd usually make one of them the guide and pick a comfortable speed for him, like 14 knots, and we'd all keep station on him.

John T. Mason, Jr.: Did you have any difficulties at any time during this tour?

Admiral Colwell: Oh, you always have broken hoses or broken highlines, and that sort of thing. We had our share of those. We had a steering casualty one time. Fortunately, it was alongside a carrier, and fortunately it jammed so that I was sheering out instead of in, so we didn't hit. It pulled out three or four highlines by the roots and broke hoses and was a mess. It took us till the next day to get it cleaned up and re-rigged. We carried spare hose and spare cable for highlines.

We were an awful mess one night. We'd been fueling since dawn, and it was about midnight. I must have been fueling another carrier because I had all my hoses over, and one of them let go right up in the top of the saddle with 100-pound pressure. It just sprayed me with black oil from midships all the way aft. We were really painted black. When we finally got a chance to work on it the next morning, we took diesel oil and swabbed the ship down with diesel oil, which would cut the black oil and left only a little film of its own. We washed down as best we could and finally got rid of it. Man, that was a mess!

John T. Mason, Jr.: What about polluting the waters? I mean, did this occur frequently when you were fueling?

Admiral Colwell: No not frequently because we spilled very, very little. Usually if you had any kind of a spill it would be the result of a split hose, like the one I just described. The hoses are sent over capped, they're returned capped. It's drippage more than spillage in one of those operations, unless you get a broken hose, and in the open ocean drippage is really absolutely nothing. An ecologist wouldn't agree, but it's a fact.

John T. Mason, Jr.: But when there is a broken hose, say, in the Mediterranean, this does become a serious matter, doesn't it?

Admiral Colwell: Well, this would ordinarily be far from land, even in the Mediterranean. You have people stationed so that you just get one good squirt out of it, if it breaks, then you get a valve closed. You don't lose very much. It's not thousands of gallons or anything like that. You might lose 50 gallons from a broken hose. It spreads out pretty fast.

John T. Mason, Jr.: When you're operating in the Mediterranean, on occasion, I would imagine, some of our NATO allies were involved with operations?

Admiral Colwell: Yes.

John T. Mason, Jr.: Then, what about refueling them at sea?

Admiral Colwell: We had standard procedures.

John T. Mason, Jr.: Are they as adept at this?

Admiral Colwell: Yes, perfectly adequate. There are standard adapters, standard procedures, standard signals. They practice it. They get the job done. They're not quite as fast as some of ours sometimes, but that's merely a matter of practice. They know how.

John T. Mason, Jr.: Did you put in at Malta when you were in the Mediterranean?

Admiral Colwell: No, I did not, I never got in there. I got in to Palma, Mallorca, Valencia, Naples many times, Athens, and I even got to the island of Rhodes one time. You probably recall we had a Voice of America ship in there with a big transmitter. They were not in the little harbor when I got there because I couldn't get in. He had come around the other side of the island and anchored in a shallow spot, and I came alongside, gave him oil and a deck load of assorted things that they'd been collecting for him in Naples sorts of odds and ends, and food and so on. I filled him up with everything that he was waiting for. It was a small ship. I've forgotten what her name was. That was just sort of an unusual chore that I picked up on.

We weren't there long enough to go ashore or anything like that. In fact, the wind started to blow up and we had to leave even before we'd given him his last couple of crates.

John T. Mason, Jr.: Such a tour is an interesting break in the ordinary naval career, isn't it?

Admiral Colwell: Yes. This was something entirely new to me and, as I said, I enjoyed it. Part of the enjoyment, I know, was the fact that I did a great deal of independent steaming.

I was my own boss. I could lay out my own schedule, make my own track, did all my own navigating, and so on. I enjoyed it; it was fun, lots of ship handling.

John T. Mason, Jr.: Where was the Service Force centered in the Atlantic?

Admiral Colwell: In Norfolk.

John T. Mason, Jr.: The command was in Norfolk?

Admiral Colwell: Yes.

John T. Mason, Jr.: Does it operate differently from what it does in the Pacific?

Admiral Colwell: No, about the same. On those jobs you get a great deal of ship handling, you learn some different kinds of seamanship that you haven't used before, kinds of rigging that you never find in a battleship. What's a Burton rig, what's a housefall rig. I didn't even know the terms before.

John T. Mason, Jr.: What's the second one?

Admiral Colwell: Housefall. They're just different ways of rigging your yards to handle different loads, situations, and so on. Most of it now is done by highline, at least for packages of any size that the highline will take and that's much faster. Something that has developed since I had the Elokomin is replenishment by helicopter, and it's a very efficient way to do it and very rapid. It reduces the time alongside, all of which is improved safety, of course.

John T. Mason, Jr.: And this is for stores and ammunition?

Admiral Colwell: Stores and ammunition, but you can't transfer oil by helicopter.

John T. Mason, Jr.: Not yet, at least!

Interview Number 4 with Vice Admiral John B. Colwell, U. S. Navy

Place: Admiral Colwell's apartment in Washington, D.C.

Date: Thursday, 1 November 1973

Interviewer: John T. Mason, Jr.

John T. Mason, Jr.: Well, Admiral, one of the high points in your career was the very significant period when you served as deputy to Admiral Raborn for the development of Polaris.* Would you take it from there, sir?

Admiral Colwell: I would certainly have to class it as one of the most important segments in my career and certainly one of the most satisfying.

I was assigned to this somewhat to my amazement. I had but recently reported to the office of the Chief of Naval Operations and had hardly gotten my feet under the desk when I was directed by telephone to report to Admiral Raborn.

John T. Mason, Jr.: Did they have something else in mind for you?

Admiral Colwell: Yes, I had been assigned to one of the offices in OP-34, but I really hadn't even found out what I was supposed to be doing. So I reported to Admiral Raborn, not knowing anything about this project at all. It had been very closely held up until that time.

John T. Mason, Jr.: This was still in 1955?

Admiral Colwell: This was in 1955, December. When I reported in, I increased the on-board count by exactly 100%. The office consisted of Raborn and Colwell.

---

* Rear Admiral William F. Raborn, Jr., USN, was director of the Special Projects Office, which developed the Polaris submarine-launched ballistic missile system. He held the post from 2 December 1955 to 26 February 1962, being promoted to vice admiral in 1960. His Polaris oral history is in the Naval Institute collection.

John T. Mason, Jr.: Fill in the background to this. You had known him before?

Admiral Colwell: I had known him, in fact, since I was a midshipman, because he was a first classman when I was a plebe. We were in the same platoon, so I saw him quite frequently during my plebe year. Then I had seen him only very occasionally during our commissioned service. Our paths had not crossed much, perhaps because he was an aviator and I was not.

John T. Mason, Jr.: The reason I ask you that is because your talents and accomplishments must have loomed large in his estimation for him to have reached out for you at that point.

Admiral Colwell: We had had some not-too-close professional relationship. I was an ordnance engineer. He had had considerable to do with aviation ordnance, so we had had some rather arm's-length professional relationships. I never asked him how I came to be chosen, whose recommendation it was. Someday maybe I will, just for fun.

At any rate, I joined the office, and we started from there. He quickly acquainted me with the circumstances and, naturally, I was immediately impressed with the importance of the project to the continued welfare and perhaps the existence of the country.

As an office, I believe that we were all continuously aware, perhaps in the back of our minds, of the urgency and the importance and the absolute necessity for success. With that sort of a brief breaking-in period we set to work to try and put together a small working organization. This involved two immediate projects. One was obtaining a nucleus of very-well-qualified personnel in the various disciplines that we required, and the other was obtaining some funding. The office, of course, beginning in December, was in the midst of a fiscal year, and we therefore had to obtain our funds from other sources—already-funded sources. This proceeded without any great difficulty, although the people who lost money by transfer to Special Projects were somewhat distressed.

John T. Mason, Jr.: These were component parts of the Navy?

Admiral Colwell: Yes, that's right. This was all Navy money. Speaking of that, there was rather a continuing bone of contention with the office of the Secretary of Defense, because the Navy had been given to understand that the Polaris, which was recognized as a very, very expensive proposition, would be funded over and above the normal Navy budget.

John T. Mason, Jr.: Was this the understanding from the beginning?

Admiral Colwell: It was, but it did not occur. So the Polaris money came from the rest of the Navy throughout.

John T. Mason, Jr.: Well, as you intimated, there must have been some squawking on the part of others.

Admiral Colwell: There was, indeed.

John T. Mason, Jr.: How did you deal with this?

Admiral Colwell: One of Raborn's most successful performances during this entire period was a salesmanship job to the rest of the Navy. You see, when we started nobody knew anything about it. It didn't mean anything to most people. I would say the majority of people did not understand the urgency of the project, and they in particular did not understand why they should have to fund it to the detriment of their own projects. So there was an enormous educational process within the Navy itself. Of course, there was an educational process throughout the United States, but I'm speaking now only of the Navy and why there was some dissatisfaction in some quarters. This eventually almost entirely disappeared. It was a matter of education, and, of course, success brings success, as the project went on and was successful.

John T. Mason, Jr.: And the urgency was not well known, you say.

Admiral Colwell: People didn't know anything about it.

John T. Mason, Jr.: Did the urgency center in what the Russians had accomplished and what you knew they were accomplishing?

Admiral Colwell: Yes. As soon as people understood it, it was quite apparent that we were at an enormous disadvantage with the Russians if we did not have this kind of long-range nuclear bombardment capability.

Now, to get back to the beginning. We were given, of course, total support by Admiral Burke and by the Secretary.[*]

John T. Mason, Jr.: That was Secretary Thomas?

Admiral Colwell: It was Secretary Thomas at the time.[†]

John T. Mason, Jr.: And Secretary Wilson was Defense?

Admiral Colwell: He was Defense, and I'm trying to think who the Secretary for Research and Development in the Navy was, but it escapes me at the moment. At any rate, we had complete support. This manifested itself first in the provision of funds by taking them away from other sources in the Navy.

Then we were given a hunting license for people, and we actually did bring in the nucleus staff from all over the world on urgent and immediate orders.

John T. Mason, Jr.: This is the men in uniform?

---

[*] Admiral Arleigh A. Burke, USN, served as Chief of Naval Operations from 17 August 1955 to 1 August 1961. His oral history is in the Naval Institute collection.
[†] Charles S. Thomas served as Secretary of the Navy from 3 May 1954 to 1 April 1957.

Admiral Colwell: Men in uniform. We picked by name people whom we knew to be experts in various branches of missiles and rocketry. And there weren't very many in the Navy at that time.

John T. Mason, Jr.: This was personal knowledge on your part and Admiral Raborn's?

Admiral Colwell: Yes, and advice from other people, say, in the Bureau of Ordnance and in the office of the Chief of Naval Operations, and so on. People who knew by name. And we then simply told BuPers who we wanted and their orders were issued, like that. The job they were doing didn't make a darned bit of difference. This was more important, and they literally came from all over the world.

John T. Mason, Jr.: There must have been squawking as a result of that?

Admiral Colwell: Not when they got there and found out what they were going to be doing.

John T. Mason, Jr.: But I mean on the part of the offices where they were.

Admiral Colwell: Oh, there was some, yes, until it was explained to them. There are no indispensable people, so everyone survived.

As soon as this small group arrived, one by one, then we set ourselves to the task.

John T. Mason, Jr.: May I ask—I hope you don't mind these interruptions?

Admiral Colwell: No, not at all.

John T. Mason, Jr.: Had you determined at the outset that it was to be a small group?

Admiral Colwell: Yes, we had.

John T. Mason, Jr.: What was the philosophy back of that?

Admiral Colwell: The philosophy was that we were to be a group of overseers. We would make the Washington decisions. The actual effort in working toward hardware would be done by industry, in order that we would not have to establish an enormous office in Washington, or wherever, staffed by the Navy. It was apparent from the outset that this was going to involve the efforts of thousands of people. We didn't want to do that.

We started out with, say, about five people and then when we finally got the nucleus of our official staff, I think it was about 14. I've forgotten exactly, but I think 14 is a pretty fair number. This permitted us to put together a top-floor organization. I can still recall, in my mind's eye, the evening we did it. This small group sat around a blackboard and we drew up some wiring diagrams of what we thought it would take to oversee the job, and as I recall, we wound up with about five divisions for the missile itself, of course: fire control, navigation, launching, training, and perhaps there were a couple more.

And, of our group, we picked then and there the people who were to head those divisions. Oh, and then there was a plans and policy group.

John T. Mason, Jr.: How far along was this after the December date?

Admiral Colwell: Within the first few weeks. I can't remember exactly. I would think within three weeks.

John T. Mason, Jr.: You and Raborn must have done a lot of homework in that period, in order to envision what was necessary?

Admiral Colwell: We did a lot of talking together, just the two of us. We didn't stay up all night, even during this initial period. We felt that it was possible to get to work on time in the morning and work hard, and go home in the evening. Several times during those first weeks we came back in the evening and worked two or three hours. But, by and large, we did our work pretty much during working hours, but everybody worked hard. We went in on Saturday mornings. At first, this was a time for review, staff meetings for review, because we were not disturbed by outside influence.

Now, I think I'll sort of start a new chapter here because, in the beginning, we were joined with the Army, and there was a joint Army-Navy committee, which was jointly chaired, as I recall, by the two Secretaries, Army and Navy.

John T. Mason, Jr.: Was this at the insistence of Secretary Wilson?

Admiral Colwell: Probably. I couldn't certify to that, but I would think probably yes. The Army had well along a liquid-fueled, very large, intermediate-range missile called Jupiter, and at the same time the Air Force had one coming along, at about the same stage, called Thor.[*] These were nominally, oh, about 1,200-mile birds, what they then called intermediate-range ballistic missiles, IRBM. We were directed, and did, the Army in a joint project where we were to take the Jupiter missile and adapt it to shipboard carriage and firing.

This Jupiter missile was the furthest thing from something anybody would choose for use aboard ship.

John T. Mason, Jr.: Its size was tremendous, wasn't it?

Admiral Colwell: Its size was tremendous. It was liquid-fueled, which made it a very dangerous animal. It also made it a very tender bird so far as longitudinal strength and bending was concerned. Its skin was very thin, and it really had no strength in it unless it was fueled.

We set ourselves to work to try and adapt it to shipboard service.

---

[*] The Jupiter intermediate-range ballistic missile ballistic missile was developed by the Army at Redstone Arsenal in Alabama under the direction of Dr. Wernher von Braun. However, in 1956 the Department of Defense limited the Army's operational employment of missiles to those with less than a 200-mile range. Thus when Jupiter became operational in 1959 it was under U.S. Air Force control. It was 65 feet, 4 inches long; 8 feet, 9 inches in diameter; weighed 109,000 pounds at launch; and had a maximum range 1,500 statute miles.

John T. Mason, Jr.: With how much enthusiasm?

Admiral Colwell: Surprisingly, quite a lot, because we were still imbued with the urgency of the project. Although, I must say, it was rapidly becoming apparent to all of us that this was a most difficult chore. We sketched literally dozens of possible configurations for various types of surface ships, adaptations to cruisers, battleships, building new hulls, methods of supporting this tender missile, how do you fuel it, how do you carry the fuel, which all had to be refrigerated to a very great degree because it was liquid oxygen.

This occupied us for quite some little time. We established a liaison office in Huntsville, Alabama, to work with the Army Missile Command, headed by General Medaris.[*] It was rapidly becoming quite apparent to us that to get a really satisfactory system, we were going to have to go underwater so that we could cruise near enough to the potential enemy's shores to have some assurance that we could get the beast there before the vehicle was destroyed. So we gave some thought to how do you put a Jupiter in a submarine.

John T. Mason, Jr.: And what about the size of the submarine?

Admiral Colwell: Well, this was going to involve a very strange-looking submarine because the bottom of the Jupiter would be inside the hull and there would have to be a huge conning-tower structure which would support it. We hoped that if we could do this at all, we could, I think, put three in a very unwieldy submarine. It was rapidly becoming apparent to us that this just wasn't going to work.

About that time, two things happened which are central to the success of the project. A group of eminent scientists were engaged in a summer project; this would have been in the summer of 1956, I guess. In the course of this project they agreed that it was possible to build a warhead which would at least approach a megaton within some greatly reduced weight—better than anything that we'd had before. So that it was possible to boost

---

[*] Major General John B. Medaris, USA.

this warhead into a proper trajectory, perhaps with a missile that didn't weigh over 30,000 pounds. Up to now we'd been talking about 150,000 or 175,000.

Incidentally, while we were engaged in the Jupiter thing we took a look at what it would take to do this job with solid rockets—solid propellant, rather than this very dangerous liquid, and that was going to be about a 175,000-pound bird.

John T. Mason, Jr.: To fly the Jupiter?

Admiral Colwell: To fly the Jupiter warhead, and its diameter was going to be some 18 feet. It was a beast, but now we had offered to us a whole new vision of what the weight of the warhead would have to be.

At about the same time there was a breakthrough in solid propellants for rockets, where the specific impulse was vastly improved, and it would therefore be possible to build a lightweight rocket to go with the lightweight warhead.

John T. Mason, Jr.: These were all concurrent developments.

Admiral Colwell: It happened almost at the same time.

John T. Mason, Jr.: But not under the aegis of the Polaris group?

Admiral Colwell: No. These were just presented to us and were central to eventual success.

John T. Mason, Jr.: Oh, yes!

Admiral Colwell: With those two offers available to us—of course, these had not been built yet; they were just theories but well substantiated by competent people—Raborn went to work and after literally months of effort succeeded in breaking way from the Army and Jupiter. Why they fought this so hard, I don't know, but they did. He succeeded in breaking way and we were on our own for the first time, and along some place in this period we chose the name Polaris, I guess because it would mean accurate navigation or something.

We had in the very beginning chosen the name Special Projects, which was supposed to be a cover. That, of course, as naive to think that that could be a cover. Although Manhattan District had succeeded, it was unlikely that it would succeed again, particularly in peacetime.[*] However, the name has continued for years.

Incidentally, this original organization that we put together held also for years. It proved to be a very workable organization. The offices were, of course, expanded so that you had enough people to get the work done, but the basic organization held.

John T. Mason, Jr.: Which indicates some sound thinking at the beginning?

Admiral Colwell: And a great deal of good luck. I would have to say that one of the hallmarks of the entire project was enormous good fortune, coupled with a lot of very good thinking. Lots of times you make your own luck, but in so many cases we had a choice of routes offered. Sometimes we were able to pursue parallel paths until the murk cleared away somewhat, but this was not always true. We were blessed with very good fortune.

John T. Mason, Jr.: Were these dilemmas sometimes hashed out on a Saturday morning?

Admiral Colwell: Oh, yes. As a matter of administrative operation, we followed what I considered to be an entirely proper scheme of operation because that was a project where time was of the essence. As Raborn's deputy, I operated with an open door. I never closed the door of my office. I was accessible at all times to the staff. Raborn was also accessible at all times. He didn't operate with a closed door for a very good reason—so that he was accessible. The division heads could talk to Raborn at any time. They didn't have to get my permission. I just insisted that they come back and tell me what they talked about,

---

[*] Manhattan District derived from an Army Corps of Engineers term connected with the U.S. program to create an atomic bomb in World War II. The overall effort is often referred to as the Manhattan Project.

whether any decisions were made. I was the vice president in charge of the budget and we held, as I remember, about monthly reviews on how goes it with the money, who's got some that they're not using, who needs some more? We would juggle this around. It just took a little persuading for some of the people at first. Some of them had the idea that when we started out on the fiscal year and you were given your budgeted amount, that that was theirs, and I finally persuaded them it wasn't theirs, it was mine!

John T. Mason, Jr.: When did you cease drawing on Navy funds exclusively for the project?

Admiral Colwell: After our first six months, then we started on a new fiscal year and we were in the budget. We had budgeted funds which were our own.

John T. Mason, Jr.: How large was it?

Admiral Colwell: I've forgotten. It seems to me that for the first six months we had a $20 million bank account, and then it went up pretty rapidly, as we were bringing on board a lot of contractors and they were hiring a lot of people, so it took a good deal of money to fund them.

John T. Mason, Jr.: I suppose simultaneously public education had progressed?

Admiral Colwell: Oh, yes. Raborn made hundreds of speeches, I suppose. We prepared, incidentally, with Tom Watson's assistance, a pretty doggone good slide presentation, and the script was very carefully prepared.[*] Raborn and I both learned it, and we both gave it to various groups. This wasn't any off-the-top-of-the-head job. It was very carefully prepared, and designed to educate people in what we were going to do, why we were going

---

[*] Thomas J. Watson (1874-1956) was an American industrialist. After working for the National Cash Register Company for 15 years, in 1914 he became president of a company that became the International Business Machines Corporation in 1924. He led the corporation from 1914 to 1956.

to do it, and how we were going to do it. One of the objectives was to answer everybody's questions before they could ask them.

John T. Mason, Jr.: Very astute!

Admiral Colwell: It's very important. I've used it ever since. It's very important to keep people from asking questions in the middle of the talk, because that disturbs their train of thought and yours and everybody else's. They'll get off on some hare-brained discussion that hasn't really got anything to do with it. So, avoid questions. Answer them before they're asked. This was a good feat. Tom Watson helped us a great deal.

We had, for the first time, gotten ourselves embarked on something that had hopes of success—the solid rocket, the lightweight warhead—and we were on our own.

John T. Mason, Jr.: And this was in the middle of 1956?

Admiral Colwell: This would have been the middle or the tail end of 1956. I don't remember these dates really very well.

At first, when we had been attempting to do this job with the Jupiter, our contractor had been Chrysler Corporation, because they had experience with the Army in building these big birds and so forth. When we broke away, one of our first decisions—I suppose the first decision—was the choice of a new contractor. We could stay with Chrysler, GE was a possibility, Lockheed was a possibility. It seems to me there were a couple more, but I've forgotten who they were. Here again, I can still see in my mind's eye the final session we had—we being Raborn and myself and the department heads, or division heads. We sat around and we drew a matrix on the blackboard and put down what we thought were the strengths and the weaknesses of the various possible contractors. These contractors were people who wanted the job.

John T. Mason, Jr.: You'd been in consultation?

Admiral Colwell: Yes. As a result of that, we finally made our choice, and it was Lockheed. There was, of course, a certain amount of wailing and gnashing of teeth about this, but the decision stuck.

John T. Mason, Jr.: What were the factors that determined this?

Admiral Colwell: You know, my memory isn't good enough to bring those back. Some of them were objective and some were subjective. There was a certain amount of opinion that went into it. We were, after all, going to attempt something that had never been done before. At any rate, we chose Lockheed, and they chose Aerojet to build the solid rocket. Westinghouse was chosen to build the launching mechanism. This came along somewhat later because a lot of thought went into this. We had a number of contractors in the navigation area because there were a lot of different techniques—that must have been GE, I think. I'm almost certain it was GE. MIT, of course, was in the heart of the missile-guidance business, with Dr. Stark Draper's laboratory.* A myriad of operations were set in motion.

Very early on, we brought in a division head for training, because it was apparent that this was going to be a very large job.

John T. Mason, Jr.: What would that entail? Training within industry?

Admiral Colwell: Primarily training Navy people to operate the system. They were going to have to live with it for probably a couple of years in order to be letter perfect, for example, in the fire-control system. So a very thorough training organization and training program was established, including a shore-based training site. We had to have hardware for training. So this was set in motion and proved its worth many times over.

John T. Mason, Jr.: How interesting! This was before the product was available?

---

* Dr. Charles Stark Draper of the Massachusetts Institute of Technology had an important role in the development of the inertial navigation systems used in Polaris missiles and later in the space missions sent to the moon.

Admiral Colwell: That's right. This was simply to establish a training plan, and, of course, it involved all sorts of modifications later on, but the idea was that we had to have a plan in hand in order so we could budget for the people and the money and the brick-and-mortar construction. Buying extra sets of hardware, all of these things had to be planned a long time ahead. This was done.

John T. Mason, Jr.: At that point, what was your time schedule?

Admiral Colwell: That's very important. It seems to me when we first went to work with these things, which would have been in 1956, we were aiming at a first operational capability, IOC, in 1965. Then we were advised that that wouldn't do, that was entirely too long.

John T. Mason, Jr.: Whose advice was this?

Admiral Colwell: This came from the powers in OpNav and in OSD, and probably with prodding from the National Security Council, but this I'm not sure of. Raborn would know.*

So we went back to the drawing board and redrew the schedule, and this was acceleration number one. Some months later, we redrew the schedule again, and this was acceleration number two, shortening the time period each time.

John T. Mason, Jr.: How much?

Admiral Colwell: I've forgotten exactly, but it seems to me that we finally came up with acceleration number three, which we called A-cubed, and this resulted in an actual first launch in 1960, as a result of these various accelerations.

---

* OpNav—the extended staff of the Chief of Naval Operations. OSD—Office of the Secretary of Defense.

The new schedules were drawn as better information became available on progress, how we were coming. The solid motors were being poured and test-fired and were giving us reason for optimism. The warhead design was coming along and it appeared that it would do what people said it would do. I think there was some reduction in the projected yield, but they were going to be able to hold the weight that was acceptable. As you know, a pound extra weight in the payload translates into reduced range, and it doesn't take very many pounds to make a significant reduction, but they were going to make their weight.

The warhead shield design was coming along and giving us cause for optimism. The launching mechanism decisions were made reasonably early and, as I recall, they gave us reason for more optimism than any of the others. It looked like that would work. It was pretty straightforward for the engineering.

John T. Mason, Jr.: Did you have any problems with BuShips with the development of the submarine?[*]

Admiral Colwell: No. I would say that our cooperation both from BuShips and BuOrd was excellent.[†] Incidentally, one of the items that made this accelerated schedule possible was that an attack submarine hull was transferred to the project. This thing was well along, so it was just cut in half, which meant cutting all the cables and all the controls. The two halves were moved apart and the missile section set in the middle and it was put back together again.[‡] This gave us the George Washington.[§] Without that, if we had had to start from scratch building a submarine, we could not have made the triply accelerated schedule.

---

[*] BuShips—Bureau of Ships.
[†] BuOrd, the Bureau of Ordnance, existed until 1959, when it was combined with the Bureau of Aeronautics to form the Bureau of Naval Weapons (BuWeps).
[‡] For another perspective on this issue, please see the Naval Institute oral history of Captain Harry A. Jackson, USN (Ret.), who was involved in the design of the first Polaris submarines.
[§] The original hull for the attack submarine Scorpion (SSN-589) was laid down on 1 November 1957 by Electric Boat. In December of that year the portion of the hull already built was split, extended, and later renamed George Washington (SSBN-598), effective 6 November 1958. A new Scorpion with the original hull number of SSN-589 was laid down at Electric Boat on 20 August 1958.

John T. Mason, Jr.: This submarine had been designed originally for a conventional torpedo attack submarine?

Admiral Colwell: That's right.

John T. Mason, Jr.: Nuclear?

Admiral Colwell: Yes. But the basic submarine was there. All they did was cut it in half, move the pieces apart, and put in a new mid section. That became the <u>George Washington</u>.

Here is something that's important, very important, in the progress of the project. We had established a plans and policy division, which included a fiscal branch, and they worked on the budget and so on. Then it appeared that we were going to need something better than that. We were going to have to have immediately available to us some fairly detailed information on how goes it. So we cast about and we hit upon the name of Mr. Gordon Pehrson. I had known Gordon Pehrson in the Bureau of Ordnance and been tremendously impressed with him.[*] At this time, he was working for the Secretary of the Army; his exact job and title I don't recall. He was a GS-17. And casting about for someone to head up this evaluation office, if you want to call it that, various names were suggested, and I think I must take credit for advising Raborn in just about these words: "If we can get him, I think we ought to go after Gordon Pehrson."

So we made a proposition to him. Gordon felt the challenge. He's a man who loves a challenge, so he agreed to come. This was just a straight transfer, no change in rating, or in salary. He obtained his release from the Secretary of the Army and came over to us. He immediately went to work on building some sort of a reporting system to report progress, which would provide to us enough detailed information on which we might make decision—a "How Goes It?" system. Who needs help? Who has excess of money? Who has, perhaps, an excess of people? Who's coming along at such a pace that he's going to be

---

[*] The recollections of Gordon O. Pehrson are in the Naval Institute oral history volume on the Polaris program.

ready well ahead of time and we can put that on the shelf? This became a continuing effort at improving the process.

As a result of this we built what we called a management center, which had in it a number of charts showing progress in all of the various areas in which we had a vital interest. These charts were in levels. Some of them were quite detailed and on up to top-level charts which merely showed you, in essence, you're in good shape, we've got a little problem here but it looks like it will be all right, or you're in trouble. We used these charts in our staff meetings. The division heads would have to talk to them, and they would have to explain to Admiral Raborn, "I'm in good shape there, and why am I in good shape? Because—I've got a little problem over here but I can handle it. Or, I've got a bigger problem over here and I need help, I need your help. Or, we've got a big problem down here and you're in trouble, you need help." In this way we were able to keep our fingers on the pulse.

Probably the most important thing that it did was to force the division heads and their assistants to make a continuous evaluation on how they were doing. None of these horrible surprises could sneak up on you. It forced them to keep track, and their people were on the road all the time, in the plants. They weren't taking the word of a contractor, "I'm doing fine," because lots of times he wasn't doing fine at all. He was hoping he was going to do fine, but he wouldn't find out until he fixed it. We tried to prevent these unpleasant surprises from occurring.

At any rate, a good deal of this doing was Gordon Pehrson's, and eventually he evolved a computer-aided system, which came to be called PERT, and variations of PERT are now quite common, I suppose, in every complex project that's going on in the United States and probably in many foreign countries.[*]

John T. Mason, Jr.: To keep the pressure on!

Admiral Colwell: Both government and industrial. It is a process which is quite complex,

---

[*] PERT—Program Evaluation Review Technique, a system of milestones for tracking the progress of a program against its schedule.

and perhaps it's oversimplified to describe it as determining the critical paths that have to be followed in hardware development in order to come out at the end of the horn with a finished product that works, and all the pieces come together at the right stage in time en route to this final solution. This is PERT.

John T. Mason, Jr.: Well, sir, at times, since this was pioneering, you had several options, several routes to pursue, and you had different industries pursuing these individually.

Admiral Colwell: Right.

John T. Mason, Jr.: When did you determine which one to select and which one to break off?

Admiral Colwell: Well, one thing that the critical-paths system provides for you is decision points at which you must decide, or you're going to be late. For instance, Equipment A up here has to follow down this line and join up with Equipment B, C, D, and E, and eventually you'll come out with total Equipment X. Now, at some point up here, if you have several side issues with Equipment A, at some point you have to make a decision. You can't continue to play with all of these things up here, because you're going to wind up out here in time in making your decision, when you should have made it back here. And the whole thing is going to be delayed by that amount, and that you cannot afford. This is what a decision point shows you. It is a very powerful management tool in complex projects.

I certainly hope that you'll be able to have a very lengthy interview with Gordon Pehrson. In the first place, I think you'll find him a fascinating man to talk to. I think he comes closer to total recall than anyone, so he should be able to fill in a lot of the blanks, and possibly correct some of the things I've given you from memory.

John T. Mason, Jr.: Now that we're interrupted at this point, I seem to recall rather vividly that Arleigh Burke said that built into your planning was the possibility of a cut-off date, if it looked like the project wasn't going to work?

Admiral Colwell : Yes, that was always there.

John T. Mason, Jr.: He also said that there was one occasion when it came near being applied.

Admiral Colwell: It may be that he was referring to the initial flight test, where they had— by this time I had left the project, but they had either five or six successive failures on the flight pad down at Canaveral. I would imagine that they perhaps were coming pretty close to a cut-off at that time. I had left the project by then and I had no knowledge of it personally. Raborn, I'm sure, would have a lot to say about it! Levering Smith would have a great deal to say about it.[*]

John T. Mason, Jr.: Why was that provision put in in the beginning?

Admiral Colwell: I don't know that it was ever written. I think it was just understood. We were trying to do something that had never been done, and I think it was just understood that if we ever came to a roadblock, for example, suppose the pilot motor wouldn't produce the specific impulse that was projected for it and you couldn't get a launch, or maybe you could only get 400 miles out of it, that would not be enough to do you any good. Or suppose the theoretical computations on lightweight warheads proved to have a flaw and they couldn't build any; that would have been a reason to stop.

Suppose, for example the proposed submarine structure was going to be unstable, though this was unlikely, that would certainly be cause for stopping. If the flight controls on the bird failed, and this is what did happen at the early launchings, so that you had a

---

[*] Captain Levering Smith, USN, was the second technical director in the Special Projects Office. He succeeded Captain Grayson Merrill, USN, when Merrill retired in 1957. The oral history of Captain Merrill is in the Naval Institute collection.

completely unmanageable bird in flight, you'd have to stop. It was nothing but common sense, really. I suspect that's what Burke was talking, about.

You will certainly want to talk to Levering Smith, if you are building a Polaris history.* He came on board very early as our technical director.

John T. Mason, Jr.: He'd been out in California, had he not?

Admiral Colwell: He had been at China Lake, and he had also been down at White Sands. Levering Smith is a scientist-engineer of very high caliber. He has retired from the Navy. He was an ordnance-engineering-duty-only officer. They ordinarily serve a specified number of years in flag rank and then are retired, in order to make some necessary advancement opportunities for the younger officers in that branch. BuShips people do the same thing. Aeronautical engineering duty officers do the same thing. It's necessary.

At any rate, he was retired and came back on active duty the next day in the same job. Levering is a very quiet, unflappable man. If something fails, as the early flight vehicles did, Levering would simply go back to work and start figuring out where the failure was, and fix it, and he did.

I guess maybe I'm coming along toward the end of my recollections about the project.

John T. Mason, Jr.: Could you talk, sir, about the letting of contracts and carte blanche you had?

Admiral Colwell: Yes. From the very beginning we were attached to the Bureau of Ordnance in a sort of arm's-length way for administrative services. They took care of all of our personnel records. They took care of our contracting. They took care of our dealings with the Civil Service Commission for rating. At one time we had a very substantial expansion, all at once, and this involved writing Civil Service descriptions for a lot of people and getting Civil Service permission to approve the assignment of grades. This

---

* Smith, unfortunately, did not do an oral history.

ordinarily is a rather difficult procedure because the commission, quite properly, guards this carefully, so that people are not given high grades just because they're a friend of Joe. On the other hand, in establishing brand-new positions with a requirement for certain skills, including high qualities, then it is very important for the office requesting these positions to get adequate grade structure, or you can't hire anybody. A top-notch engineer isn't going to work as a GS-9, when he can get a GS-14 somewhere else.

John T. Mason, Jr.: Simply for love of country!

Admiral Colwell: That's right. So at this one particular time, Raborn, I believe personally, went to the head of the Civil Service Commission—I'm a little hazy on this, but Red will remember it—and got the assignment of two or three or four Civil Service examiners to come into our office and work with us, listen to the story of what these people had to do, and work with us in the establishment of these positions so that we would be able to get on with the job. The reason, I think, Red went personally to the head of the commission was that he had to give him what we called the dog-and-pony show in order to impress on him the urgency the project.

John T. Mason, Jr.: What did you call that?

Admiral Colwell: The dog-and-pony show. This was the slide speech.

John T. Mason, Jr.: Why dog and pony?

Admiral Colwell: Red invented that phrase. It just sounded good, I guess.

With an understanding of the urgency of the project, why, this went along, certainly as smoothly as you could expect. That was just at one point when we had a sudden increase in the number of people.

One of the things that we kept in front of us all the time—and we'd explain this to all the new people who came on board, I'm talking about people in uniform—was that this was a project of sort of indeterminate length. We didn't know how long it was going to take, but it required total dedication to the project, it required some loss of mobility for the people involved. People when they arrived were going to have to be prepared to stay. This was at variance with the established procedure for moving officers around in order to give them varied experience and presumably enhance their chances of selection to flag rank.

John T. Mason, Jr.: How did you deal with that particular problem?

Admiral Colwell: We got agreement from the Bureau of Personnel and the Chief of Naval Operations that this was the way it was, that people were going to have to stay. There could be some exceptions. I turned out to be, I guess, the first exception. I was in the zone for selection to rear admiral. Red was very understanding about this. I can't remember whether I asked if I could go or whether he suggested that I ought to go. He may have suggested it. As a result, I was detached to command the Galveston, which was the first Talos cruiser, and was being put together and was eventually commissioned in Philadelphia.

I therefore left the Special Projects office in January of 1958, after something over two years in it. In hindsight, I would say that the deputy director could probably be more easily spared for rotation than one of the division heads, because I was not so intimately involved in technical development and particularly in technical decisions. I was the deputy and assistant to Admiral Raborn, and I could be replaced.

John T. Mason, Jr.: And since your selection was imminent, you had to have that duty in command of a cruiser?

Admiral Colwell: Well, without a major command behind you, it was pretty difficult to be selected, no matter what you'd been doing. This wasn't a rule, but it was darned close to one. This sort of a rule has been greatly relaxed recent years, and properly so.

John T. Mason, Jr.: And you really couldn't get them to relax it at that point?

Admiral Colwell: This is the way a selection board works for flag rank. The Secretary of the Navy issues letter to the president of the selection board, and this selection board consists of an admiral, a four-star admiral, at least two three-star admirals, and the rest of them two-stars. They have a letter of instruction which tells them roughly the way he wants them to work. He cannot direct them to do a particular thing or to select a person by name. That is not the way selection boards work. They are free to operate within the rules that he has established for them.

Therefore, there was no assurance that I could ever be selected if I stayed in this field and didn't have my major command. This is the reason Raborn let me go, or at least I assume it was. At any rate, I left Special Projects in January of 1958. That concludes that chapter.

John T. Mason, Jr.: I want to ask you a few things. The Congress got very enthusiastic about this project?

Admiral Colwell: Oh, yes.

John T. Mason, Jr.: During your period with it, did you have anything to do with the education of the Congress?

Admiral Colwell: Raborn did that by himself, and he did a beautiful job. No one should ever take away from Raborn credit for—you can call it a sales job, if you will, but that's not a very good term—the educational job that he did. I don't know how many speeches he made all over the country explaining to people why and what and how. I don't know that we ever had any difficulties with the Congress at all. I don't think so.

John T. Mason, Jr.: Is he to be credited with the great success in the industrial world, in developing this tremendous enthusiasm and sense of dedication?

Admiral Colwell: Yes. Yes, indeed, he is. He should receive full credit for that. He traveled. He was on the road a great deal, going to the various plants, talking to the people, talking to the people on the benches, workmen.

John T. Mason, Jr.: Whose idea was it to have the various industries separate the Polaris project from the rest of what went on in the factories? What did you call it—fragmentation?

Admiral Colwell: Yes. That was pretty much a decision that we made in the Special Project office. We felt that it was the only way to assure that the people who worked on Polaris didn't work on anything else, and that they stayed with it.

John T. Mason, Jr.: Based on what? Experience with that?

Admiral Colwell: Just our determination that it was the right way to do it.

John T. Mason, Jr.: Did this entail a larger expenditure in order to accomplish it?

Admiral Colwell: Perhaps. We took this view, and this may sound as though we were careless with our funds, but that I would contest. We took the view that each one of these missiles that we were going to build and each part of the system that we were going to build was so vital to the well-being of the United States, each missile in flight was worth so much that we could afford to build it with jewelers' tools, if necessary. That doesn't mean that we were careless with money, because I deny that we were. We used a great deal of money. We pursued parallel courses in many cases, but this was all part of the urgency of the project and the very short time scale in which we had to produce the final product.

We spent a lot of money, but we produced an awful good system, and well ahead of the time anybody thought it could be done.

John T. Mason, Jr.: Tell me how you were able to circumvent the traditional way of letting contracts?

Admiral Colwell: Well, of course, there has always been available a process of going sole source. This was not new.

John T. Mason, Jr.: Sole source?

Admiral Colwell: Sole source, rather than going out on the street and asking everybody till kingdom come to bid on something. We've always been able to go sole source, and properly so, if you could justify it, and we could justify it.

John T. Mason, Jr.: That had been infrequently used, however?

Admiral Colwell: That's right, and properly so, infrequently. It can lead to excess pricing, it can lead to all sorts of unsatisfactory conditions. But it can still be used if it is properly justified.

John T. Mason, Jr.: Were there any protests as a result of the route you chose?

Admiral Colwell: Not that I recall. There may have been, but I don't recall them. Red would probably have a better idea about that. Levering Smith would probably have some ideas about it. He's still with it, so he's been with it now for 17 years.[*]

John T. Mason, Jr.: Tell me how you chose the number of 41 as the number of submarines?

---

[*] His tenure continued beyond this interview. As a rear admiral, Smith eventually served as director of the Special Projects Office/Strategic Systems Projects Office from 16 February 1965 to 14 November 1977. He thus took over the billet originally held by Admiral Raborn.

Admiral Colwell: That's a good question. As part of the planning process, it was, of course, necessary to project what the total Polaris force should be. Incidentally, a part of this was deciding how many birds should be in each submarine, and I can remember going through that process. A lot of people think it was pretty much waving a magic wand and coming up with 16. Actually, we gave it a lot of thought. Naturally, they were all even numbers, so that you could put them in two rows down the spine of the submarine. We started with a number like eight, and it seemed as though that wasn't enough for the price of the submarine and the fire-control system could handle more, so we got up to a number like 24 and that required a bigger submarine than we wanted. Today, of course, with the Trident they're talking about one much bigger, but the submarine construction people didn't want to build one that big.* So we started backing down, and we arrived at 16, which I still think was frankly a pretty good decision. You could build a submarine, you could build a fire-control system that could handle it, and so on.

Now, where was I?

John T. Mason, Jr.: At how you arrived at 41.

Admiral Colwell: Oh, yes. There began to be a lot of figuring on many Polaris missiles there ought to be. So we started with 16 per ship, and we worked out on rotation schedules how many submarines we felt could be kept at sea continuously, how many you could add to that in times of tension. This, of course, had to look at overhaul schedules, overhaul frequency, time of overhaul, time to give the crews a rest at home, training, all of these things. So we finally came up with the number of 45 submarines. This would provide for X number at sea all the time, which would provide 16X Polaris birds in position on the job, and this would menace so many Soviet and Red Chinese targets. To put that many targets at risk with that many birds at sea.

---

* The Trident submarine-launched ballistic missile entered the fleet in 1979; the USS Francis Scott Key (SSBN-657) began the first deterrent patrol with Trident in October of that year. The first submarines specifically designed for Trident constituted the Ohio (SSBN-726) class; the Ohio was commissioned 11 November 1981. The first version of the Trident missile, the C-4, was 34 feet long, 74 inches in diameter, and weighed about 65,000 pounds. It had a range of approximately 4,000 nautical miles. Each Ohio-class submarine carries 24 missiles.

This began to involve lengthy and, at times, acrimonious discussions and arguments with the Air Force proponents arguing, how they could do it better and cheaper and quicker, instead of building all these expensive submarines, of which only part could be ready to go at any one time. Well, that particular argument you can't fight. It's true. But you could provide a certain number of missiles at sea all the time, and therefore put at risk that many targets.

The number we finally came up with, we—and this included a lot of people in addition to the SP office over in OpNav—came up with was 45 submarines, and a building schedule was projected on that number. This, again, appeared to be a reasonable building schedule, and you would get the total force within a reasonable number of years, so that you weren't talking about getting the last boat in 1985.

You need to talk to Red on why that number went down to 41 because it escapes me. There was some kind of a compromise number, and it went from 45 down to 41, but I can't remember what it was.

John T. Mason, Jr.: But it was related to the pressure from the Air Force?

Admiral Colwell: I'm sure it was. There was a tremendous battle for money in this entire program, you see. The three elements of the strategic system, total strategic system, were bombers, Minuteman, and Polaris, and you had to add the funding for all three of them together in order to present it to the Congress and to the country as a U.S. investment in strategic preparedness.[*] So there was, quite naturally, a competition for money among those three strategic systems.

John T. Mason, Jr.: Now, the fact that the Air Force was arguing and applying pressure implies that they were cognizant of developments within your shop?

Admiral Colwell: Oh, yes, always.

---

[*] Minuteman was a land-based intercontinental ballistic missile under Air Force control.

John T. Mason, Jr.: How was this accomplished?

Admiral Colwell: There was a continuing exchange of information between the Air Force and the Navy. We had a liaison man in the Air Force headquarters in Los Angeles, in the ballistic missile division.

John T. Mason, Jr.: What about the element of secrecy surrounding the project, to wit, the broad effort at selling to the nation much of what you were doing had to be revealed?

Admiral Colwell: Yes. It was, of course, impossible to conduct this in anything approaching the Manhattan District system. In the first place, that was wartime and we had all kinds of censorship. It was perfectly apparent this was not going to be any secret to anybody, and the best we could do was to maintain secrecy on the vital elements. We tried to maintain secrecy on what kind of range we expected to get with the first generation. That turned out to be, I think, within 1,100 to 1,200 miles. We were hoping for 1,500. We did maintain secrecy on the warhead yield. That secrecy has long since been broken, but we maintained it at the time. The accuracy that we expected to get was carefully kept secret for a long time, and the accuracy we did get. A lot of these things have been given away over the years, I think improperly.

So, there were only certain vital bits of information we were able to maintain in secrecy, or that we tried to maintain. Launching was kept closely held for a long time. That's long since been broken. The speed of the submarine for the Polaris missile, that's been given away.

I think I'm about running dry on Polaris.

John T. Mason, Jr.: When did your training division decide upon the necessity of double crews?

Admiral Colwell: That was not a training division decision. That was one that was generated really during the deliberations on what the size of the force should be. An essential part of keeping X percent of the boats at sea all the time is the double crewing. Otherwise, the percentage of boats at sea constantly would be considerably smaller. So it was part of that.

John T. Mason, Jr.: Did the problems loom early in the development of the project, the problems of personnel, and endurance, and boredom, and that sort of thing? On long cruises?

Admiral Colwell: Yes. They loomed up very early and were given a great deal of thought. I don't think that there is any way that you can eliminate it. The Polaris submarines on long patrols are provided with the best food, with individual types of entertainment, with mass entertainment, and do-it-yourself projects, hobbies, and, above all, a great deal of work.

I have talked to submarine people from time to time in fairly recent years, because I had this question in my mind weren't these people getting awfully tired of spending half of their lives under water.

John T. Mason, Jr.: And away from families.

Admiral Colwell: Away from families and seeing the same people all the time. The answer is, yes, they are. They are, indeed. Of course, there isn't any way to hold a man who says, "I don't want to do that anymore."

John T. Mason, Jr.: Yet a lot has gone into his training for it!

Admiral Colwell: Yes, indeed. They watch psychological matters very, very carefully, but, of course, they do in all submarine operations. But in these in particular because a 60-day patrol imposes an entirely different set of factors on a person, and knowing that when you get back you get 30 days off, and then you spend 30 days retraining ashore, then you're off again, this can get to be kind of a grim thing to look forward to. It's a problem. One solution might be, and I've talked about this too to various people—I don't find very many people accepting it—to stop the business of maximum boats at sea continuously, since we've had the National Security Council-Presidential decision and a very important one. It would amount to a lowering of the active deterrent. Perhaps if the détente continues and actually improves with the Russians, we might come to this some day, where we wouldn't try to maximize the number of Polaris submarines on patrol.* This would give the people a lot better break on home life. It might even come to the point where you wouldn't have to double crew any more. This, of course, is a national decision of great magnitude.

John T. Mason, Jr.: Has the problem lessened with the development of Holy Loch and Rota?†

Admiral Colwell: Yes, the problem was lessened, but perhaps even more importantly it made possible a maximizing of sea patrols to the point where the force as a whole was much more effective. It lessened the problem.

John T. Mason, Jr.: When did the satellite come into use as a means of directing the submarines?

Admiral Colwell: We've had communication satellites now for—time passes so quickly—what, four or five years, and we've had navigation satellites for longer than that, so that's about the only answer I can give. Navigation for the Polaris boats is, of course of vital importance. They have to know where they are when they launch. They use every possible means at their disposal to pick their positions, including bottom-contour navigation. Satellite navigation is a beautiful system. It has one fault as far as Polaris is concerned. It requires the exposure of a sensor. They don't like to do that. If you had any positive assurance that there wasn't going to be anybody there to see it, why, you could go right

---

* In the 1970s the United States and Soviet Union experienced a period of détente, that is, a relaxation of previously strained relations.
† During the years of operation by Polaris-armed submarines, they had forward bases at Holy Loch, Scotland, and Rota, Spain, so they would be relatively near their patrol areas in the periods between patrols. With the subsequent development of longer-range submarine-launched ballistic missiles, the submarines are based in the United States.

ahead. Or, if you were in extremis, and you did not know where you were, this might be a chance you had to take.

John T. Mason, Jr.: It's not that large, is it?

Admiral Colwell: It's not too big, no. I don't know what they've got that dish down to now, 18 inches, maybe.

John T. Mason, Jr.: Would it loom up on a radar ever?

Admiral Colwell: Yes, it could, if there was anybody there to see it. Communications with the Polaris boats, of course, have been a cause for concern from the very beginning. It was one of the first things we had to start thinking about. How do you talk to them? You have very-low frequency, and those are waves which will penetrate a certain amount of seawater so that you can be submerged and receive. If you wanted to call high frequency, then you have to poke out an antenna, and high frequencies are not too hard to jam.

All sorts of exotic schemes have been proposed for communication with the boats, primarily in extremis. Suppose you were faced with certain destruction of a large part of your transmitters in the U.S. or allies, or whoever uses them, then what do you do? All sorts of schemes have been proposed. I don't even know what they are. I've been out of this business so long.

You have no doubt read about a proposal to build a very large grid, it was first in Wisconsin, now I think they're talking Texas, for ultra-low frequency, because these waves will penetrate water to a considerable distance. This would be better. This would be great. Also very hard to jam. It would be nice if that were classified information, but it's been all over the newspapers.

I'd like just to add a sort of a postscript to this.

The first generation of the Polaris birds could fly about 1,100 to 1,200 miles. It was obvious to everybody that the more range we could get out of these things, the better off we would be, because if you could add 500 miles of range then you add millions of square miles of water that the enemy has to be concerned about. That was called the A-1 bird. The A-2 bird took it out to about 1,500 miles.

John T. Mason, Jr.: When did he come into being?

Admiral Colwell: I've forgotten just what the timing was.* A couple of years later, I suppose.

Then, as the technique of manufacturing the solid-propellant motors improved, we were able to make them bigger, that is fatter. The birds were made a little bit longer, as much as the submarines could stand, and, of course, there was some improvement in specific impulse as the result of experience.

Then they came up with an A-3 version, and this, I think, would get you about 2,200 miles.

John T. Mason, Jr.: I would imagine that, as range increases, the need for Holy Loch and Rota would decrease?

Admiral Colwell: That's true, but we're still using them. They still have an advantage because it will shorten your transit to the patrol areas. Instead of going this way directly toward Russia, why, you can go this way, a little farther away.

You perhaps have been reading recently that the trouble with the Poseidon bird is that its reliability has not been as good as everyone hoped, so we're going to have to go back to re-work.† This is not a cause for alarm. They're going back to rework. I think they've already found out what the problem is.

John T. Mason, Jr.: And Levering's there!

---

* The A-2 version of the Polaris ballistic missile was 31 feet long; 4 feet, 6 inches in diameter; and weighed about 30,000 pounds. It had a range of 1,725 nautical miles. It first flew in November 1960.
† The Poseidon C-3 ballistic missile, which had initially been designated Polaris B-3, was 34 feet long; 6 feet, 2 inches in diameter; and weighed about 65,000 pounds. It had a range of about 2,500 nautical miles. Flight tests began in August 1968. The first submarine to deploy with Poseidon was the James Madison (SSBN-627), which fired the first Poseidon C-3 in August 1970.

Admiral Colwell: Levering is there. He is there.

I went down to Canaveral a year ago last summer to watch a Poseidon shot. It was a fascinating experience. It was the first one I'd ever seen.

John T. Mason, Jr.: And it's now called Canaveral again, isn't it?*

Admiral Colwell: Yes, it is.

---

* Cape Canaveral, Florida, has been the site of many U.S. missile launchings, including the earliest in the space program in the early 1960s. In November 1963, following the assassination of President John F. Kennedy, it was renamed Cape Kennedy. The name was changed back to Cape Canaveral in 1973 in deference to the wishes of Floridians. It is the site of the John F. Kennedy Space Center.

Interview Number 5 with Vice Admiral John Barr Colwell, U.S. Navy (Retired)

Place: Admiral Colwell's apartment in Washington, D.C.

Date: Tuesday, 20 November 1973

Interviewer: John T. Mason, Jr.

John T. Mason, Jr.:   Good to see you this morning, Admiral. Last time, you talked about your two years with the Special Project, the Polaris project. That was an interesting time, indeed, and a high point in your career.

I wonder if you would tell me what was the relationship between the Special Project and the Ballistic Missile Committee in the department?

Admiral Colwell: When the Special Projects Office was first formed, you recall that we were partners with the Army in their ballistic-missile project, known as the Jupiter, and a Ballistic Missile Committee was formed which was joint Army and Navy. This joint Ballistic Missile Committee, as I recall, was jointly chaired by the two service secretaries, and it was the authority to whom both the Army and the Navy ballistic missile project managers reported. That would have been General Medaris for the Army and, of course, Admiral Raborn for the Navy. It was designed to keep the top people in the two services informed of progress and, looking back on it, I would assume that it was designed to improve and to ensure an adequate joint effort.

As far as OP-51 was concerned, OP-51 was the Special Projects Office contact in the office of the Chief of Naval Operations, and they gave us substantial support, which is really rather hard to define or to describe.[*] We obviously needed a contact in CNO, and OP-51 was it. Raborn additionally, of course, had completely free access to the CNO and to the Secretary.

That, I think, is a brief description of what the relationship was.

---

[*] See the Naval Institute oral history of Commander Paul H. Backus, USN (Ret.), who was involved in the OpNav end of the Polaris development program.

J. B. Colwell, Interview #5 (11/29/73) - 160

John T. Mason, Jr.: Did they in any sense control your finances?

Admiral Colwell: Perhaps "control" isn't the exact word, but OP-51 was the channel for Special Projects's budget submission, in order to feed it into the Navy budget and get it into shape. The actual hearings on the Hill for the SP budget were handled by Raborn, but there did have to be a process by which SP's budget requests were fed into the overall Navy and Department of Defense budget.

John T. Mason, Jr.: This is the channel where, in a sense, it was regularized?

Admiral Colwell: That's correct.

John T. Mason, Jr.: Did they have anything to do with the developing policy, for example?

Admiral Colwell: Yes, I would say that they did. In addition to the technical chore of producing the Polaris weapon system, there was, of course, a necessity to produce the policy, the doctrine, the justification for end-strength, and various types of things that are normally handled within CNO and the various branches of it.

OP-51 was the channel. Of course, we had dealings with the plans and policy people, 06, and so on.*

John T. Mason, Jr.: Was 51 of any use to you in dealing with the bureaus? Admiral Raborn said at one point early on there was opposition in the Bureau of Ordnance. Were they helpful to you?

Admiral Colwell: I would say yes. I don't recall any particular instances where they were helpful, but I'm sure they were, again through this mechanism of being our channel within OpNav.

---

* OP-06—Deputy Chief of Naval Operations (Plans and Policy).

J. B. Colwell, Interview #5 (11/29/73) - 161

John T. Mason, Jr.: Did they have a representative present when you had your weekly sessions?

Admiral Colwell: You know, I can't quite remember whether they did all the time or not, but they had a representative in and out of the office a great deal. I can't remember whether they attended the Saturday sessions or not. They probably did.

John T. Mason, Jr.: Another thing I wanted to ask you about, another person I wanted to ask you about, if he then was prominent and played quite a part in one aspect of the Polaris submarine and continues prominent, and that's Admiral Rickover.[*] What was his role? What are your recollections of him?

Admiral Colwell: As I recollect, his role was almost entirely restricted to the submarine vehicle itself. I don't recall that he took any part in the development of the weapon system. Certainly not the missile. Raborn might have some different recollections on this, but it seems to me that Admiral Rickover confined himself to his particular field almost entirely.

John T. Mason, Jr.: Did you personally have any direct dealings with Admiral Mumma in the Bureau of Ships?[†]

Admiral Colwell: Yes. We dealt regularly with various people in BuShips, as in BuOrd. I would say that these were almost on regular basis, perhaps not scheduled regularly but quite frequent.

John T. Mason, Jr.: While you were still there, did that changing of the schedule occur? That was in 1957.

---

[*] Hyman G. Rickover was considered the father of the nuclear Navy. He ran the U.S. Navy's nuclear-power program for many years, from 1948 until he eventually left active duty in 1982 with the rank of four-star admiral on the retired list. Rickover Hall at the Naval Academy is named in his honor, as is the nuclear-powered attack submarine Hyman G. Rickover (SSN-709), which was commissioned 21 July 1984.
[†] Rear Admiral Albert G. Mumma, USN, served as Chief of the Bureau of Ships from 1955 to 1959. His oral history is in the Naval Institute collection.

Admiral Colwell: Yes. One of the accelerations occurred while I was there. You remember last time we talked about accelerations 1, 2, and 3, which we called A-1, A-squared, and A-cubed. As I remember, one occurred while I was there, and the other two after I'd left. But that's a little hazy.

John T. Mason, Jr.: Well, Admiral, you got a very fine assignment when you left the SP. You went up to Philadelphia to commission and take to sea the Galveston.* She was the first of her kind.

Admiral Colwell: Yes, that was a very fine assignment. Fitting her out was really a very interesting and a very pleasant time.

John T. Mason, Jr.: Tell me about that.

Admiral Colwell: Well, the Galveston hull had been built as a light cruiser towards the end of World War II, but she was never quite finished. She was at least 95% complete, something like that, at the end of the war, and she was immediately tied up in mothballs.

John T. Mason, Jr.: She was put in limbo.

Admiral Colwell: She was never commissioned, never quite completed.

John T. Mason, Jr.: What was the rationale behind a policy like that?

Admiral Colwell: She wasn't needed. The war was over.

---

* The light cruiser Galveston (CL-93) was launched 22 April 1945, and her construction was suspended 24 June 1946. After being held in reserve for several years she was reclassified a guided missile light cruiser, CLG-3, on 23 May 1957 and commissioned on 28 May 1958. She was armed with six 6-inch guns, six 5-inch guns, and was fitted with one twin launcher for Talos surface-to-air missiles. She had a full-load displacement of 14,600 tons, was 608 feet long, 64 feet in the beam, had a maximum draft of 25 feet, and a top speed of 33 knots.

John T. Mason, Jr.: But she could have supplanted some older ships.

Admiral Colwell: Well, they weren't that old, so I would assume—I'm inventing this now, but I would assume that the reason was we might as well get all the mileage we could out of ships that were actually in commission, operating, had crews. And ships such as Galveston, which were brand new, could be tied up and kept in limbo for several years with no deterioration. Then, when we wanted them, why, we'd have brand-new ones. I would guess that was the reason. They were very fine ships. They were pretty well standardized. They produced a whole train of them and were just alike.

John T. Mason, Jr.: What tonnage?

Admiral Colwell: They were nominally about 10,000-ton ships. As I remember, after conversion when we went to sea, they were a little heavier and, full load, they were around 14,000 tons, or something like that. They had a superb power plant, reasonably simple in terms of plants, but an excellent, reliable plant.

I spent several months in Philadelphia with the nucleus crew, which was gradually increased as we came closer to completion. I had a superb crew. The officers were all very carefully chosen. The missile people were practically the entire naval force of Talos missile people.* I had almost all there were in our Navy. They'd been working on this missile for a long time.

John T. Mason, Jr.: The fact that she was the first of her kind, a missile cruiser, must have entailed some special work at the shipyard. Tell me some of the problems there.

Admiral Colwell: She was not the first missile cruiser.† She was the first Talos missile cruiser. Talos is a very large bird, long-range, originally built as a 50-mile antiaircraft

---

* Talos was a long-range ramjet missile used by surface ships in the antiair mission. Its first successful intercept of a drone target was in October 1952. It entered fleet service on board the Galveston in 1958 and from then until 1979 was the U.S. Navy's most impressive shipboard antiair missile.
† USS Boston (CAG-1), which had previously been a conventional heavy cruiser, was recommissioned on 1 November 1955 as the world's first guided missile cruiser.

missile, and as more powerful fuels were developed, why, it would reach out in the neighborhood of 100 miles. For a missile of this size, obviously, with all of the handling gear, the loading gear, and the launching gear was massive. As I remember, this was built by Northern Ordnance. We had a twin-arm launcher, and we kept some 6-inch guns forward; she was built as a 6-inch cruiser. Then we had the two vitally necessary, very large, very heavy, and very powerful tracking and guidance radars for the Talos, and these were, built by Sperry.

Additionally, we had a very-long-range search radar, which could pick up the target initially, and then the contact would be transferred over in weapons control to guidance radars, and eventually the launch would be made. One of the difficulties that we had was the extreme complexity of the entire system, so that there were miles and miles and miles of wires, and the switchboards were enormously complicated. Just putting one of these things together and getting all the wires checked out was a job of many, many months. At one time, this was complicated by a fire in the switchboard which set us back quite some while, because large sections of it had to be rewired.

Another difficulty that we encountered was in the storage space for the reserve missiles. We had a ready storage from which we could load and reload the launcher in a fairly rapid cycle. Then there was a sort of a dead storage in a large, large room on the main deck. The plans for that were either not carefully drawn or not carefully executed, because when the stanchions were put in so that we could store the missiles in racks, they didn't fit properly, and these all had to be torn out and remanufactured and reinstalled. That was another delay.

Of course, the ship could operate without that, but it wasn't much of a missile ship without that.

John T. Mason, Jr.: How many missiles of this size could the ship accommodate, in storage and in readiness?

Admiral Colwell: You know, I don't remember the exact number, but it must have been somewhere around 100, I would think.

John T. Mason, Jr.: Quite an armament!

Admiral Colwell: Oh, yes. I don't remember exactly, but it seems to me it must have been somewhere around there.

John T. Mason, Jr.: Adding all of that to a cruiser hull which had been planned for quite a different kind of armament, did you have a problem of weight on the upper decks?

Admiral Colwell: We tended to be a little top-heavy, yes. One of the later ships, which was a sister ship, for some reason which I do not know, had more of a top-heavy problem than we had. Ours was never serious, and I don't know why theirs was. It seems to me we had extra ballast added down in the bilges.

John T. Mason, Jr.: Would that reduce the speed potential?

Admiral Colwell: Not noticeably. It made the ship heavier, but it also helped the top-heavy condition. At any rate, we finally got ourselves in condition so that we could be commissioned.

John T. Mason, Jr.: You spoke a little bit ago about the fact that you ran into some difficulties with the racks for storage, which were inappropriate in size. This leads me to ask were the Talos people present during this period of construction or were they not?

Admiral Colwell: Oh, yes. We had fairly continuous contact with not only the missile people but with Sperry on the fire control and Northern Ordnance on the massive launching and handling gear.

John T. Mason, Jr.: Then, the obvious question, if the Talos people were present, why did they permit the inadequacy of that storage?

Admiral Colwell: This was not the fault of the Talos people. It was an error within the Navy. As I said, either they misread the blueprints or the blueprints were wrong. At any rate, these large stanchions that were supposed to hold the missiles didn't fit. This was strictly a Navy yard responsibility.*

John T. Mason, Jr.: How much license did you have, as the potential and the future skipper, to reorganize things and make changes?

Admiral Colwell: Very little, except for cause. It's absolutely necessary to control this sort of thing very tightly. Otherwise, if people were permitted to make any changes that they wanted to, you'd wind up with heaven knows what on your hands.

John T. Mason, Jr.: A potpourri of some kind!

Admiral Colwell: Yes, and the prices would be uncontrolled. They'd go out of sight.

If I found something in the ship that I felt ought to be changed for cause, then I could and did submit letters to the Bureau of Ships, the CNO, and whoever was concerned about the particular piece, requesting changes, which might or might not be approved. This is a standard procedure for the commissioning of a ship. But you are not, and quite properly not, permitted to just go and tell the yard, "Hey, I want to do it this way." And if the yard does it, he quite properly gets slapped down and told that isn't the way we run the railroad.

John T. Mason, Jr.: But you, as the future skipper, had a very special kind of knowledge for a new ship?

Admiral Colwell: Well, if there were changes that appeared to be required in the missile system, these would be discussed thoroughly with the cognizant offices in Washington,

---

* The conversion of the ship was done by the Philadelphia Naval Shipyard.

with the Navy yard people, and, if the changes were agreed to be necessary, then they went ahead.

John T. Mason, Jr.: I assume that there were special training courses for crew, as they assembled?

Admiral Colwell: Oh, yes.

John T. Mason, Jr.: Tell me about that.

Admiral Colwell: I had a nucleus crew in the engineering force who worked with the Navy yard in getting the engines and boilers together. A nucleus of missile people in various categories who were there for many, many months. Lots of them were there before I arrived. Then, the commissioning crew was assembled several weeks before commissioning under the executive officer in Norfolk. These people went through such regular schools as the firefighting school, and antiaircraft school, and so on. These were the non-missile specialists. These people all arrived in Philadelphia very shortly before commissioning and were put up in barracks.

Then, as I remember, the day before we commissioned they all moved aboard, started serving meals and living aboard—the entire crew. This part all went very smoothly and we commissioned her on, I think, it was the 28th of May 1958, a very hot day in Philadelphia.

John T. Mason, Jr.: How much voice did you have in the selection of the key people?

Admiral Colwell: None, and I didn't ask for any. I took the attitude that the people in the bureau had access to better information than I had.

John T. Mason, Jr.: Did that prove to be the case?

Admiral Colwell: Yes, they were all very good. I was very pleased with the crew, both officers and men, very pleased.

After we commissioned, then we had the summer in Philadelphia. We went to sea a few times on trials. As the ship became ready, we would go out on trials. The engineering plant worked very well from the beginning. As I remember, the ship was so new that when we commissioned and started actually steaming, I think the boilers only had six hours on them or something like that. She was a great joy to take to sea, very nimble, quick acceleration, high speed.

John T. Mason, Jr.: What speed?

Admiral Colwell: Well, we went out for a full power trial in her, which was one of the requirements before the ship was delivered. Commissioning is not delivery, you know. She still belonged to the Navy yard, but I was permitted to drive her. So we went out for a full-power run and made it with no difficulty whatsoever. The ship was running so beautifully and the weather was excellent, the chief engineer said, "Why don't we open her up?" We'd already made her designed full power, and we still had more power available. We still had not reached the rotational limits on the turbines. That is actually your limit on the speed of a ship, as long as you have boiler power. So we opened her up till we got up to the limit and we ran off the revolutions-versus-speed curve. I would estimate that we were somewhere over 34 knots. She was a great pleasure to drive.

John T. Mason, Jr.: What was her designed speed?

Admiral Colwell: Thirty-three. She made that very easily, with lots to spare.

I did get to take her to sea several times on trials. I didn't get to stay until she was actually delivered to the Navy and accepted.

John T. Mason, Jr.: And you left in November?

Admiral Colwell: I was selected for rear admiral and thus promoted out of my job.

John T. Mason, Jr.: That selection came in July and then, I think, you continued on for a little while

Admiral Colwell: Yes, I left in November. That's right.

John T. Mason, Jr.: Tell me about the practice use of missiles for a unit like that of the fleet.

Admiral Colwell: Actual firings are very few, because the birds are so terrifically expensive. Well, a Talos missile in those days cost something like $200,000 apiece, so you don't shoot very often, and when you do you make every effort to have a fully instrumented shot so that you can find out exactly what happened. In case of a miss, why, you want to know why. In case of a missile failure, you particularly want to know why. In case of a hit, you're jubilant,

John T. Mason, Jr.: What kind of a target do you use?

Admiral Colwell: Usually drone aircraft because you can get maneuvering, you get fairly good speed and altitude, and you can actually use the warhead without danger to anybody else.

John T. Mason, Jr.: This adds to the expense, however?

Admiral Colwell: Oh, yes, that's right. You don't shoot very often. You do an awful lot of dry runs in practice, a great deal of practice with any targets you can get. We used targets of opportunity any time we could—commercial airliners, just for tracking and for training the fire-control crews. Of course, there would be no missile for this.

John T. Mason, Jr.: There's no possibility of using the missile without the warhead, so to speak?

Admiral Colwell: Yes, you can use what they call a telemetering head. In fact, most of your shots are not warhead shots. It's a lot better to get information back than it is to watch it go bang.

Just to finish off on Galveston, I was relieved by a very good friend of mine, Dave Scott, and he actually took delivery of the ship when she was completed and took her down to the Caribbean for shakedown training, and so on.* In the meantime I had been ordered into OpNav.

John T. Mason, Jr.: She was destined to be a unit in the Atlantic Fleet,

Admiral Colwell: I think that's correct. After Dave got down south with her, he continued to have trouble with his search radar. I had had some trouble with it while I was still with the ship. It was a pretty intricate radar, and the trouble was in the screen presentation, where it was very difficult to pick the targets out of phantom pips on the screen. In fact, I remember one time when I looked at the screen, and it looked as though someone had thrown a handful of rice at it. It was covered with pips. The ship continued to have trouble with that particular radar.

John T. Mason, Jr.: In battle, that would be very confusing, wouldn't it?

Admiral Colwell: It sure would.

Admiral Burke then ordered me to go down to join the ship at Roosevelt Roads on temporary duty from OpNav.†

John T. Mason, Jr.: This was after you were in the bureau?

---
* Captain David D. Scott, USN.
† Roosevelt Roads is the site of a U.S. naval station on the island of Puerto Rico.

Admiral Colwell: Yes, and report back to him on this radar condition which was so troubling, and recommend what ought to be done. So I did go on down to Roosevelt Roads, went aboard the ship, and we went out for the first Talos practice—actually, the very first, and I pulled the trigger on the first shot. This, of course, was very exciting, but it wasn't my primary mission down there. So I did examine this particular radar. It obviously was completely inadequate, so I sent a message back to the CNO recommending that no further efforts be made to try to fix this machine. Any attempts had been completely fruitless, and I recommended that the machine be removed and replaced and no further efforts be made to try to fix it. And that eventually is about what happened.

John T. Mason, Jr.: Was it a new type of radar?

Admiral Colwell: Yes, it was.

John T. Mason, Jr.: Has it been duplicated since?

Admiral Colwell: I'm not sure exactly what happened to it. I suspect that it was redesigned. I honestly don't know what the final result was. I merely mentioned that because it gave me an opportunity to have a little special fillip pulling the trigger on the first Talos shot at sea.

John T. Mason, Jr.: Well, the missile itself, did it operate according to expectation?

Admiral Colwell: Yes, it did.

John T. Mason, Jr.: Over a distance of 100 miles?

Admiral Colwell: No, that actual shot was about 45 or 50, I think.

John T. Mason, Jr.: Many of the bases on the islands in the Caribbean were granted to the U.S. at the time of the destroyer deal have been known as missile-tracking stations.* Would they come into play for a shot like this?

Admiral Colwell: Not those. Those are associated with the Atlantic Missile Range for launches primarily from Canaveral, the long-range ballistic missile type. Our guided-missile range in the Caribbean is based on Roosevelt Roads, which is at the eastern end of Puerto Rico, and Culebra—this area, and that's where these shots were taking place. The pilotless aircraft that we used, the drones, for targets can be launched from Roosevelt Roads. It's a very large airfield, as you know. They had their own tracking facilities down there for this particular type of work. The missile-tracking stations along the island chain are not for this purpose.

John T. Mason, Jr.: That leads me to a question which is in the nature of a footnote, a question asking for your comments on the use of Culebra and Vieques and their essential nature for the Navy.†

Admiral Colwell: There is no doubt in my mind whatsoever that they are essential to the Navy and, therefore, essential to the country. There isn't anyplace else to go. The arguments to boot the Navy out of these range areas have been primarily based on hysteria. There are some people in the Caribbean area who keep this issue alive for their own purposes, in my opinion, and a number of people in the U.S. have been misled and do not understand the necessity for retaining them. Nor do they understand that our use of these ranges does not really cause any great difficulty to the people who live down there. It's a very small number of people and the Navy ranges cause them very little inconvenience, if any. The islands are practically without fresh water, they are not suitable for large-scale development.

---

* In September 1940 President Franklin D. Roosevelt concluded a deal with Prime Minister Winston Churchill of Great Britain whereby the United States transferred 50 destroyers to the Royal Navy for use against German submarines. In return the United States received 99-year leases to British bases in the West Indies, Bermuda, and Newfoundland.

† For decades the U.S. Navy has used these islands as targets during shore bombardment training.

The impact area for gunnery down there can be used without danger to the natives, and has been for years and years. The loss of these range facilities is a very great loss, and they are something which cannot be replaced. There isn't anyplace else to go. If it causes some pain to the number of people who are trying to get them for their own purposes, this is just one of the charges that must be made to national defense. They can be compensated, and it's a bill that has to be paid.

John T. Mason, Jr.: Why did we permit it to become such an issue as it has been?

Admiral Colwell: I think that a number of people were badly misled and were persuaded by what I considered to have been improper arguments, non-factual arguments.

Numerous surveys were made as to the need to retain these facilities. None of the Navy's arguments were accepted by the people who were promoting closing down, and they seem to be quite happy to accept anybody else's arguments as to why they should be closed down.

These are my views.

John T. Mason, Jr.: So what's the prognosis?

Admiral Colwell: I think the prognosis is that they're going to be closed down.

John T. Mason, Jr.: Then what?

Admiral Colwell: I don't know. There isn't anyplace else to go.

John T. Mason, Jr.: Well, sir, after that testing experience with the Galveston, you came back to your duties in the department. Tell me about that job. That was OP-93, wasn't it?

Admiral Colwell: That was later. When I first went into OpNav, after I left Galveston, I was an assistant to Admiral Holmes in OP-90, which had a great deal to do with planning the budget.* I was then ordered to OSD in the office of the Director of Research and Engineering, with a very fancy title as the principal naval advisor to the Director of Defense Research and Engineering.

John T. Mason, Jr.: Before you deal with that, tell me about your time, and was it a brief one, in OP-90.

Admiral Colwell: Oh, yes, that was pretty much of a temporary assignment while they figured out some place to send me.

John T. Mason, Jr.: How long were you there?

Admiral Colwell: Three months, maybe, or something like that.

John T. Mason, Jr.: Enough to take a gander at budget-making, then?

Admiral Colwell: Oh, yes, it was a very instructive period.

John T. Mason, Jr.: Tell me some of the details of how a budget is put together for the Navy.

Admiral Colwell: That's a pretty complex subject! This particular period we were sort of getting broken in, this business of how you start out preparing a budget. First of all, you get an indication of just about how much you can take a shot at for a first cut.

John T. Mason, Jr.: What do you mean by that?

Admiral Colwell: Suppose you got $20 billion last year, and then the Secretary of the Navy, after conferring with the Secretary of Defense and various other people, perhaps

---

* Rear Admiral Ephraim P. Holmes, USN.

even with the President, might say, "Well, let's prepare a budget of 25 for the coming year." Then all the various claimants who want a piece of the budget will put together what they think they ought to have. That will probably come to be 30, or so or something like that.

Then you have a rather agonizing period of give and take, and cut and slice, till you get down to what the Secretary of the Navy said you can start with, 25 billion, knowing that you're not going to get that. And you have to prepare in very big detail your justifications. There are forms for this, so it can be managed. All the time you're having discussions back and forth with the people down at OSD. What are they going to support? It isn't any use going in for a widget if you know the people down at OSD are going to say "no widget" this year.

So there's a great deal of back and forth, and eventually you'll come up with a budget submission.

John T. Mason, Jr.: All of this is done without any kind of consultation with the Congress?

Admiral Colwell: Pretty much so, yes. You may get some indications from the Congress on what they're going to stand for.

Eventually you will make a budget submission to the Secretary of Defense. The Secretary of the Navy said you could shoot for 25, and you do that, but by the time you get around to it the Secretary of Defense maybe says you can go for 22. So you have to go back and juggle and re-do. It's a very long, difficult, and tiring process. I'm sure there must be a better way to do it, but we haven't found it yet.

John T. Mason, Jr.: Yes, you could, it seems to me, go directly to the Secretary of Defense to begin with and get your figure and work from that?

Admiral Colwell: Well, yes, this I highly recommend. Now, when McNamara came in, we did just the opposite.[*] He made the statement, "Any service can have anything they have to have as long as they convince me they have to have it." Of course, this was wide

---

[*] Robert S. McNamara served as Secretary of Defense from 21 January 1961 to 29 February 1968.

open. If you got 20 billion the year before, why, this would let you put in for 40 billion. But, of course, the joker in that was "as long as you convince him that you have to have it," and he insisted that he had no preset totals, which of course is utter nonsense. Of course, he had preset totals. He can't go up to the Congress with an outrageous statement. But he always maintained that he didn't have any preset totals, which, I maintain, is an impossible way to run it.

John T. Mason, Jr.: Why did he give such latitude?

Admiral Colwell: I haven't the vaguest idea. I consider him to have been nothing but a total disaster the entire time he was there.

At any rate, I spent a little time in that business.

John T. Mason, Jr.: That was educational, I'm sure!

Admiral Colwell: Oh, yes, it really was. Then I went down to OSD to be an advisor to the Director of Research and Engineering, where I stayed for about a year, I guess.

John T. Mason, Jr.: Yes. You had a fancy title, and what did you actually do?

Admiral Colwell: Not very much. It was not a rewarding assignment. As it turned out, I was not in the mainstream of things. I was out here on the side, as an advisor, and very seldom asked to give any advice. It was not a rewarding assignment at all, and eventually I made this fact clear and I was detached.

John T. Mason, Jr.: Ideally, as it was set up, it could have been a useful assignment, couldn't it?

Admiral Colwell: Yes, if the person to whom you reported chose to make it useful for you. With the setup that we had, it was very difficult to insert yourself in anything that was going on if people didn't invite you in. In fact, it was very difficult to find out what was going on, unless people chose to tell you.

There was one from each service in this job, and I think all three of us pretty much agreed that it was not working out well. Whatever had been planned for us wasn't working. The Army man left, I guess, first, then I left, and I think finally the Air Force man left. It was just not a very useful period.

John T. Mason, Jr.: Weren't there committees and sessions and so forth which you were obligated to attend so that you would be cognizant of what was going on?

Admiral Colwell: There were meetings, yes, but usually you didn't know about them until they were all over, because you hadn't been invited.

John T. Mason, Jr.: Were there not certain kinds of meetings where you were automatically expected to be present?

Admiral Colwell: Routine staff meetings, which weren't held very often and which did little to really bring you into the day-to-day operations.

John T. Mason, Jr.: What kind of advice would you be called upon to offer? Can you give me an illustration?

Admiral Colwell: No I can't even remember any. I don't know that I ever gave any. I did perform one fairly useful function. While I was in this job I would attend routine meetings in OpNav, the CNO's weekly meeting, and so on, and I was able to keep up with what the Navy was doing and gave them some feeling for what they might expect from the DDR&E people, also some feedback—suppose there had been a Navy presentation to DDR&E and this would be preparatory to a budget request, perhaps, and I could give the Navy some feedback on what the reception had been.* This was useful to the Navy. I did perform a useful function for the Navy, but not really for DDR&E.

John T. Mason, Jr.: Did you have any contact with the Joint Chiefs?

Admiral Colwell: No.
    Well, eventually the job was abolished.

John T. Mason, Jr.: That seems logical, doesn't it?

Admiral Colwell: Yes. I went back into OpNav and back into OP-90 for another temporary period much like the first one that I had. The actual timing of this now sort of gets away. OP-90 was the general planning group.

John T. Mason, Jr.: That was November of 1960. More budget planning?

Admiral Colwell: Yes.

John T. Mason, Jr.: Can you think of any of the interesting, highlights to that tour?

Admiral Colwell: No, not really, except it was an awful lot of hard work, tremendous long hours. The business of doing, undoing, redoing, time and time and time again, with mountains of paper.

John T. Mason, Jr.: When is the Navy budget required to be presented? What season of the year?

Admiral Colwell: It seems to me that the final presentation to OSD of the clean copy has to be in there about the first of December. By this time, the various adjustments have

---

* DDR&E—Director of Defense Research and Engineering.

already been made, so this doesn't mean that the people in OSD are going to start reviewing your budget for the first time. That's when you give them the clean copy so they can put it all together and the Secretary of Defense can present the budget to the Congress.

John T. Mason, Jr.: Well, now, the process that leads up to the clean copy entails how long a period?

Admiral Colwell: Oh, a year and a half.

John T. Mason, Jr.: Leading up to that?

Admiral Colwell: Yes. You're always working on three budgets: last year's, this year's, and next year's.

John T. Mason, Jr.: That must be confusing! It sounds like one alone is confusing, enough.

Admiral Colwell: That's correct.

John T. Mason, Jr.: Why are you working on the one that's already in operation?

Admiral Colwell: There have to be adjustments to it from time to time, reprogramming. Your budget cycle is so long, and there is no kitty that you can draw on. You're not allowed to have a bank account.

John T. Mason, Jr.: No contingency fund?

Admiral Colwell: The Secretary of Defense has a contingency fund, and you can go to him. Suppose a brand-new idea shows up, you can go to him for some development money. You don't have any, and he may tell you, "All right, I can give you something to start with, but that isn't going to be enough so you're going to have to find it." And usually he'll tell you to go find it, and this calls for re-programming. This is more blood-letting.

John T. Mason, Jr.: You mean putting the pressure on a given bureau for this project, to get some money away from them?

Admiral Colwell: That's right. This is the way we got our first 20 million for Polaris. We took it away from other people.

John T. Mason, Jr.: I would think this was extremely difficult.

Admiral Colwell: It is, indeed, very difficult. And along late in the fiscal year it's hard to find such a relatively small amount as one million dollars out of many, many billions, because they're all already committed. They're just not lying around loose.

John T. Mason, Jr.: What about the supplementary appropriations which the Congress makes from time to time? What do they cover?

Admiral Colwell: If you have unexpected expenses—for example, you go into South Vietnam, and all of a sudden you have to buy $100 million worth of ammunition. It is not budgeted. You can't find $100 million dollars lying around loose. This is an unexpected requirement, so then you may be permitted by the President to go to the Congress for a supplemental. That would be an example of something that they might support, but it has to be submitted by the President. Nobody else can submit a budget except the President.

John T. Mason, Jr.: Well, Admiral, the budget-makers or budgeteers, or whatever you want to call them, must have their own list of priorities over and above, what a given bureau has?

Admiral Colwell: Oh, yes, there's a list of priorities.

John T. Mason, Jr.: How do you establish that list?

Admiral Colwell: There's a great deal of give and take in it.

John T. Mason, Jr.: Whose wisdom goes into the establishment of the list?

Admiral Colwell: For things that are really important it becomes the CNO's decision, his personally. He will listen to all the arguments, pro and con. This may, and probably does, involve in a series of meetings between the CNO, the Vice Chief, the various deputies, the Chief of Naval Material, and the heads of the principal offices. This is the board of directors, and you meet for hours and hours and hours many, many times during the budget process. There will be a great deal of give and take and argument, some of it pretty violent. And eventually, the CNO will say, "All right, this is the way we're going to do it," and he may get pretty violent too, to the point where he may tell the assembled company, "This is the way we're going to do it, and if there's anybody that doesn't like it, he can leave!"

John T. Mason, Jr.: Roughly, what takes precedence?

Admiral Colwell: I couldn't give you an example because these are all matters of judgment. The people that are involved in that, the group that I call the board of directors, are very knowledgeable people. They've been around for a long time. A nonaviator will know a lot about aircraft matters and vice versa. These are very knowledgeable people, and they are there for the express purpose of advising the CNO and they give him their best advice.

John T. Mason, Jr.: They see the Navy from the overall view, rather than a parochial one!

Admiral Colwell: That's correct. All the time I was there, of course, there were many, many violent arguments, and people could be accused of parochialism from time to time.

I'm sure there was some, but in general these were people who were trying to do the very best they could for the Navy the way they saw it.

John T. Mason, Jr.: So they weren't black shoes and brown shoes!*

Admiral Colwell: Well, sometimes, but largely they—they're very responsible people, lots of experience and a good education.

John T. Mason, Jr.: Where do the experts in the Bureau of the Budget come into this picture, or do they?

Admiral Colwell: Throughout. They conduct their own reviews of programs and projects. Some of them get to be pretty knowledgeable in technical areas. Some of them don't. They can cause you a good deal of trouble. You're talking about the Office of the Budget now?

John T. Mason, Jr.: Yes, because I understand that they do have teams of experts.

Admiral Colwell: They do. They do, indeed, and we used to talk to them at length and frequently.

John T. Mason, Jr.: Did you find them helpful?

Admiral Colwell: In lots of cases yes. I didn't always agree with them, but they have a very important function to perform also.

John T. Mason, Jr.: The General Accounting Office, and its functions are after the fact.

---

* In the early days of naval aviation, the aviators wore brown shoes with their khaki uniforms and green uniforms. They thus acquired the nickname "brown shoes" to distinguish them from the traditional surface ship officers, who are known as "black shoes."

Admiral Colwell: That's an entirely different kind of a function. The GAO is an arm of the Congress. It is the investigative office for the Congress. It's a large organization. They investigate all sorts of things, I suppose usually at the behest of a congressman or a congressional committee chairman, or whatever.

John T. Mason, Jr.: But largely in terms of funds that have been spent?

Admiral Colwell: Largely in terms of funds that have been spent, that's right, or are in the process of being spent for an ongoing program. They may investigate one that's going on now, or they may investigate one that has just been closed up and charges have been made of improper functioning. The GAO performs this investigation and they submit their report, and that report goes to the outfit that was investigated. For example, if they're unhappy with a certain shipbuilding contractor, the GAO reports will come to the Navy for comments. They're usually pretty difficult to comment on. Sometimes you will find that the GAO investigation has been incomplete; they haven't taken testimony from all of the people who should have been represented. Other times you will find that it's petty daggone good. You have to comment on it, and if you've been caught out, why, you have to explain what you're going to do to correct the matter so that it doesn't happen again. They're a watchdog outfit.

John T. Mason, Jr.: So, when you draw up a budget and go through the total process, you still have to be cognizant of this other outfit?

Admiral Colwell: As long as you are able to sustain your request for budgeting funds before the Congress and they go ahead and pass the appropriations bill, and then you go through the apportionment process, just because the Congress has passed your appropriation doesn't mean you've got one single cent. OSD still has to apportion it to you, and he may give you all of it, or he may give you part of it at one time.

As long as you have gone through that process and satisfied the Congress so that they presumably give you what you were asking for for a certain purpose, then it is your responsibility to see that those funds are properly expended for that purpose and for no other, unless you are given permission to reprogram, those funds into a new project. If you don't discharge this responsibility correctly, then you can expect that you're going to find the GAO on your back. But if you do the job correctly which you have been told to do and given the funds to do, then you have nothing to fear from the GAO. They perform the same function for the Congress that the Inspector General performs for the CNO.

John T. Mason, Jr.: I think of that large area of Navy business which is conducted through contracts and industry, in framing a budget I know it's the responsibility of the bureau to submit the initial figures, but in your office how do you take into consideration potential contracts that haven't been let and that might vary quite widely in amounts?

Admiral Colwell: This becomes what baseball umpires refer to as a judgment call. If the bureau has a new project which is just getting started, they make an estimate of how much money they are going to require in the next fiscal year to bring this project along at a given speed. Now there are a few elements of judgment involved here. Is the given speed of progress reasonable? Is it too fast? Is it too slow? If it's too slow, they ought to have more money. If it's too fast, they shouldn't have that much.

The second area of judgment is actually how much money does it take to produce that speed? This is a judgment call, and if the bureau comes in requesting X million dollars for such and such a project, which may be one of these new ones just getting started, they have to justify that to the CNO. He has a sponsor in CNO. For example, when I was in OP-03 I was the shipbuilding sponsor, and the Bureau of Ships would come in with—we would tell them what ships we wanted built, now you give us an estimate of what it's going to cost, and they would have to justify their estimate of what those costs would be.

John T. Mason, Jr.: And I suppose there's a matter of judgment involved in what is the correct speed for the development of a project so that waste and costs won't rise too high?

Admiral Colwell: That's quite true. Polaris, for example, is something that has a great deal of money expended on it in order to achieve speed, of production, and this was because it was considered to be vitally important to the well-being of the country. You will find other projects which are proposed for acceleration.

Well, for example, in the most recent budget, you will recall that the Trident project was proposed for acceleration, and you will recall the violent arguments that were reported in the newspapers, pro and con.

John T. Mason, Jr.: Yes.

Admiral Colwell: So the speed of advance on a project is something which is a judgment matter and has to satisfy the people who eventually pass on it. First of all, you have to satisfy the people in the Navy and you have to satisfy the people in OSD. In the Trident business, obviously, you had to satisfy the people in the President's office before it was ever submitted. And then you've got to satisfy the Congress.

John T. Mason, Jr.: While you were there, of course, Polaris was blossoming, and funds were necessary. Would you tell me about that aspect of the budget?

Admiral Colwell: The estimates for requirements of funds were made by Raborn's office and were submitted through the CNO, and Raborn had to go through the justification process. He didn't receive quite as rough treatment as some, I'm sure.

John T. Mason, Jr.: No, because he carried A-1 priority.

Admiral Colwell: That's right, and he used to carry that little piece of paper around with him just in case anybody wanted to argue.

He would make his estimates based on the estimates of the people in his office. This process was no different from that followed in any other office. You start with the working engineers, and you work up to the office head and then you work up to Raborn.

He submits it to the CNO and if the CNO says, "Yes, that's reasonable," why, that's the figure that goes in the budget. So this was no different from any other budgeting process, except as I mentioned it may have been a little bit easier for Raborn because of the super priority that was attached.

John T. Mason, Jr.: This is such a complicated subject, the making of a budget.

Admiral Colwell: We could discuss this for weeks!

John T. Mason, Jr.: Well, it leads me to ask a question about the preparation of a naval officer for this is kind of duty. Where do you acquire your preparation?

Admiral Colwell: On-the-job training! If you have duty in one of the bureaus as a younger officer, a lieutenant on up through commander, you get introduced to it there in a very small way.

Then, almost everybody who goes into OpNav, and this accounts for the vast majority of naval officers, then you are involved in the budget, whether you choose to be or not. Some of the people in 06, for example, don't do much budgeting, but 03, 04, 05, 02, the various 90s, they are all involved in it, almost as a daily function, practically every day. So you get a pretty fast breaking in.

John T. Mason, Jr.: And I take it that BuPers is cognizant of those that excel in the process, and they get assignments such as you got?

Admiral Colwell: There are some people who have had more than a modicum of experience in it, and they usually get tagged for such jobs. Not always. Once in a while you find some people who haven't been in it before. I can recall one case only a few years ago and it was a complete mis-assignment. The man didn't stay very long. He was given another assignment for which he was better qualified.

John T. Mason, Jr.: This throws light on one facet of the responsibility of the CNO. It's one that I didn't think of necessarily in terms of a man who's eligible for service, but it's a very important facet, isn't it?

Admiral Colwell: Oh, yes. It's almost inconceivable that a man who would even be considered for CNO would not have had enough experience of this kind to set him on the right road. It's almost inconceivable. You just can't get that high without having considerable experience in this area.

John T. Mason, Jr.: You told me, off tape, a little about the establishment of the Office of Navy Planning.

Admiral Colwell: The Office of Program Planning. This was an office which was established, I guess it was during the period while I was there in OP-90, to give a better staff a more powerful focal point for handling all of these budget matters. As I recall, Rivero was the first one to occupy this office, and he was succeeded by Ephraim Holmes, with whom I had worked in OP-90.* That office still exists and is a very, very powerful office.

John T. Mason, Jr.: It's a centralization?

Admiral Colwell: It's a centralization point for these never-ending budget problems. In the existing year you have three programming problems almost continuously. You're working on the next budget—these are just day-in day-out functions, and the Program Planning Office runs it. They don't have final decisions. A deputy, for example, can always appeal to the CNO, and this is as it should be. But somebody has to run this thing, and that's what that office does. It's a very powerful office, a very hard-working office, and a very difficult job.

---

* On 1 October 1963 Vice Admiral Horacio Rivero, Jr., USN, reported as Director of Navy Program Planning and held the job until July 1964, when he became Vice Chief of Naval Operations as a four-star admiral. The oral history of Rivero, who was a Naval Academy classmate of Colwell, is in the Naval Institute collection.

John T. Mason, Jr.: It seems to me, as you talk about this whole area, there are certain obvious lines of development, and yet the human personality enters into the picture largely?

Admiral Colwell: Oh, yes, it does, and I'm sure that this isn't any different from industry. They have a board of directors, and we have a board of directors in the Navy.

John T. Mason, Jr.: You have an obdurate kind as a bureau head, and you have few problems that you wouldn't have otherwise!

Admiral Colwell: That's right, and the CNO may get sufficiently provoked with him that he fires him. I've seen that happen. Get somebody else that you can deal with. And this doesn't mean that the CNO is looking for a yes man. He's looking for a way to get the job done. You can't get the job done if you have a roadblock sitting there.

This is somewhat the same as a fleet commander removing a commanding officer because he just doesn't like the way he does his job. I know that when this happens the civilian press almost invariably is up in arms about this ruthless performance. That's a lot of hogwash. The President of Sears, Roebuck doesn't put up with a branch manager if he can't get along with him. He fires him.

John T. Mason, Jr.: But his branch manager is not a public servant, and I suppose this makes the difference!

Admiral Colwell: But you do the same thing with a commanding officer if you don't like the way he runs his ship.

John T. Mason, Jr.: That brings up a question about the press and the budget-making process. How interested are representatives of the press in this?

Admiral Colwell: And they should be. This is a great deal of the public's money, and they are entitled to be very interested in it, but they are not always very competent in their interests. And that's unfortunate because you'll certainly find news stories that are based on inadequate or inexact information, and sometimes completely false information. That's too bad. Some of the people in the press are quite knowledgeable.

John T. Mason, Jr.: And how interested are they in the budget process?

Admiral Colwell: They're very interested, not in the budget process so much as in the final product. They don't much care how you arrive at this, if you don't make a jackass of yourself, but they're vitally interested in the final product, and properly so.

John T. Mason, Jr.: How available to them is the information that goes into the development of it.

Admiral Colwell: It's not. You could never get your work done if you had the press looking over your shoulder during the formulation process. There's too much in-and-out flow and back and forth and bloodletting. You would find yourself faced with special pleaders of all kinds. You would never get your work done. No, you couldn't have it. Special pleaders in the budget business are the bane of your existence. They take up your time and refuse to be anything but parochial. Well, that's a lot of philosophy about budgets!

John T. Mason, Jr.: Well, that goes into the budget-making, does it not?
    Admiral, when Secretary McNamara came in, he had a, new concept of budgetary matters. He insisted upon a total cost figure.

Admiral Colwell: Yes, that's correct, and it was under this sort of costing scheme that a number of very large contracts were in practice. It was a paper monster, and I'm sure that the Department of Defense is still suffering, from that, even though portions of it have been canceled. In time, maybe they'll get it down to the point where it is fairly easily handled and where it will still perform the function for which it was designed. It was a monster when I was there.

John T. Mason, Jr.: How did the Congress receive it?

Admiral Colwell: They were never too involved in the huge paper exercise. They'd hear complaints from somebody about it, I suppose. I don't think they had too much to do with that. There were a number of congressmen who did not approve of Mr. McNamara. I didn't approve of him either. On the other hand, there were a number of congressmen who thought he was the White Knight. He had brought this huge Department of Defense under control. He almost brought it to stagnation with this paper mill that existed, which he never intended. But it got away.

Interview Number 6 with Vice Admiral John Barr Colwell, U.S. Navy (Retired)

Place: Admiral Colwell's apartment in Washington, D.C.

Date: Wednesday, 12 December 1973

Interviewer: John T. Mason, Jr.

John T. Mason, Jr.: Admiral, today I believe you are ready to resume your story with an account of your command of Amphibious Group Four.

Admiral Colwell: Yes. At this time, I had not yet flown my flag at sea, which, of course, is one of the early high points in any flag officer's career. I was ordered to command Amphibious Group Four, which comprised about half of the amphibious force of the Atlantic Fleet. The Amphibious Force, Atlantic Fleet, is based in Norfolk, a good part of time at the amphibious base at Little Creek. During this rather short period that I commanded Group Four, I was in the flagship part of the time, and part of the time I was operating out of an office at the amphibious base.

John T. Mason, Jr.: This was from October 1961 to September 1962?

Admiral Colwell: That's right.

The reason for not being aboard a flagship, although I was technically at sea all the time, was simply a matter of the availability of flagships.

My principal duties during this period of command were, of course, training, inspection of my ships, and a continuing process of preparing and updating contingency war plans. This, as I said, was a continuing process. Superimposed on top of that was the preparation of actual exercises.

John T. Mason, Jr.: Would you give me an idea, sir, of the ships and the men included in the amphibious group?

Admiral Colwell: Well, I have a little trouble remembering that. I would guess that I must have had about 25 ships, and this might have totaled between 6,000 and 8,000 men. I'm guessing now because I can't remember.

It was a very enjoyable period. It was my first experience in the amphibious business. I found that the people in my command were quite competent and extremely helpful in teaching an uninitiated flag officer how to run his business. I had a good staff, and I enjoyed it very much.

John T. Mason, Jr.: You were under the command of CinCLant?

Admiral Colwell: Second removed. My immediate commander was Commander Amphibious Force, who at that was Vice Admiral Ward, later four stars and now retired.[*]

This command lasted less than a year because I was then ordered back to Washington.

John T. Mason, Jr.: Tell me about some of the training exercises. Where were they conducted?

Admiral Colwell: There were two general training grounds for the Atlantic Fleet in amphibious warfare, which, of course, is a combination of Navy and Marines. Well, actually, there are three. The one nearest home and the most minor of these was right there at the Norfolk-Little Creek area, where we could use the beaches for primarily training exercises and beaching. A very important area to both the Navy and the Marines for amphibious warfare is Camp Lejeune in North Carolina. And the third area is at the island of Vieques in the Caribbean.

During my short tour as ComPhibGroup 4, my ships and my staff and I operated in all of these areas. One that stands out is a demonstration exercise that we conducted at

---

[*] Vice Admiral Alfred G. Ward, USN, served as Commander Amphibious Force Atlantic Fleet from August 1961 to October 1962. The oral history of Ward, who retired as a four-star admiral, is in the Naval Institute collection.

Camp Lejeune for President Kennedy. During this one we were blessed with superb weather, and it went off without a hitch.

I wouldn't say that aside from that very pleasurable experience anything of any great interest went on during this period of somewhat less than a year.

John T. Mason, Jr.: The techniques employed in the amphibious operations were those of World War II, were they?

Admiral Colwell: Very generally so, yes. Not only the techniques but the equipment. I'm happy to say that in the past two years the amphibious force has been almost entirely reconstituted with new ships. We are in excellent shape now, as far as equipment goes. The numbers are far less; the numbers needed are far less. The ships are bigger, faster, and altogether much more competent.

John T. Mason, Jr.: Based as you were at Norfolk, did you have any relationship with the service fleet?

Admiral Colwell: I would say only indirectly. The ships of the Service Force operated with us at sea, yes, in exercises.

John T. Mason, Jr.: The reason I asked that is because some time before, of course, the amphibious forces were under the Service Force.

Admiral Colwell: During the time that I was in the Amphibious Force, both Atlantic and Pacific, we were, of course, a separate type and had our own type commander. It's a proper break, really. There's no reason why they should be joined.

John T. Mason, Jr.: It was just involvement.

Admiral Colwell: Yes.

John T. Mason, Jr.: Did you have foreign observers for any of your operations?

Admiral Colwell: Not that I recall. If we did, I have no recollection of it. The exercises that I directed were not particularly large scale, although one exercise in the Caribbean involved most of the ships that were then available on the Atlantic coast. We maintained, of course, at that time a fairly sizeable amphibious force in the Sixth Fleet in the Mediterranean at all times, so that for operations along the Atlantic seaboard we had to subtract the ships that were actually in the Sixth Fleet at the time, plus those that were in overhaul or perhaps had just returned from deployment. This happens to everybody. It wasn't unique to the amphibious forces.

John T. Mason, Jr.: Since you were there as an aftermath to the Bay of Pigs episode, did the Amphibious Force show any concern about operations from, say, Swan Island and that area?[*]

Admiral Colwell: No, we had no connection with that. We were involved, of course, in contingency plans for possible operations in Cuba, in the Cuban area. That was the only connection that we had after the Bay of Pigs.

John T. Mason, Jr.: Did you have any connection with the SACLant command and the North Atlantic forces of the Atlantic Alliance?[†]

Admiral Colwell: No, not really. Of course, when I was there we were not engaged in one of the multinational exercises which occur from time to time. I did not participate in any of those. That was just a happenstance of timing.

---

[*] In mid-April 1961 a force of 1,400 Cuban exiles, secretly trained by U.S. personnel in Guatemala, landed in the Bay of Pigs, on the southwestern coast of Cuba, in an attempt to overthrow Fidel Castro, that nation's Communist dictator. The invasion attempt was a disaster. President John Kennedy decided that U.S. naval intervention would worsen the situation, so ships and aircraft offshore were prohibited from taking part.

[†] SACLant—Supreme Allied Commander Atlantic, a naval command in the structure of the North Atlantic Treaty Organization (NATO).

John T. Mason, Jr.: Yes, they occurred without any regular schedule, I guess.

Admiral Colwell: Yes.

John T. Mason, Jr.: Did you enjoy amphibious operations as a command?

Admiral Colwell: Oh, yes, very much.

John T. Mason, Jr.: What made it unique?

Admiral Colwell: Well, there's an awful lot going on. In many operations at sea in which I had previously engaged, I would be in a ship or perhaps even commanding a ship, and you were just one of a large number of units. And you might not actually see very much in the way of activity, particularly things of great interest. In the Amphibious Force all the units are right there. You're at the beach, and you have the unloading and the movement to the beach and exercises ashore. There's a great deal going on all the time, and there's a lot for the group commander to do, rather than just sit there, in addition to the operation of the amphibious forces themselves involving the movement ashore, resupply, and so on. And, of course, we had the pseudo enemy to contend with. He would mount air attacks, attempted submarine attacks, attempted PT boat attacks, and these all had to be contended with day and night. It was a busy period and instructive.

John T. Mason, Jr.: Who comprised the enemy? Units of the Second Fleet?

Admiral Colwell: Oh, yes. We'd be divided up into the reds and the blues, or whatever you choose to call them.

John T. Mason, Jr.: Well, sir, did you want to come back to Washington?

Admiral Colwell: I can't say that I wanted to, but I did come back to a good job.

John T. Mason, Jr.: It was an extremely important job, wasn't it?

Admiral Colwell: At that time, yes. The job was later consolidated with activities in OP-06, and I think properly so. There was some reorganization and OP-93, as the former planning group was called, was sort of overtaken by reorganization.

John T. Mason, Jr.: What was it when you were there?

Admiral Colwell: When I was there we prepared annually what might be called a prognosis or a forecast of what the Navy should be some years hence. Some people like to talk about 15 years. I always said I couldn't see that far, and I thought ten years was a pretty far stretch for your vision. This didn't make an awful lot of difference really.

John T. Mason, Jr.: For this age that's a long stretch!

Admiral Colwell: Right. The information that you had to work with was in some cases factual and in some cases manufactured out of your own imagination. In preparing this kind of a forecast for the Navy in particular there is a constraint which is not felt in some areas, and that is the generally long life of ships, so that a ship which is fairly new today is probably going to be with you ten years from now. This provides you with at least a nucleus of the fleet, so that you know what it's going to look like.

Now, to lay on top of that new ships, here again you have a constraint, which is that it takes a long time to design, draw plans for, build, commission, and put into the fleet any ship, even a relatively small one. It's a long process, in terms of years. So that if you're talking about what the fleet is going to look like ten years from now, you can pretty doggone well draw a picture of it today. As an example, in today's ship technology what do we have that's new? We have, of course, rather than propeller-driven ships, jet-propelled ships, which is a new type of propulsion. This doesn't really add an entirely new dimension to ship construction. It's simply a different sort of a teakettle that pushes it around.

John T. Mason, Jr.: Admiral, is there not another factor that you consider, however, even though a ship will be in existence ten years hence, in many respects it may be obsolete?

Admiral Colwell: Yes, if you don't do anything about it. Ships generally have growth potential in terms of the substitution of new weapons, or the addition of new weapons. There is growth potential built into a new hull. Also, you may find it quite expedient to remove an old weapon and put on a new one, so that you get a substitution of weight and specs. It is not economically feasible to throw a ship away at the end of ten years. You just cannot afford to replace the entire fleet at the end of something like ten years. You must keep it. It's very expensive. And it is entirely feasible to keep it, if you modernize it from time to time. I think our experience in the past has been with today's ships you have to modernize about every ten years. This is the result of new developments, weapons, missilery, for example, and simply what has been called the velocity of invention. We had gone to solid-state electronics and micro-technology, self-diagnosis. This sort of thing permits you to take an old weapon off, which has perhaps been obsolete in ten years, and put a new one on, and it probably will be an exchange of missile for missile in today's world. I don't know what it will be in tomorrow's world.

We were talking a little bit earlier about what types of new ships might be available. If you were trying to make a prognosis of what the ships of the fleet would look like, let's say, in 10 to 15 years, as of today, there are two types that show promise. One is the hydrofoil, which, so far, is somewhat limited in size and tonnage. I don't know what the upper limits might be. My personal belief is that they're fairly small, which limits the amount of payload that you can put on, although they behave very well at high speed and fairly high sea states.

John T. Mason, Jr.: What limit do you put on their speed?

Admiral Colwell: Oh, I think for fleet operations and high reliability we're probably talking about 50 knots. But still, that's very good, and they behave well in fairly high sea states.

The other type which I think shows promise, although it has a lot of development work still to do, is the surface-effect ship supported on an air bubble.

A lot of work is being done on both of these, and one can visualize that they may, in time, greatly change the appearance of the fleet. But one must be cautious here because surface-effect ships, proved out, of oceangoing size, are probably 15 years away. So I can tell you what the fleet is going to look like ten years from now. I know what it'll look like, because most of it's sitting in the harbor right now.

Anyway, this was the primary function of the OP-93 office. It was a very small office, only a small number of people.

John T. Mason, Jr.: May I ask something else which is sort of concomitant with your planning, long-range planning? You also had to consider the planning and development of, say, the Russian fleet, did you not?

Admiral Colwell: Yes.

John T. Mason, Jr.: In terms of what we were doing?

Admiral Colwell: You have to look at what the competition is, that's right, as well as what you think you can do. We worked, of course, very closely with the research and development people. What did they think was going to be coming along? The intelligence people, what did they think the competition was going to have, and with our own shipbuilders.

The Naval Ship Systems Command maintained a small group that produced what they called sometimes "the spring styles." These were unusual hull configurations which might confer particular advantages on a ship. One of them that I recall looked like a submarine under the surface of the water connected by a strap to another submarine which rode above the surface of the water and had a submarine shape. This, it was hoped, would confer some advantages in stability in high seas and so on. That's just an example.

We worked with all these people and tried to distill something that would indicate real progress and, not stultified thinking, but at the same time we'd remain in contact with the real world.

John T. Mason, Jr.: There's always a danger there, isn't there?

Admiral Colwell: There sure is. It's easy to go off into left field. I suspect—I think I have a basically quite conservative nature—that the material we turned out while I was OP-93 was perhaps a little on the conservative side, but I do think we had kept in contact with the real world.

John T. Mason, Jr.: Let me ask, sir, that was a little more than ten years ago when you were drawing these plans and making these prognoses. Did they work out pretty well in terms of the present?

Admiral Colwell: Yes. The real world may hold up.

John T. Mason, Jr.: This long-range planning, how much credence was given to it by other parts of the Navy?

Admiral Colwell: I believe it was pretty well accepted. People could look at it and relate it to what they could see around them. I'm, sure that there was some feeling that maybe it was overly conservative, but generally accepted, yes. It was in fact, the basis for the submission of the annual shipbuilding program in the budget, modifications accomplished, of course. Some types of ship dropped out completely, which was largely forced by economics.

John T. Mason, Jr.: How did Secretary McNamara and his special group look on it?

Admiral Colwell: I honestly don't know. I had very little direct contact with him. Part of which was by choice. I don't know how to tell you. They were not knowledgeable in the area. I don't know how they felt about it.

John T. Mason, Jr.: The appropriate committees of Congress must have been cognizant of your forecasts, and how did they react?

Admiral Colwell: They were generally receptive. They didn't have direct dealings with this office, but they came in contact with it sort of secondarily in considerable detail as a result of the submission of the shipbuilding bill. There, of course, was as an entirely direct relationship some years later when I was OP-03, and one of the congressional committees asked the Navy for a letter which would set forth their views on what the shipbuilding program should be for the following five years. This was the same type of thing that OP-93 prepared. A letter was actually prepared and was cleared by the Office of the Secretary of Defense and did go forward to the congressional committee.

A rather odd result of that was that a year later I asked about some of the submissions which we had made and why they did not agree with the letter that was given them a year before. There were some people who were really quite exercised about this, but, of course, there was a very simple explanation. The previous year the shipbuilding bill, as passed and funded, bore no relation whatsoever to what the Navy had said they'd like to have. So that a year later and two years later and three years later the prognosis was completely outmoded and had to be redone. I had a little trouble explaining that. It seems very simple, but they didn't get it.

A little aside about the OP-93 office was it had not been in existence for very many years. It was established for this particular purpose of taking a look into the future, at what the fleet ought to consist of.

John T. Mason, Jr.: Whose wisdom was it that established it?

Admiral Colwell: I believe it must have been Admiral Burke. I'm not sure. I'm not at all sure, but my predecessors in the office—well, my immediate predecessor was Tom Moorer, and before him I believe it had been Don Griffin.[*] Before him was Roy Johnson.[†] I think there was one before that, but I can't remember who it was.

John T. Mason, Jr.: They were all four star.

Admiral Colwell: Every one of them got four stars. I broke the model. I only got three.

John T. Mason, Jr.: As you observed somewhere else, OP-93 was being downgraded, gradually.

Admiral Colwell: It was gradually running out not of usefulness but out of necessity for its continued existence, and I agreed with this. I agreed that there should be a consolidation of this business, and it looked to me as though OP-06 was the right place for it.

John T. Mason, Jr.: You said a little bit earlier that you were required to make yearly reports, yearly prognoses?

Admiral Colwell: Yes, we published a yearly forecast.

John T. Mason, Jr.: Did it differ materially year by year?

Admiral Colwell: Not greatly, no.

John T. Mason, Jr.: It was a matter of updating?

Admiral Colwell: Very largely, yes.

---

[*] Rear Admiral Thomas H. Moorer, USN; Rear Admiral Charles Donald Griffin, USN. The oral histories of both are in the Naval Institute collection.
[†] Rear Admiral Roy L. Johnson, USN. His oral history is in the Naval Institute collection.

John T. Mason, Jr.: Was there any contrast between your first yearly report and what had gone before with Admiral Moorer, or did you simply build on his report?

Admiral Colwell: I wouldn't say that any differences were major. Perhaps they were more just a reflection of our personalities and the way we put things together and the way we liked it written. Nothing major that I recall.

John T. Mason, Jr.: A forecast, then, could reflect the personal philosophy of the man in command?

Admiral Colwell: That's true, up to a point. The final document, of course, had to be approved by the Chief of Naval Operations, and the next-to-the-last step in the annual preparation was the exposition of the entire plan to the CNO, the VCNO, and all the deputies, which I used to refer to as the chairman of the board and the board of directors, at which full discussion would be held and changes would be suggested or directed. Then we would finally publish, and it would be signed.

John T. Mason, Jr.: In the early 1960s when you were operating in 93, did you emphasize in your planning and forecasts any particular ship developments, any particular line of ships, reflecting your own personal experience?

Admiral Colwell: Not so much personal experience, I think, as what I considered to be recognition of the most important types the way my staff and I saw them. First of all, we visualized the U.S. Navy as a deep-water navy and emphasis was therefore given—of course, setting aside the strategic forces, which were and still are in a class by themselves because, they certainly relate directly to national survival. Setting those aside, we gave high priority to the carrier force escorts, and again in particular nuclear power, high-quality carrier force escorts, and again in particular nuclear power, the attack submarine force, nuclear-powered. Then, as rather a separate group, the modernization of the amphibious force, which at the time I was there was already well under way, and something that had been too long neglected primarily for economic reasons was the full modernization of the service force.

I think that pretty well covers the period in OP-93. This was an interesting time. I was, of course, included in many of the sort of inner sanctum meetings with the CNO and the Secretary, so it was a time of great interest, primarily desk work and book work.

John T. Mason, Jr.: Since you put such great emphasis on nuclear power, what role did Admiral Rickover play in any of your planning?

Admiral Colwell: I don't recall that I had very much in the way of direct contact with Admiral Rickover during this period, probably because I was in basic agreement with what he wanted to do. It was reasonably apparent, at least to me, what ships ought to have nuclear power in order to give us an adequately size nuclear-powered fleet. It was apparent that the carriers all ought to be nuclear. We participated in a number of studies trying to determine what a proper number of nuclear-powered escorts should be, that is, nuclear frigates. In general, most of these studies seemed to conclude that about four per carrier would be a proper number. Some lesser number could be accepted and has since been accepted. There's a limit to how much you can build in terms of money.

We participated in all those studies, and we finally reached pretty good agreement throughout the Navy Department on what kind of numbers we would like to ask for, what would our druthers be.

John T. Mason, Jr.: You worked out proportions, then?

Admiral Colwell: Yes

John T. Mason, Jr.: For the conventional forces how did this work out?

Admiral Colwell: Here again, we had an automatic restraint and that was the one of what was in existence, how long were they going to be good for, assuming that they were modernized, and that this had in fact happened.

We were sort of handed a number on a platter for the conventionally powered escorts. We had extreme difficulty at that time in trying to forecast what we would do when the time came to replace those conventional-powered escorts. This was sort of left in limbo, because it was very difficult to see that far and certainly it was extremely difficult to get any consensus on it.

John T. Mason, Jr.: Was it feasible to think at all in terms of an all nuclear-powered Navy?

Admiral Colwell: This was considered and was actually proposed by some people. I can't remember who they were. But if you ran the dollar numbers out on it, why, it was not feasible.

John T. Mason, Jr.: How could you anticipate, say, what the Congress was willing and able to appropriate in terms of money for the Navy ten years hence?

Admiral Colwell: Well, actually we couldn't; we only had to make some guesses. We had years of experience behind us which showed peaks and valleys of enormous size. We had to be optimistic and at the same time try to be realistic. This is way we approached it.

The shipbuilding proposals were always larger than we were going to get, and we knew it. But we tried to be somewhere near the real world.

John T. Mason, Jr.: This long-range planning was predicated on, say, a peaceful world or semi-peaceful? You couldn't anticipate any major events that might aid your cause?

Admiral Colwell: No, that's right, and we did not. We based our projections on first of all what would be a reasonable size for U.S. Fleet divided into Atlantic and Pacific based or two things: one would be the contingency that we would have to fight a potential enemy, and this was obviously Russia because nobody else had any navy of any size that we thought we would have to fight; the other consideration was continuing deployments, which have in fact happened. We had available to us a fairly good rule of thumb for continuing deployments, and that is one in three, that is you spend a third of your time deployed in a ship, something which is acceptable in terms of ship maintenance, ship training, navy yard overhauls, and, above all, personnel. Anything shorter than that, if the turn-around period is shorter than one in three, is unfair to your personnel. It puts a great strain on them and on their family lives, and you will find that it will result in eventual disaster.

We certainly ran into this difficulty all throughout the war in South Vietnam, and it was terrifically accentuated by the length of that conflict. Our Navy deployments during that period just worked a frightful hardship upon our people and also a frightful hardship upon the mechanical condition of the ships, but primarily people. And this resulted in something we have suffered from for years, a terrific turnover of people, failure to retain career people.

John T. Mason, Jr.: You saw the need for dealing with this problem in terms of Polaris, didn't you, with the double crews?

Admiral Colwell: Oh, yes, but that had sort of a different genesis, which was—I think we've mentioned this before—what was determined to be a necessity to maintain a maximum number of Polaris missiles at sea, and this is the way we did it, with two crews. So that was slightly different kind of a concept. Over the years many proposals have been made to have two crews for carriers so that you could keep them on the line more of the time. This I consider to be impractical, both from the people point of view and from the mechanical condition point of view.

John T. Mason, Jr.: Even with a nuclear-powered carrier?

Admiral Colwell: Yes, things just wear out. In a carrier, the catapults take a tremendous beating, the arresting engines, even the decks themselves take a beating. Your electronics all have to be refurbished from time to time; just day-to-day repairs probably won't be sufficient. You can't keep a ship at sea forever, working hard. If you want to send him on a pleasure cruise, he can go a long way, but you can't operate a carrier almost 24 hours a day for very long, or it will break down. You have to give it a rest.

John T. Mason, Jr.: Was it necessary for you to consider one of the ramifications of your study in terms of the economic development of the country, of the prosperity of the country, all of this as it related to personnel?

Admiral Colwell: I think maybe the only answer I have to that is that we had to be optimistic. We had to assume that the economic conditions in the country would continue to support a navy of adequate size to do the things that we projected, and that we would be able to get the men to man the ships. Otherwise, what have you got? What do you deal with? I think we had to be optimistic, and we were. Not overly optimistic, but we just assumed that the country could pay for a fleet, and we assumed that we would be able to get the men to man it.

John T. Mason, Jr.: When you were considering what you might be able to obtain ten years hence from the Congress in terms of appropriations, you had to put into the hopper any increases in pay for enlisted men and all that?

Admiral Colwell: No. We perhaps should have, but we didn't. Here again, I think we simply worked on a matter of optimism that all things inflated at an even rate.

John T. Mason, Jr.: Did you tie in your studies in any way with the Office of Information, the Chinfo people, and their educational program in the country at large as to the value of the Navy and promoting the Navy and Navy ships?

Admiral Colwell: I think the only answer that I have to that is that everybody in the Navy Department was involved in this sort of thing. We all took our turns at making speeches and so on. I wouldn't say that there was a direct involvement with the office of Chinfo in the preparation of our annual forecast. It was just a general involvement of everybody in that sort of thing.

John T. Mason, Jr.: Looking at it in a negative sense, as in recent days we have had to, the anti-militaristic factor in the country, would this have a bearing on long-range planning?

Admiral Colwell: I think it would. We were not suffering from that at that time, or at least if we were I didn't recognize it. Aside from the customary potshots that people take, there certainly was not an extreme antimilitary feeling among the young. We didn't have that to contend with.

John T. Mason, Jr.: You were there during the period of the Cuban Missile Crisis.[*] Did this have any bearing on plans drawn up subsequent to that crisis?

Admiral Colwell: You mean insofar as OP-93 operated?

John T. Mason, Jr.: Yes

Admiral Colwell: I guess maybe that didn't occur on my watch. I was only there about 15 months, so I think any changes that came about would have been put in by my successor.

John T. Mason, Jr.: You would anticipate changes?

Admiral Colwell: Some perhaps.

---

[*] The Cuban Missile Crisis was triggered in mid-October 1962, when a U.S. reconnaissance plane photographed a Soviet nuclear missile site in Cuba and the presence of Soviet bombers. On 22 October President John F. Kennedy went on national television to announce a naval quarantine of Cuba, to be implemented on 24 October. On 28 October Premier Nikita Khrushchev of the Soviet Union notified President Kennedy that he was ordering the withdrawal of Soviet bombers and missiles from Cuba.

John T. Mason, Jr.: Of what nature?

Admiral Colwell: I'm inventing now. You might feel that there was a need for increased emphasis on the strategic forces, for example. Perhaps they needed to be enlarged; perhaps they needed to be changed in form. I don't know that this happened but you can visualize that such a thing might occur. You might feel that there should be a greatly increased emphasis on antisubmarine warfare forces, and this, in fact, may have occurred. I don't know really, but this is the sort of thing that I think you can visualize coming into consideration.

John T. Mason, Jr.: You mentioned previously national survival as a part of your consideration. Did this bring you into contact with the Air Force and developments that . . . ?

Admiral Colwell: Not in the form of across-the-table discussions. We knew, of course, what the air forces consisted of—their strategic forces, that is—what they were proposing, what they requested in their budget submission, what the various discussions were with OSD. These were all facts of common knowledge to us, just as our plans were known to them. The general attitude within the Navy Department during all this period was that we should not have all of our strategic forces in one basket of a single type, and that there was indeed room for submarines, bombers, and missiles in the strategic forces—not only room but a requirement, in order that the competition would not be able to concentrate on a single type of countermeasure.

There was, of course, competition within the U.S. for funds, naturally because there was never enough to go around for everything anybody wants. The military are perhaps notorious for asking for a lot more than they can expect to get and some people think a lot more than they need. So there was competition for funds, but this competition was not in a vacuum. Everybody concerned was aware of what the true facts were, and, of course, the intelligence was disseminated on a need-to-know basis among all of the services and all the Secretaries and so on.

This was what I would call a friendly rivalry. Some people didn't think it was very friendly but—

John T. Mason, Jr.: At times it seemed to get beyond the bounds of friendliness.

Admiral Colwell: Well, it got a little acrimonious at times, but this was usually a matter of personalities. I never came to blows with any of my Air Force counterparts.

John T. Mason, Jr.: During your time there, was there not some effort under the aegis of the Department of Defense to have a meeting of minds and to have the long-range planning groups of the different services meet together and discuss common problems?

Admiral Colwell: No, I don't recall that any such suggestion was ever made. Maybe my memory is faulty, but I don't think so. I don't recall it.

John T. Mason, Jr.: In your time there did you consider in your long-range planning the possibility of using the merchant marine in terms of national defense, of putting missiles, say, on board merchant ships?

Admiral Colwell: Suggestions of this type came in from time to time, and usually they would give them a very decent reception. Studies were made as to the possibilities and so forth. It was the type of thing that certainly was not going to be accomplished in the absence of a real emergency. This involved enormous amounts of money, but they were examined, yes, and some of them showed good feasibility—the use of helicopters in merchant ships under convoy conditions for ASW work. These were all examined, and there was a great deal of feasibility there. But it's not the sort of thing that you can afford to do in the absence of a real necessity, and that holds true today. Something that is being done today somewhat along this line is the actual use of merchant tankers as substitutes for fleet oilers. This is something that is much more easily done. It requires relatively small amounts of money to provide the necessary rigging.

John T. Mason, Jr.: Because the tanker serves in two capacities. What was the role assigned to the U.S. Merchant Marine in your planning?

Admiral Colwell: Two, I would say. One would be the well-known role of expansion of the service force facilities in the area of direct support to forces overseas, and these may be land forces, sea forces or air forces, whatever. Absolutely essential, because it is impossible to maintain within the Navy a service force which is adequate to that kind of a task because of the enormous tonnages that are involved. The same thing we had in World War II, Korea, South Vietnam, you name it. The other primary role of the merchant marine is associated with it and would be, as in the past, in support of our friends, including civilian populations, because they would certainly not be self-sufficient in food, oil, and munitions. At least, we expect that they would not. These are really the two traditional or historic roles of the merchant marine, and they are exactly whey we need an adequate merchant marine.

John T. Mason, Jr.: Were you intrigued at all by the role of the Russian merchant marine as it seems to be vis-à-vis their Navy?

Admiral Colwell: Yes, indeed. They use parts of their merchant marine as semi- or quasi-naval vessels, both in direct support and operating by themselves. They use their merchant marine in the export of propaganda very effectively. Yes, we observed this with very great interest.

John T. Mason, Jr.: And a feeling of envy?

Admiral Colwell: A certain amount, yes, especially the role of their merchant marine worldwide in the export of propaganda and in other matters where they were directly under government control, as differentiated from the free-enterprise system where a merchantman is under control of his company. There are two different kinds of horse races.

John T. Mason, Jr.: Yes, accept the disadvantage of the democratic system as well as the advantages.

Admiral Colwell: That's right, and I'll take them any time!

John T. Mason, Jr.: In your role as a long-range planner you obviously had to be cognizant of the State Department thinking, did you not?

Admiral Colwell: Yes, and the input from this kind of source really came to us through OP-06. Of course, they had direct connection with the Assistant Secretary of Defense's office for political affairs. They had a direct input from the deliberations of the Joint Chiefs. Their views were fed into us in this way, that degree of thinking was applied.

John T. Mason, Jr.: How important was it to your planning?

Admiral Colwell: I think it's a very necessary input, just as our discussions with the research and development people formed a necessary input. They didn't provide a very large section of the annual report, but it was a necessary input so that we weren't working in a vacuum.

The long-range elements of U.S. policy, U.S. strategy, and so forth certainly were important, and this I would say now, in hindsight, was what led me to the conclusion that actually the long-range planning group, the long-range planning office or function really belonged in OP-06, rather than as a separate group.

John T. Mason, Jr.: How important did you deem the intelligence input and so forth that came to you?

Admiral Colwell: Oh, yes, very important.

John T. Mason, Jr.: Were you in touch with the CIA and cognizant of their operations?

Admiral Colwell: No, we were not. I didn't have the special clearances that would be required for a lot of intelligence activity, and I didn't feel they were necessary, nor did anybody else. I never asked for them, and they were never offered. I don't feel that I needed them, not for what I was doing.

John T. Mason, Jr.: In retrospect, were you, would you say, optimistic in your long-range planning or did you reflect some of the attitude of one of your successors in that job, George Miller, who is always kind of Cassandra-minded?[*]

Admiral Colwell: I would think that I was probably a little more optimistic that George. As I said earlier, I'm basically a conservative. Certainly the numbers that we talked about in future years, the numbers of ships, were optimistic. They weren't bad numbers, but they were optimistic from an economic point of view, no question about it.

Here again, there was a saving factor. So long as you maintained within your projections a balanced fleet designed to do, or to perform, all of the prime functions which we envisaged as Navy responsibilities, then it was not difficult to cut back in terms of numbers. This would not necessarily be an even cut across the board, where everybody took the same kind of a 20% slash; it might be but not necessarily so. There were some functions that could be determined by necessary discussions and agreement with the CNO as less important than others, and they might take a bigger cut. Historically, this has always been the fate of the mine forces, simply because the ships involved are small, they can be built faster, and you can reconstitute them somewhat faster. At least, I guess that's the thinking.

---

[*]Rear Admiral George H. Miller, USN, served as Director, Long Range Objectives Group in the OpNav staff from January 1964 to January 1967. His oral history is in the Naval Institute collection.

John T. Mason, Jr.: And they're only essential in times of war?

Admiral Colwell: That's right. Then they can be vital. But you can reconstitute a mine force faster than you can reconstitute anything else, I think. I believe this to be true. The same way with the service forces. This is one of the reasons why the service forces were not modernized at that same rate as the others. It is possible to use merchant hulls.

John T. Mason, Jr.: But the ordnance that goes into the mine-laying force is another matter:

Admiral Colwell: Mine-laying, yes. We have never maintained a mine-laying force in peacetime of any real consequence. We have maintained a nucleus of minesweeping force because this is really more essential to us. We must keep our ports and facilities open.

John T. Mason, Jr.: Admiral, in this time we hear discussed the fact that the preponderance of units in our fleet are overage.

Admiral Colwell: This has been true in the past, but there has been, I think—I was going to say "remarkable," but I guess that's the wrong word—there's been very substantial progress made in the reduction of age of ships, not as fast as a lot of people would like to have it. But, here again, you must face the real world, particularly in regard to money.

Today a $3 billion annual building bill will produce a vastly smaller number of ships than it used to, for two reasons: inflation, of course, and secondly, an individual ship and its equipment is vastly more complex today than it used to be, and it just costs more to build one. Therefore, it is not reasonable to expect that the Navy can replace old ships on a one-for-one basis. It's just not reasonable.

There is also another argument that can be advanced against any such process, and that is that, by our own statements, our new ships are vastly more capable than our old ships, and that's quite true. Now, the fact remains that the competition is vastly more capable than it used to be also, so that isn't a complete plus. You may be just running along the even line, but the fact remains it is not possible to replace outmoded, broken-down ships on a one-for-one basis. You cannot expect to decommission a World War II destroyer, or decommission all of them, say, to the number of 200—I've no idea what the number is—you can't expect to decommission 200 of those and commission 200 brand-new guided missile ships. It's just not reasonable.

However, to get back to the basic subject here, the quality of the U.S. fleet has been going up. A lot of new ships have been added. The guided-missile fleet is a high-quality fleet, basically quite young. I suppose the average age on those is somewhere around ten. years, maybe it's 12. I don't know what it is, but they're not 25 the way the destroyer force used to be.

We're about to start taking delivery on a new group of big destroyers conventionally powered, big enough to go with the big carriers, and go for a long time.[*] They have long legs. We're about to start building a new group of small escorts called patrol frigates which appear from what I know about them to be very good ships.[†] They take over the function of escorting an amphibious force, service force, merchant convoys, oilers, whatever.

We certainly were in dire straits a few years ago with the aging of the fleet. Today I think we're in a lot better shape, but part of that improvement has been achieved at the expense of a very considerable cut in numbers. The old worn out ships have been simply tied up, and we have accepted the fact that we don't have 900 ships any more, we only have 550, or whatever today's number is.

John T. Mason, Jr.: And how important has the long-range planning of the Navy been in the development of this situation?

Admiral Colwell: I really don't know. You see, I've been retired for a little over four years, and at the time of my retirement we still had in the neighborhood of 900 ships. But

---

[*] USS Spruance (DD-963), lead ship of the new class, was commissioned 20 September 1975.
[†] The Navy eventually built 51 guided missile frigates of the Oliver Hazard Perry (FFG-7) class. The first of them was commissioned in December 1977. They were originally classified as patrol frigates; in 1975, before the commissioning of the lead ship, they were reclassified guided missile frigates.

we were still talking, and quite correctly, about our aging fleet. Within the past year or so, the Navy has been forced to take large cuts in the number of units, and this has resulted in an automatic lowering of the general age of the fleet.

I don't know what role long-range planning has had in that. It may have been something that was just simply forced on it. I don't know.

John T. Mason, Jr.: What role did mothballing of units of the fleet play in your long-range planning?

Admiral Colwell: We maintained in inventory, of course, the ships that were in the mothball fleet, divided by categories, and the categories were supposed to represent general condition and, as I recall, was usually expressed in terms of the number of days that would be required in order to put them to sea. These were our strategic reserve, would be one way to express it, and very important because this is the only way we could make up the shortage in numbers of what we actually had and the numbers that we presumed that we needed in order to accomplish all the functions the Navy was supposed to do. That strategic reserve is today very largely dissipated. We have simply worn those ships out. The ones that are tied up, except for the ones that have been decommissioned within the past year, would take a long time to put into operation.

John T. Mason, Jr.: And then the degree of their seaworthiness, once they were in operation?

Admiral Colwell: Yes. They can be made to run. They can be repaired so they could safely go to sea. It would be an enormous job. First of all, they have not modern communications. Their weaponry is certainly obsolescent, except for gunfire support. One thing that we have found in the reserve fleets is that even though a ship is dehumidified, the insulation of the wiring eventually goes. There would have to be an enormous amount of rewiring on these ships.

To talk about putting one of these ships into commission in 30 days, in my opinion, is sheer nonsense.

Today is a great deal different from what it was ten years ago in terms of counting on mothballed ships as a strategic reserve. Time marches on. It's merely a matter of old age.

John T. Mason, Jr.: Yesterday I listened to a two-minute lecture to our board of control on the age of specialization in the Navy and the need to be prepared for it and to include it in all their planning and so forth. Was this also a factor in your long-range planning?

Admiral Colwell: I would say ten years ago it probably should have been and was not. At that time, I guess, most of us really thought a naval officer should be the whole man, probably incorrectly.

John T. Mason, Jr.: You told me off-tape, and this was at the time when you sat in the seats of the mighty, you sat among them, at least, and this was an indication of the importance of your office.

Admiral Colwell: Well, this is rather a matter of hindsight, I think, but here I can certainly recognize that for the first time in my career I was sitting among the mighty. I wouldn't say that I sat in the seats of the mighty because I didn't. But I was included in large numbers of meetings, discussions, and conversations with the top people in the Navy Department and sometimes with people from the office of the Secretary of Defense. So, for the first time, I was reaching a position, or had reached a position, from which I might reasonably expect to move into positions of greater importance. I recognize that today.

John T. Mason, Jr.: Thank you for a very interesting session.

Interview Number 7 with Vice Admiral John Barr Colwell, U.S. Navy (Retired)

Place: Admiral Colwell's apartment in Washington, D.C.

Date: Tuesday, 15 January 1974

Interviewer: John T. Mason, Jr.

John T. Mason, Jr.: Admiral, for interview number seven, chapter number seven, the locale changes. You assumed command in January, as a matter of fact on January 17, 1964, of the Amphibious Forces in the Pacific. Do you want to take up the story at that point?

Admiral Colwell: Well, this quite obviously was a very high point in my naval career, because it meant that I put on my third star, and I suppose anyone starting out in the Navy never expects to get that high. When you do, it's a tremendous emotional lift.

John T. Mason, Jr.: But it could not have been such a great surprise to you, sir, could it?

Admiral Colwell: That's really pretty hard to say. When you get up in that bracket, it's a case of many are called and few are chosen. There aren't very many jobs available, and even though you may feel that your qualifications are superb, there just aren't very many jobs available.

As I was saying, in addition to this great emotional lift of being promoted to three stars, I was greatly pleased with the job that was being given to me. It was a very large sea command. It was based in a very pleasant area, San Diego, Coronado, and extended to the remote regions of the Pacific actually. All in all, it was a day of great rejoicing. That's a pretty poor way to say it, but that's what it was when I took command of the Amphibious Force Pacific.

John T. Mason, Jr.: You were under the over-all command of Admiral Felt, were you not?

Admiral Colwell: Yes, once removed. Admiral Felt was CinCPac, an area command under the Joint Chiefs.* My immediate commander—you see, the Amphibious Force was a type command under the Commander in Chief Pacific Fleet—was Roy Johnson.† A type command, or perhaps I should say that particular type command, is a combination administrative command and an operational command. Not all type commands are so. For instance, cruisers/destroyers, at least it was at that time, strictly an administrative command. You did not take your forces to sea. The amphibious command, on the other hand, involved all of the same administrative duties but, in addition, I commanded the Amphibious Force when it went to sea as a total force. I had two group commanders. You will recall that I had commanded a group in the Atlantic.

John T. Mason, Jr.: Yes, and rather enjoyed it!

Admiral Colwell: Oh, very much, very much indeed. I liked the Amphibious Forces. I did from the beginning. Commanding the entire Pacific Amphibious Force just enhanced my view of the competence of the people who worked in the Amphibious Forces. We had at that time a lot of rather ancient ships, many of them conversions from the merchant types not designed for the exact chore, but by and large the men of my force performed just admirably.

John T. Mason, Jr.: I expect many of these ships were veterans of the Korean War, were they not?

Admiral Colwell: Oh, and World War II. They were pretty old. I'm happy to say that almost all of those, I suppose, have been retired now and replaced by new construction designed for the job. But at any rate I thought they did a great job, and I enjoyed my work with them and with the people.

---

* Admiral Harry D. Felt, USN, served as Commander in Chief Pacific from 31 July 1958 to 30 June 1964. His oral history is in the Naval Institute collection.
† Admiral Roy L. Johnson, USN, served as Commander in Chief Pacific Fleet from 30 March 1965 to 30 November 1967. His oral history is in the Naval Institute collection.

I had a very competent staff. My commanding officers were generally high caliber, and their crews performed well. So, all in all, it was a most enjoyable time, professionally. In addition to that, it was a very enjoyable time from a personal point of view. We had government quarters in Coronado on North Island, the air station.*

John T. Mason, Jr.: Was this the first time you'd had government quarters?

Admiral Colwell: No. I had government quarters when I was on shore duty in Dahlgren, but that was quite some time past. All in all, it was a most enjoyable period. One of the things that added greatly to the enjoyment of it was the sort of combination of professional and personal social affairs.

We, of course, came into contact with and got to know as friends a large number of the civilian community, primarily the business community, of San Diego and Coronado, and these people, I would say without exception, were just delightful people, and we were more than happy to be able to claim them as friends.

John T. Mason, Jr.: It was a bit unusual, was it not, to branch out beyond the naval circle?

Admiral Colwell: Not in a job like that one, because this was a ranking job in the San Diego area. There were three vice admirals in San Diego, of which I was one, so that we represented the Navy at the top. So in a job like that it was not unusual that we should come to know the civilian community. The same thing would be true in Norfolk.

John T. Mason, Jr.: You represented big business, too, in that community?

Admiral Colwell: We did, indeed. A very large part of the local income came from the Navy in many different ways. Part of it was the pay of personnel and we, of course, purchased supplies locally, not only food but hardware and so on. The air station on North Island had an employment number in the thousands.

---

* North Island Naval Air Station is on the end of the Coronado peninsula, across the harbor from San Diego.

So, yes, the Navy was tremendously important and still is to San Diego. In addition to that, we had the Navy Recruit Command, Marine Recruit Command, and just up the road a few miles we had Camp Pendleton, which housed an entire Marine division. A little farther up the road we had the Marine Air Station at El Toro, the Naval Air Station at Miramar. The entire area was dotted with defense installations.

Professionally, as I think I said earlier, I count this tour most rewarding. During my tour there we became heavily involved in South Vietnam, to the extent that we maintained an entire amphibious group deployed out there from then on for several years.

John T. Mason, Jr.: That was the beginning of the year 1964?

Admiral Colwell: Yes. The huge supply complex, airfields, Marine base at Danang and Chulai were established during this period. I, of course, visited out there professionally several times.

John T. Mason, Jr.: When did you first go out?

Admiral Colwell: I can't remember what the date was.

John T. Mason, Jr.: Actually, our first operations, I believe, began in September of that year with the Yankee Station, the photo reconnaissance.*

Admiral Colwell: Yes, and then we began going in to Danang. Of course, Danang in the beginning was just sort of an open roadstead. There was a harbor of sorts. There's the river there and some sort of dockage, but it was truly an amphibious operation to even land supplies in the beginning.

---

* During the initial stages of involvement in the Vietnam War, the U.S. Navy maintained aircraft carriers on two stations based on Civil War designations—Yankee Station off North Vietnam and Dixie Station off South Vietnam. The latter, which began on 16 May 1965, was dropped 15 months later once airfields were available ashore in South Vietnam.

A man who had been my operations officer, Tom Weschler, was selected to flag rank and he was sent out there and built the base.* He did a tremendous job. This was later on.

During that entire period, of course, there was amphibious activity not only in the Western Pacific but also in the Eastern Pacific. We intensified our training and training exercises, some of them quite large scale, in the Eastern Pacific in order that the ships and the people whom we deployed to Southeast Asia would be as near a peak as we could get them. I think with no modesty at all I can say we were pretty successful.

John T. Mason, Jr.: What were our objectives, limited as they were at that time, in terms of amphibious operations?

Admiral Colwell: In South Vietnam?

John T. Mason, Jr.: Yes.

Admiral Colwell: Well, sort of broadly speaking we were there simply to be ready at hand to move the Marines, mostly the Marines, any place that the overall commander in the area might want them. This involved actually landing Marines over the beach; it involved the amphibious construction battalion, airfield building, etcetera; it involved a series of movements of Marines when they were pulled out of the field and sent back to Okinawa to regroup, refit, rest, retrain, and then come down for another operation. I can't remember how many operations there were while I was there. Actually, not too many because I didn't stay so awfully much longer after that. After only 16 months of command, I got a most unattractive phone call one morning.

B. J. Semmes called me from Washington and said, "You might as well brace yourself. You're coming back immediately."† And that's exactly what happened, much to

---

* Rear Admiral Thomas R. Weschler, USN, served as Commander Naval Support Activity Danang from February 1966 to February 1967. The oral history of Weschler, who retired as a vice admiral, is in the Naval Institute collection.
† Vice Admiral Benedict J. Semmes, Jr., USN, served as Chief of Naval Personnel from 1 April 1964 to 31 March 1968. His oral history is in the Naval Institute collection.

my dismay. I loved what I was doing, and I had hopes of moving on to command the First Fleet, which was something that had been happening with fair regularity out there. But unfortunately it didn't come to pass.

John T. Mason, Jr.: Would you concentrate a bit on that period and on Vietnam, recalling any details that might be interesting and useful historically?

Admiral Colwell: I'm not sure that I have anything that would be of historical value. I did not actually participate in any of the Vietnamese amphibious operations. Those were carried out by one or the other of my group commanders who remained there on the spot with the ships.

Our principal job in the type command, that is, my staff and I, was, of course, continuous training, logistics, and repair, and these came to be of vital importance. The ships in the Western Pacific could be repaired in Subic or in Yokosuka, and, of course, we made continuous use of both of those bases and their repair facilities. Those same two ports were about all that were available to us as rest and recreation areas, and Yokosuka was a very long way away and wasn't used too much. Subic, as a big bustling base, offered very little in the way of recreation.

John T. Mason, Jr.: Hong Kong was not available to you?

Admiral Colwell: Not freely.

John T. Mason, Jr.: What do you mean by that?

Admiral Colwell: Well, we were politically restricted to small numbers of ships in Hong Kong at any one time, and as I recall we were somewhat restricted in return visits by the same units. The Communists frequently attempted to make propaganda from the fact that we were using, as they claimed, Hong Kong as an operating base. That was not true. We were using it as a recreation base, but perhaps that gets to be semantics when you're in this kind of field of international politics. So Hong Kong was not freely available to us. It was the best liberty port that we had.

John T. Mason, Jr.: What about Bangkok?

Admiral Colwell: Too far away. You had to go clear down and all the way around the Indochinese peninsula, and it was just too far. These old ships, you see, were pretty slow. We didn't have 20-knot ships, except for very few.

We had some use of Kaoshung in Taiwan, but this didn't offer very much really in the way of recreational facilities.

John T. Mason, Jr.: And not a very pleasant climate, is it?

Admiral Colwell: The climate wasn't too bad, but it just didn't offer very much.

The lack of liberty ports for any kind of decent recreation became one of our most serious problems. It was something that continued throughout the Vietnamese War, and it was something that the people just had to learn to live with.

I do have something which I think is of historical significance. One of the things that came out of the employment of amphibious forces in Vietnam was the development of a quite sophisticated system of handling battlefield casualties. We finally got off Vietnam a hospital ship, but, of course, it could only be in one place. The Vietnamese coastline is rather long, and battles were taking place in a lot of different areas. The amphibious ships had some rather rudimentary medical spaces designed to handle casualty evacuation and a certain amount of treatment. Under the strong leadership of my staff physician, Dr. Honsik, a captain in the Medical Corps, these medical spaces in the larger ships such as the helicopter carriers were expanded and built up in terms of available equipment.[*] Medical teams were built up so that more skills were available, and helicopter evacuation from the battlefields to good surgical care became the order of the day.

---

[*] Captain Cyril J. Honsik, MC, USN.

After I came back to Washington this system had really come into full play. Captain Honsik visited me here in Washington and brought me some figures on how they had been able to make a miraculous reduction in losses from battlefield casualties, and also a miraculous reduction in the number of amputations. It was not unusual at all for the battlefield casualties to be on the operating table getting high-grade surgical care in 15 minutes. Previously these people were certain fatalities.

John T. Mason, Jr.: Yes.

Admiral Colwell: Because the best that could be offered was a forward medical post where they really had no opportunity to give proper surgical care. This was really a very dramatic development. I would like to have seen a documentary made on this, but I was never able to stir up any real interest in doing it.

John T. Mason, Jr.: What type of injuries predominated? Were they largely to the limbs from land mines, that sort of thing?

Admiral Colwell: Very heavily so. Injuries from fragments, I believe, predominated. Injuries from, say, rifle fire, bullets, were not a very large percentage. The enemy out there was very proficient in the use of ground mines, land mines, and they resulted in, I believe, the majority of the casualties and very severe casualties.

I remember seeing back here in Washington a film that was produced on the treatment of these severe casualties. It was the closest thing that was made, I guess, to a documentary, but it didn't stress what I wanted to stress. It did show quite graphically the extent of some of these fragment injuries. It was just frightful.

John T. Mason, Jr.: One would have thought the Medical Corps might have been interested in a documentary.

Admiral Colwell: Well, they did make this one film that I saw, and they may have made others, but I thought that the real gripping story that would have caught the imagination of the American public was this matter of speed of treatment which resulted in saving lives. I wish that had been done because to me it was most dramatic.

John T. Mason, Jr.: Were there lots of casualties and treatment necessary because of tropical disease? They were operating in the jungles.

Admiral Colwell: Oh, they had the usual things that you associate with jungle warfare and tropical climates. Yes, lots of tropical diseases. These were not so much the province of our amphibious medical people as base hospitals, and of course many of those were evacuated.

Incidentally, the medical evacuation service which was run by the Air Force through their MATS operation was fantastic.[*]

John T. Mason, Jr.: Again in proficiency and speed?

Admiral Colwell: Oh, yes. They did a magnificent job. And, of course, for the first time they had the airplanes that could do the job.

John T. Mason, Jr.: The helicopters specially?

Admiral Colwell: The helicopters to make the first jump, and when they were ready to move, why, they put them aboard these huge jet aircraft and they were back in Honolulu or the States in a full-care hospital in a matter of hours. A magnificent operation.

John T. Mason, Jr.: Did your amphibious forces have any brush with drugs and that sort of thing that you came to know of?

---

[*] In World War II the Army Air Forces operated MATS, the Military Air Transport Service. By the time of the Vietnam War the title had been changed to Military Airlift Command. In 1992 it became known as the Air Mobility Command.

Admiral Colwell: Not in the time that I had the amphibious forces, because this was very early in the business. They all did later, I guess.

Another development that fell in the lap of the Amphibious Force later on was riverine warfare. This really developed after I left the Amphibious Force and came back to Washington. You see, I left there in May of 1965.

John T. Mason, Jr.: Yes. Were there some intimations that it was going to be necessary to develop this technique when you were there?

Admiral Colwell: Yes. It was quite apparent that something was going to have to be done. There were some riverine warfare craft actually in operation down there. There were old French craft that were being operated, quite ancient, and only marginally satisfactory, but they did form a basis for us to work on. The new boats that we built and sent down there, some of them followed that kind of planning in the way of armor and so forth. That all came later.

I was down in the delta on one of my trips out there, at Can Tho, flying over that area and it looks as though most of it's under water. At certain times of the year I guess it is. There was an airfield at Can Tho, where we landed, and went down in a South Vietnamese DC-3 transport.* We landed there and looked around. The airfield was ringed by riflemen about every 50 yards, and so forth. It wasn't very reassuring, completely surrounded by tall grass. I don't know whether they call it elephant grass or what they call it, but it afforded perfect cover for anybody that wanted to come and take a potshot at anybody else.

On this same trip, we also flew up to a place not too far from Saigon, called Benhoa. Driving into the camp, we came to a barbed-wire roadblock, and that really brought home to me that I was in the middle of the war zone. Barbed-wire roadblocks

---

* The Douglas DC-3 went into service in the mid-1930s as perhaps the first really successful commercial airliner. Designated C-47 by the Army and R4D by the Navy, the plane was a much-used transport and cargo plane during and after World War II.

were something that I hadn't seen. They were frequently attacked by Viet Cong with rockets, small-arms fire, and satchel charges, which they used to use quite frequently.[*]

John T. Mason, Jr.: Satchel charges?

Admiral Colwell: Yes. These were just chunks of plastic. They might even be in a brown bag, and they'd throw it into a window with a fuze on it. It was like throwing a few sticks of dynamite. Fortunately, this didn't happen when I was there, but it happened about a week before.

The entire country, of course, was a battle area. You never knew where the enemy were. There was no way to find them. They all looked alike, dressed alike.

John T. Mason, Jr.: There were pockets here and there?

Admiral Colwell: Yes. Jungle warfare was brutal in the extreme. The Viet Cong—you see, this was early in the game, before they tried to mount any frontal assault. It was all guerrilla, so they operated largely at night. They all dressed the same, they all looked like farmers or fishermen. They'd be villagers by day and guerrillas by night, and they operated on a system of terror. The numbers of assassinations and brutalities were in the thousands, eventually, I guess, in the tens of thousands. A very tough war, indeed.

John T. Mason, Jr.: I know the hamlet program, which we initiated and which General Krulak was so very interested in, was somewhat removed from the amphibious command, but did you have any involvement?[†]

Admiral Colwell: Not really. That was run by the Marines. Of course, the Marine medical people are all USN, so there was a Navy involvement from that point of view and a very

---

[*] Viet Cong is a derogatory term for Vietnamese Communists in South Vietnam. This was an irregular force, as differentiated from the North Vietnamese Army.
[†] Major General Victor H. Krulak, USMC, served in the early 1960s as special assistant to the director of the Joint Staff; his area of concentration was counterinsurgency and special activities.

important one. The corpsmen were most important in these teams. Krulak, incidentally, had the Fleet Marine Force, Pacific, at the same time that I had the Amphibious Force.* We worked together; we were partners.

John T. Mason, Jr.: Did you have anything to do with CarDiv 3?

Admiral Colwell: Only insofar as you almost always had carrier support in amphibious operations. It's just another branch of the Navy that you work with, and the same way with the destroyers and cruisers. It was all part of the total Navy team. In our training exercises along the California coast we worked with all the other branches of the Navy, including submarines. One of the things that you must train for in the amphibious business is protecting your forces when they are in an objective area. You have to stay there for a while in order to land your troops and all your supplies, and you have to come back to it, so you must have reasonable safety for your ships while they're getting the job done. This involves primarily the destroyer force and the ASW forces, of course, particularly the ASW aircraft.

An operations order, an operations plan, for the amphibious force always must include all of these branches of the Navy in order to get the job done. You have your own aircraft to protect you against enemy aircraft, ASW aircraft to assist in the protection against submarines. The destroyers are there for antisubmarine and also for gunfire support, which is most important in amphibious forces. Gunfire preparation to let you get on the beach without getting murdered in the surf, and then gunfire support to permit the Marines to make their advances and take their objectives. That's most important.

We had a certain amount of developmental work around Coronado, that is, in the form of different types of boats or different types of equipment to try and get the job done better.

The place where people get killed early in the game in the amphibious business is in the surf, trying to get ashore. As an amphibious boat grounds on the shore, the men have to wade out of it and get under some kind of cover so that they can group and proceed with

---

* In 1964, as a lieutenant general, Krulak became Commander Fleet Marine Force Pacific Fleet.

their business. So it has always been one of the hopes and one of the objectives of people working in the amphibious business to speed up the ship-to-shore movement so that defending gunfire couldn't knock out your boats on the way in, and in particular to get out of the surf in a hurry.

One of the things that has been under development for quite some time now and we had a little bit of work with is the surface-effect ships which are truly amphibious in that they ride on a cushion of air over the water, over the surf, over the beach, and inland, that is, until you meet some sort of an obstacle like a grove of trees or a wall or even a bluff. They'll climb a reasonable grade, but they won't handle a vertical height of more than two feet. Work continues to be done on these, and I'm reasonably hopeful that this will result in a ship-to-shore movement much faster and much safer than anything we've had before.

John T. Mason, Jr.: And you actually worked with prototypes of those?

Admiral Colwell: We didn't actually work with them, but we knew what was going on and we kept track of tests that were being run here in the Atlantic, primarily using some British types. Then, I guess it was after I came back to Washington, we actually sent out to the Mekong Delta three very small air-cushion types that were built by the Bell Company on a British design, and these operated down there in the delta for quite some months with what I'd call limited success. They couldn't operate in the rice paddies because the boundaries of the paddies were, in effect, dams, and they were high enough so these very small ships couldn't get over them.

John T. Mason, Jr.: When you say small, how many tons?

Admiral Colwell: I've forgotten what the exact size was, but they would carry maybe five or six men, which is very small. They're fast and they're very light.

One time—and I m sure this was after I came back to Washington—they operated in a place called the Plain of Reeds, which was sort of made to order for these people because it was flat, it was marshy, and there wasn't any other kind of a vehicle that could move there. In this area, they track down infiltrators. They could track down people in dugouts and attack them with machine guns. They could work on the rivers, of course, but this was not always a successful kind of operation because they were subject to ambush. The enemy could hear them coming and they were, of course, forced to follow the river, and the guerrillas could hide on the river bank and fire on them as they went by.

John T. Mason, Jr.: They really announced their approach!

Admiral Colwell: Oh, they did, indeed. This was sort of a mixed bag of blessings that we got with those things.

John T. Mason, Jr.: Are these the ships that impressed Admiral Zumwalt when he was out there?*

Admiral Colwell: He knew about them. I don't know how much impressed he was with those in that kind of an operation. I think their true worth is really in the amphibious business, the business of getting through the surf and organized into operations on the beach.

Some other things that came to our hand during this period were a type of amphibious truck that was developed by the Army. You remember the World War II DUKWs?†

John T. Mason, Jr.: Yes, I do.

Admiral Colwell: Well, we had some of those, which were used mostly by the Seabees and amphibious construction battalions, and we got some newer ones from the Army which were called LARCs.‡ They came in various sizes, and they were in some ways an

---

* Vice Admiral Elmo R. Zumwalt, Jr., USN, served as Commander Naval Forces Vietnam/Chief of Naval Advisory Group Vietnam from 30 September 1968 to 14 May 1970.
† DUKW was the designation of an amphibious truck used by the U.S. Army in World War II. The name was pronounced like that of an animal capable of operating on both water and land, the duck.
‡ LARC—lighter, amphibious resupply, cargo.

improvement on the DUKWs, but these were still in the developmental stage when I was out there. They needed more work done on them.

We also got an entirely new development to test, which was a very large barge with gas turbine engines. This was moderately successful while I was there, and later on there was a plan to re-engine it because the engines that we had weren't satisfactory for one reason or another. I've lost track of it since. I don't know what went on with that. But that's an example of the type of developmental work we did.

John T. Mason, Jr.: In this area, the use of these prototypes for development purposes, were you involved with ComOpTEvFor?

Admiral Colwell: Sort of peripherally. Some of these things were done for OpTEvFor because he didn't have any staff to do it.* I would say that more OpTEvFor work was done by the Amphibious Force Atlantic, because they were close at hand. It was just easier administratively to do it that way.

John T. Mason, Jr.: Did a Seabee unit come under your cognizance?

Admiral Colwell: The amphibious construction battalion did, yes, and of course there was a large Seabee base at Port Hueneme. We also had an outfit that has always gotten lots of favorable publicity and rightly so, underwater demolition teams. They belonged to me, and their base for operational training was there in Coronado, right at the amphibious base where my headquarters were.

John T. Mason, Jr.: What sort of use did you put them to in Vietnam?

Admiral Colwell: Oh, they were about as hard working as anybody in Vietnam. They did all sorts of operations, really. I guess they really came into their own down in the delta when they began operating with the riverine forces. It's a most tremendously competent

---

* OpTEvFor—Operational Test and Evaluation Force.

outfit, magnificently trained. I used to fuss with them a little bit because their bust-out rate on trainees was so high. I felt that maybe they were carrying it a little bit too far.

John T. Mason, Jr.: Becoming too much of an elitist group?

Admiral Colwell: Yes.

John T. Mason, Jr.: Why was this?

Admiral Colwell: It was a matter partly of pride with them. Oh, they put them through hell. I used to accuse them of continuing to do this just because they had to go through it themselves, and they wanted to perpetuate this sort of hazing. I never was able to get very far with them on that! But I must say they were magnificently trained, and the results would seem to bear out their training plans.

John T. Mason, Jr.: I would think that duty would call for a very alert man, a very intelligent man.

Admiral Colwell: It does, and a particular type of man, self-reliant in the extreme, one who cannot become flustered under conditions of extreme stress and extreme personal danger. One of the training exercises that they ran routinely would be a night swimmer attack on a ship that might be anchored off the Coronado strand there a mile or so. This would involve swimming out there, in pairs, underwater, and carrying mock demolition charges or whatever for making their mock attack on the ship and returning to shore at night, undetected. This they did routinely. We lost two men at night while I was there, never found them.

John T. Mason, Jr.: The enemy also had people of this sort, did they not?

Admiral Colwell: Yes, quite well trained too. They were a big danger to us, to ships in the harbor.

John T. Mason, Jr.: How would you say they developed their ideas and techniques?

Admiral Colwell: They probably did. They practiced and thought them up themselves. They were pretty good at it.

John T. Mason, Jr.: It seems to me one of the leaps forward in terms of our involvement in Vietnam came in February of 1965 when you were still there, with the big mortar attack on the air base at Pleiku and President Johnson then ordered our retaliation which was the beginning of what were called the Flaming Dart missions.[*] Did this mean a step up in your own activities?

Admiral Colwell: I can't remember exactly when we began reinforcing our amphibious position in the Western Pacific, so I really can't answer your question. I don't recall just when that happened. I would think it would have been about that same time, yes.

John T. Mason, Jr.: What was your relationship with the Seventh Fleet command?

Admiral Colwell: No direct relationship, but my group commander stationed in the Western Pacific was, of course, a part of the Seventh Fleet so he reported directly. My principal relationship with the Seventh Fleet was attempting to keep him satisfied in terms of logistic support and upkeep and repairs for the amphibious ships. This involved the budgeting process, the disbursement of repair funds, the pursuit of special types of

---

[*] Lyndon B. Johnson served as President of the United States from on 22 November 1963 to 20 January 1969. On 7 February 1965 the Viet Cong hit the Pleiku airbase in South Vietnam with mortars; they killed eight men and wounded 109. The United States launched retaliatory air strikes on 7 and 11 February under the codename Flaming Dart. Aircraft from the carriers Coral Sea (CVA-43), Hancock (CVA-19), and Ranger (CVA-61) hit targets in North Vietnam. The commander of the operation, CTF 77, was Rear Admiral Henry L. Miller, USN, whose oral history is in the Naval Institute collection.

equipment through repairs, and so on, the usual sort of logistic support, the kind of thing that we'd all been doing for a long time.

John T. Mason, Jr.: How many ships did you have out there in your groups?

Admiral Colwell: In the entire amphibious force I had roughly 75 and about 25,000 men. At any one time, it might be anywhere from a third to a half would be in the Western Pacific. The higher numbers would be associated with turnover periods when the new ones and the old ones were all there at the same time.

John T. Mason, Jr.: Duplication.

Admiral Colwell: There was a certain duplication. One of our main problems, of course, was rapid repair of the ships when they came back from the Western Pacific. They'd been run pretty hard, and they were very old. We would put them into regular overhaul or restricted availabilities or whatever was required, get them out again, put new crews aboard, and get them ready to go. They actually spent about half of their time in the Western Pacific. We were never able to achieve a one-in-three rotation, which was highly desirable for morale purposes and material upkeep. We were much closer to one to one.

John T. Mason, Jr.: What was the status of morale with the amphibious forces? Was there any reluctance that early in the game to serve in the Western Pacific?

Admiral Colwell: No, there was not. People had some difficulties later, which I think was perfectly understandable, but not that early on.

John T. Mason, Jr.: As long as you provided adequate R&R the morale stayed high?[*]

---

[*] R&R—rest and recreation.

Admiral Colwell: If we had been able to provide adequate R&R, the morale problem would have been vastly improved. We were never able to provide adequate R&R. But that early in the game people were able to live with it. It later became much more of a problem. After people had been back and forth for half a dozen tours out there, leaving their families and putting up with this unutterable boredom associated with most wars, where a few moments of terror are interspersed with large periods of boredom, people began to have some trouble with morale, as is quite understandable.

John T. Mason, Jr.: In this period we saw the rapid development of a new approach to warfare, the sending of specific commands for operations from the White House in Washington. Did this involve the amphibious forces in your time?

Admiral Colwell: Not to my knowledge. It may have but, if so, it didn't come to my attention. It probably did indirectly, in that Commander Seventh Fleet, was being told exactly what to do 24 hours a day, and I wouldn't be at all surprised if my group commander or my squadron commanders over there got orders from the Seventh Fleet which had been given directly from Washington.[*] This, I think, would be most likely, but I don't recall that there was anything that came to my attention.

John T. Mason, Jr.: So you were spared the sense of frustration that some of the commanders in the field had?

Admiral Colwell: Oh, yes, because I was far removed from them. Washington couldn't be very much bothered with what I was doing at San Diego, as long as I didn't bother them too much about trying to get more money for upkeep.

John T. Mason, Jr.: I know, a little earlier, the various component parts of the Pacific Fleet were involved with SEATO demonstrations and that sort of thing. Were you involved in

---

[*] Vice Admiral Paul P. Blackburn, Jr., USN, served as Commander Seventh Fleet from 1 March 1965 to 7 October 1965.

that during your command?

Admiral Colwell: Not with SEATO, as I recall. Training exercises were conducted in the Western Pacific. It wasn't all war operations. Training exercises were also conducted, and these involved the Chinese and the Filipinos and the Thais, but none of these had any SEATO connections. I was not directly involved because those exercises were scheduled in the Seventh Fleet and the plans were drawn there. I was not directly involved, and I didn't need to be.

John T. Mason, Jr.: One other thing. Since we know the CIA was operating out in that area, were you in touch with them? Did they make demands upon you?

Admiral Colwell: Well, we actually furnished them some high-speed craft that operated out of Danang. This was a very hush-hush operation. I assume it was CIA. I didn't have any direct connection with it because it was all run out there. I knew it was going on, and we had the logistic support of these high-speed boats. That was the extent of any involvement.

John T. Mason, Jr.: At the end of 18 months, very reluctantly you had to come back to Washington and give over your command. To whom did you give that?

Admiral Colwell: I gave it to Vice Admiral Brute Roeder, a classmate and old friend of mine.[*] He kept it with great pleasure and success, and he did go on to become Commander First Fleet, also based in San Diego. So he got the second tour in San Diego that I had always hoped for and didn't get.

    I came back with great reluctance, not because I wasn't pleased with the Washington job that had been given to me because I considered it to be one of the best jobs in the Navy side of the Pentagon, but I did hate to leave that Amphibious Force

---

[*] Vice Admiral Bernard F. Roeder, Jr., USN, served as Commander Amphibious Force Pacific Fleet, 1965-66.

John T. Mason, Jr.: You came back as Deputy Chief for Fleet Operations and Readiness.*

Admiral Colwell: That's correct.

John T. Mason, Jr.: What were your specific qualifications that caused them to pull you out of the Pacific and bring you there?

Admiral Colwell: Oh, I really don't know. I suppose the Chief and Vice Chief and the Chief of Personnel, who actually did the slating, as we call it, felt that I was sufficiently experienced in the varying broad areas of all sides of the Navy, and I can only assume they thought my administrative capabilities were adequate to handling this task.

John T. Mason, Jr.: And at this point we were very well aware of the fact that we had a bear by the tail out in Vietnam. What was the prevailing attitude in high Navy ranks when you came back as it pertained to the war out there?

Admiral Colwell: As far as I know, our involvement in Vietnam was not being questioned. There was general acceptance that were doing something that we were supposed to be doing. We had answered the anguished call of an ally with whom we had assistance treaty, but I think even more strongly people felt that we were fighting the Communists in a very important area, and it was something that needed to be done. This was before the feeling of frustration really set in that we were fighting with our hands tied because we were not allowed to go ahead and fight to the full extent of our strength. That was not yet apparent because we were really just getting started. So there was a sort of straightforward feeling that, yes, we're involved in a scrap out here, it's something we're supposed to be doing, it's worthwhile, so let's get on with it.

---

*In the shorthand designation used at the time, Deputy Chief of Naval Operations (Fleet Operations and Readiness) was OP-03.

John T. Mason, Jr.: Was there any real fear that the Red Chinese would step into the picture?

Admiral Colwell: I'm sure that some people had that feeling. I didn't. I never did think so. I think it fairly rapidly became apparent to most of us that we were fighting the thing all wrong.

John T. Mason, Jr.: All wrong in what way?

Admiral Colwell: Well, we were fighting with our hands tied. We were not permitted to carry the fight to the enemy. We were not permitted to do the fairly obvious things that I'm still convinced would have brought the thing to a successful conclusion in six months.

The program was given the code name of Rolling Thunder guess it was rather aptly chosen because this was the code name for a method of fighting which involved "give them a taste and if that doesn't convince them, give them a little bigger taste, and eventually they'll be convinced and they'll quit."[*] This, of course, anybody who has ever read any military history knows is utter nonsense and ridiculous. This is why I said in one of our earlier interviews Mr. McNamara and his gang can only be classed as an unmitigated disaster.

John T. Mason, Jr.: That reminds one of the old rhyme about "my darling daughter, hang your clothes on a hickory tree but <u>don't</u> go near the water"!

Admiral Colwell: Yes. Any students of history know that trying to fight in that fashion simply intensifies the resistance on the part of the other guy. The only way to fight a war is to hit as hard as you can with everything you've got and knock the guy loose from his back teeth, and then he quits. But you don't give him time to steel his nerve and build up his

---

[*] Operation Rolling Thunder was the term applied to the periodic U.S. bombing of North Vietnam. It was interrupted by a number of bombing halts with the hope that these would induce the North Vietnamese to make peace.

resources and find ways to hide from you. This is not the way you fight a war. We should have learned that in Korea, but we didn't.

John T. Mason, Jr.: To be a bit analytical, how and why did this attitude develop in the highest echelons?

Admiral Colwell: It was a new theory of how you fight a so-called limited war. The theory was that you fight limited wars in fashion for a limited objective. You don't do any such thing. It's just false theory, that's all.

John T. Mason, Jr.: It was certainly not born of the military?

Admiral Colwell: No. Oh, no, no, this was dreamed up by the civilian heads and was sold. I've heard people say, "Why didn't the military make it known that this was happening?" Well, the fact is they did. The Joint Chiefs made their views known. They didn't receive wide publicity in the press, but their views were made known, their dissatisfaction.

In retrospect, one could say that some of the military leaders, perhaps including me, should have chosen to retire in protest, which would have attracted attention to what was going on. I do not believe that it would have changed the way it was being handled, because it was attractive to the civilian leaders who were guiding the team. I don't think that would have changed it.

John T. Mason, Jr.: Now, there seems to have been a change of attitude, because early in the 1960s, as I remember it, they did draw on the wisdom of, what was his name, General Thompson, the British general who waged such a successful guerrilla campaign in Malaya. We did draw on his experiences early in the '60s, with the intention, perhaps, of using him?

Admiral Colwell: I think this was more in the area of training, anti-guerrilla training. I'm not sure about that, but I would suggest that that was it.

The basic fault was that we were never allowed to hit the enemy at home where it really hurt. There was bombing in North Vietnam, thousands of sorties, millions of bombs, some of them on worthwhile targets, but unfortunately I would say that the majority were on targets of very little importance. It's very hard to hit a very small target which is pretty well concealed by jungle, in the first place, which is very hard to find because there aren't any real well-known landmarks around it that would guide you to it, so that a very high percentage of these sorties really went for naught. And we were never allowed to hit the really important targets in North Vietnam, which would have brought them to their knees, and that's what we needed to do.

John T. Mason, Jr.: The intimation is often made that there was actually a Red Chinese involvement?

Admiral Colwell: Oh, I'm sure there was within North Vietnam. I think there was a sort of paranoia at some levels in the State Department about the Red Chinese coming in. Just as during the Korean War there was the paranoia about Russia coming in, which is the last thing in the world Russia would have done. They would have let North Korea go down the drain before they came in. The Red Chinese wouldn't have come in in Korea, except that they guessed right that we were going to be suckers and not hit them where it hurt. They would have gone back home in a hurry if we'd given them the treatment. We weren't even allowed to bomb on the other side of the Yalu River, their airfields sitting over there. We did the same thing over again in North Vietnam. A terrible way to fight a war.

John T. Mason, Jr.: Various men have told me about Secretary McNamara attending CinCPac conferences in the early years of the 1960s, and from their reports it would seem that the Secretary was very much interested in pursuing it with vigor, I mean our involvement there.

Admiral Colwell: Yes, but only under his own terms, where they finally got to the ridiculous point where he was not only picking out the targets, but he was telling you how many bombs to drop on such targets. That's jackass.

John T. Mason, Jr.: Since we're looking at this and in this way, this whole problem as it developed, to what extent would you think that domestic political considerations entered into this picture, this attitude of restraint in warfare?

Admiral Colwell: I can't answer that. I have attributed it to a mistaken theory of warfare. What else contributed I have no way of knowing.

Also, the thing that compounded it, after it became quite apparent that this theory of warfare was a broken theory, even then there was never any indication that it was going to be changed. The refusal to admit that he could possibly be wrong, this is the basic defect of the man's professional character.

John T. Mason, Jr.: As you observed the scene, what role did General Taylor play in this?[*]

Admiral Colwell: He was blowing his "uncertain trumpet" most of the time. I think he must bear some of the blame in this. His rather optimistic reports of how things were going in South Vietnam certainly were misleading. No, I don't think he comes off very well in it, nor did General Westmoreland.[†]

John T. Mason, Jr.: Was the role of the Joint Chiefs diminished as this theory developed?

Admiral Colwell: I would have to say yes. The role was still the same but it didn't function. Their advice was not taken.

---

[*] Even though he had retired from active duty after serving as Army Chief of Staff from 1955 to 1959, General Maxwell D. Taylor, became Chairman of the Joint Chiefs of Staff on 1 October 1962 and served in that post until 3 July 1964. He was then U.S. Ambassador to South Vietnam in 1964-65. Taylor had come to President John F. Kennedy's attention through his book The Uncertain Trumpet (New York: Harper, 1960).
[†] General William C. Westmoreland, USA, served as Commander U.S. Military Assistance Command Vietnam from 20 June 1964 to 2 July 1968.

John T. Mason, Jr.: Did they continue to give traditional military-type advice?

Admiral Colwell: I would say so, yes, as far as I know. I never sat in on any of the Joint Chiefs' meetings. As far as I know, their advice continued to be given how the operations should be pursued, but in many cases they were overruled. This is obvious from the way things went.

Interview Number 8 with Vice Admiral John B. Colwell, U.S. Navy (Retired)

Place: Admiral Colwell's apartment in Washington, D.C.

Date: Tuesday, 5 February 1974

Interviewer: John T. Mason, Jr.

John T. Mason, Jr.: Well, sir, today we begin chapter eight. You were returning to Washington once again. You'd been out in the Pacific in command of the amphibious operations, and you were notified in June of 1965, perhaps a little before that, that you were to be assigned as Deputy Chief of Naval Operations, OP-03, Fleet Operations and Readiness, in Washington.

Admiral Colwell: That's correct. I think I mentioned earlier that I was particularly disappointed to leave the Amphibious Force and the Pacific Fleet after what seemed to me like a very short tour. But I had to admit to myself that I was coming to Washington in certainly one of the finest assignments that one could get.

John T. Mason, Jr.: And at a very strategic time!

Admiral Colwell: Yes, a very busy time certainly. I was experienced in the ways of the office of the Chief of Naval Operations, of course, from previous Washington duty, but in spite of that, naturally there was a tremendous amount to learn on the new job. It was vastly more important than any that I had ever been exposed to in Washington. I was somewhat surprised and, I think I should say, pleased, delighted, to find that OP-03—in particular of the deputies—was involved in practically everything that went on, with one possible exception. I had very little to do with the functioning of the Joint Chiefs of Staff and no direct involvement with the strategic business of OP-06. There was, of course, an indirect involvement, just as there was with all of the other deputies.

John T. Mason, Jr.: Well, the Joint Chiefs were a province of the CNO himself?

Admiral Colwell: That's true, and, of course, his right-hand man in Joint Staff dealings was and is OP-06, that's his job. That's what his charter calls for. But, aside from that, OP-03 was involved and fairly heavily in practically everything else that went on.

One of my chief concerns was, of course, the matter of shipbuilding. I was the sponsor, as they called me, for the shipbuilding and conversion bill before the Congress, and this took up a very considerable portion of my time throughout the year. It takes a long time to put that part of the budget together. There were many iterations and many changes back and forth before it was finally solidified within the Navy, and then more before it was solidified with the Secretary Of Defense, and then a continuing series of preparation of position papers and so on in support of the shipbuilding bills as finally submitted to the Congress. Then, of course, the series of hearings that's necessary to support this particular bill before four committees, two authorization committees, Armed Services committees, and the two appropriations committees. As with aircraft and missiles, ships must be authorized in one bill, and the appropriations bill is separate.

John T. Mason, Jr.: How similar or dissimilar is the testimony you have to give, the information you have to present, in the House committees and again in the Senate committees?

Admiral Colwell: I would say almost identical, if not identical. The prepared statements are, in fact, identical, or were when I was there. The questions are quite similar, in fact to the point where if it were feasible to do so there's no reason why you couldn't testify before both houses at the same time.

John T. Mason, Jr.: It's kind of redundancy, isn't it?

Admiral Colwell: It is a redundancy, but it would not be practical to try and combine them, I'm sure, simply because it would be too unwieldy. The individual committees have a lot of members, so that you may be questioned by anywhere from half a dozen to 20 people.

John T. Mason, Jr.: I suppose there are some angles that are developed in debate, say, if a bill is before the House Armed Services Committee and then is before the House, there are angles of it that develop into debate which had not been brought out in the hearings and therefore new material for the Senate to deal with.

Admiral Colwell: That is true. This is something that could happen at any time. You may not have anticipated a certain line of questioning that is quite a valid line and useful to the committee. Then you simply have to prepare the material and answer the questions and so on.

In one of these hearings, in addition to your direct answers to questions, there are almost invariably a number of questions that may involve rather extensive ancillary preparation of tables, costing, statements, and this sort of thing, and you simply request permission of the chairman to submit your answer to that question for the record, and you supply it to him in writing.

John T. Mason, Jr.: Was your Polaris experience of great help to you in these presentations?

Admiral Colwell: Yes, it was helpful because I learned what the routine is before one of these committees, how they proceed, the form, what kind of questions you can get. I even got an insight into the nature of certain members, as revealed by their method of questioning. So, it was helpful, yes. I just went to school!

John T. Mason, Jr.: I was thinking of the expertise in public relations that Mr. Watson had while working with the Polaris project and the graphic displays and so forth used in presenting the Polaris story?

Admiral Colwell: This, of course, was some more of my schooling. Raborn was almost always, if not always, the principal witness for Polaris. I used to accompany him because it was necessary for me to be aware of questions, answers, positions, and so on, in case I should have to appear in Raborn's absence. So this was a schooling period for me and very useful.

John T. Mason, Jr.: Did you work at the JAG office in preparation for your presentations?*

Admiral Colwell: I don't recall that it was necessary to work with the JAG in preparing these presentations. The form was fairly well set, and you would just move from here to here following that form, pretty much, because it was a form that was familiar to the committees, they were happy with it, and there didn't appear to be any good reason for changing to a new format. In fact, there was a pretty good reason not to. But I don't recall that we were involved with JAG.

John T. Mason, Jr.: Did your interest in the shipbuilding program extend as far back as the Ship Characteristics Board? Did you sit on that board?

Admiral Colwell: Yes, I did at one time.

John T. Mason, Jr.: During this period?

Admiral Colwell: No. During this period the chairman of the Ship Characteristics Board was actually in my organization. He worked for me. So I did attend meetings of the Ship Characteristics Board in the preparation of final recommendations for the CNO.

My earlier connection with the Ship Characteristics Board was primarily during the time when I was OP-93, head of the Long-Range Objectives Group. I had had an interest in the total shipbuilding bill for many, many years. It was a matter that interested me, so it was really a very pleasant labor for me to work on the shipbuilding bill as its sponsor. I really had final responsibility for the recommendations that went to the CNO on what we ought to do in what years.

---

* JAG—Judge Advocate General, the Navy's legal arm.

John T. Mason, Jr.: You were now in the age of nuclear-powered ships, so it meant a proliferation of new types. Tell me about that.

Admiral Colwell: There were not really so many new types. In fact, it was pretty difficult to get very many new types in the shipbuilding operations because of the length of time involved in the design and construction of ships. And then, very fortunately, the long life that they have thereafter. These are very expensive propositions and your initial approach to new shipbuilding, say, you want to establish a five-year program, and that was a pretty sensible thing to do, in addition to the primary concern of how much money you think it might be possible to expend, about the first thing that you have to start with is what is your current inventory of ships. This, then, relates to what your actual needs are in terms of tactical and strategic plans. So you take your needs and you take your inventory and what your inventory will be in five years, because you have ships that are continually being retired, and you then arrive at a differential, and this presumably is what gives you a lead on what you ought to be building.

Then, with that, you can attempt to determine what types of ships you should build to fill the gaps—reproductions of current types, evolutions of current types, brand-new types, and what should the mix be within the funds that you can reasonably expect to have. It's ridiculous to go in with a one-year building plan for $5 billion. It's silly. You know you're not going to get it. You very probably could not spend it if you did get it because there wouldn't be shipbuilding capacity. It just doesn't make any sense. So you must force yourself to be as reasonable as possible.

John T. Mason, Jr.: I would gather that there was a constant feed-in from the battle area in South Vietnam on ship requirements and so forth?

Admiral Colwell: Yes, that's true.

John T. Mason, Jr.: How did that reach your desk?

Admiral Colwell: Well, the CNO always expects, and gets, recommendations from the two fleet commanders, Atlantic and Pacific, as to what types they think should be built and how many. These usually turn out to be very large numbers, so that you have to do a great deal of cutting on what they suggest, and they expect you to because they're telling you what they think they need, which sometimes doesn't have any very great resemblance to what you can logically expect to get. But it does give you a very good lead on both types and numbers of what they think they ought to have to improve their total position. As far as Vietnam was concerned, the primary change was brought on by our movement into the new field of riverine warfare. This was something that we had not really done before. To begin with, we and the South Vietnamese had a few ancient French riverboat conversions of various kinds. Some they called monitors and so on. These would do some of the jobs, but it was apparent that there needed to be some very considerable improvements and additions. These were all worn out anyway.

So we went into a design and building program for riverine craft. Some of them were conversions of amphibious craft, which was a pretty logical thing to do. These were pretty good boats, they had good engines, and we armored them and put small turrets on them and flame-throwers, and grenade-launchers, and various types of things, some of them very ingenious.

We also had the advantage of some fairly recent developments in propulsion in water jets. We built some small, fairly-high-speed riverboats using water jets. All in all, these boats turned in a very good performance out there.

John T. Mason, Jr.: Did we also have some hydrofoils of foreign make?

Admiral Colwell: No, we didn't have any hydrofoils, but we did have three small surface-effects craft built by Bell on license from a British firm. They moved over the water and swamps, and that sort of thing, at only a few inches above the surface, and therefore their use was limited in that particular area. For example, in rice paddies you couldn't use them, because dams would separate them which might be a couple or three feet high, and these craft would just come up against that, and there you were. All you could do was turn around. They did see some usage, but in general not terribly useful.

John T. Mason, Jr.: Were they not the ones that impressed Admiral Zumwalt?

Admiral Colwell: I think he was impressed by them, yes. He was very much impressed by all the riverine warfare. And those people did a great job. The craft worked out well, and they were operated by a much of real hell-for-leather guys.

John T. Mason, Jr.: Were some of the sturdier sampans also used?

Admiral Colwell: Oh, yes, they used almost anything that would float.

John T. Mason, Jr.: Did they do conversion jobs on the sampans?

Admiral Colwell: I don't remember that the sampans were converted much. They were just used for transports. There's a particular type of sampan down there that's useful in very shallow water. It's a long, slender boat with an outboard motor on a very long shaft, 15 feet long. With this long leverage, you can lift the propeller out of the water so that it's just barely fanning the surface and your boat is probably drawing only a few inches. This sort of thing was used for personnel transport for very small numbers of people.

A great deal of the riverine warfare down there was done at night, of course. Any boat on the rivers down there was very seriously subject as ambush. The enemy could hide in the undergrowth and levees along the sides of the rivers and ambush boats as they went by. They used all sorts of things in that business. Recoiless rifles of 57 millimeters and 75 millimeters were particularly useful to guerrillas, because they're light and easily carried. You could hide the barrel down your pants leg.

The boys fought a pretty tough war down there.

John T. Mason, Jr.: When you went before the Congress asking for funds for some of these more exotic types, did it not entail an educational process on your part?

Admiral Colwell: Yes, to a certain extent. I don't recall that that was ever very difficult. This was a pretty intriguing business, and the idea of buying 100 boats for a relatively small amount of money was very pleasing to the Congress. They were used to having me ask for $100 million for one ship! That's a little facetious, but, no, I don't recall that we had any difficulty with this. It seemed to be very easily understood.

John T. Mason, Jr.: Your interest in shipbuilding must have taken you through the avenues to MSTS and merchant auxiliaries.* Tell me about that phase of it.

Admiral Colwell: Well, ships for MSTS were part of the total shipbuilding plan, because they belonged to the government. They were not USS, but they did belong to the government, and they were operated by the Navy, by the government so that replacement ships for MSTS were a part of the overall building plan.

John T. Mason, Jr.: Were they operated by Navy crews or by civilian crews?

Admiral Colwell: They had both, some of both. Along toward the end I think they were all civilian. The people who were in charge of MSTS were continually unhappy with the lack of building to replace their old ships. They got a few now and then, but not very many, because when the slashing started to come on the shipbuilding bill, as we worked through the budget process, these MSTS types were usually the first ones that fell out. The next ones that fell out were usually the auxiliaries such as repair ships. We did build a few new tankers now and then because they had to accompany the fleet, but repair ships didn't fare very well. They were tied up most of the time anyway. We did get some new tenders for

---

* MSTS—Military Sea Transportation Service, a part of the Navy that operated ships for support functions. In some cases it chartered the ships, and it some cases it ran the ships directly with civil service mariners. In 1970 MSTS was renamed Military Sealift Command (MSC), the current title for the command.

the submarines and destroyers, but this became a matter of necessity. The nuclear submarines and the guided-missile destroyers, frigates, cruisers, required substantially greater shop space and entirely different types of shop space. The older tenders could just no longer be modified to handle the problem, so we got some new tenders.

John T. Mason, Jr.: In reviewing the naval events for the period when you were there as Deputy CNO, I noted several appeals from MSTS for additional auxiliaries, some apparently to be constructed in foreign countries. Did you have cognizance of that program?

Admiral Colwell: No. When it became apparent that MSTS was not really going to ever have very much success in replacing their fleet through the naval shipbuilding program, just because of a shortage of funds, then the head of MSTS initiated a program of persuading ship owners to build ships of the type which he needed and then he would take them back on long-term lease, charter them, let's see, for either five or ten years. I really had nothing to do with it. This was a thing that was generated by and engineered by the head of MSTS, so that took it out of the naval shipbuilding program. I think he was successful in getting approval for a program for several tankers and maybe some reefers, cargo ships, and so on.

I knew about it because I discussed it from time to time, but it was not one of my responsibilities.

John T. Mason, Jr.: Again in the realm of shipbuilding, in October of 1965 when you were well in the saddle, there was a minor upheaval in the Bureau of Ships when the chief and the deputy both asked for retirement because they were dissatisfied with the total-package concept for the design and construction of a fast logistic ship.* Do you recall that?†

Admiral Colwell: Yes. There was a long continuing argument, I guess is the best way to describe it about the total-package concept for shipbuilding as a whole.‡

John T. Mason, Jr.: First, you might give a definition of the total-package concept?

Admiral Colwell: The total-package concept was one that was devised by Secretary McNamara and his staff, and the intent was to establish a system whereby production items for the Department of Defense would be planned from cradle to grave, and the total cost of the entire program would be known within reasonable limits before it was ever approved. So that you would start with a design, build the engineering models, and eventually go into production. You would predict the total life of the system, the cost of spares, the cost of personnel training, everything in the world would be bound into the total package, so that presumably you would have a pretty fair handle on what the cost of a given program was going to be over the years.

John T. Mason, Jr.: You couldn't be surprised suddenly by a huge cost overrun?

Admiral Colwell: This was the hope, and a very reasonable hope. The program, I think, will work for certain things. There were a lot of us who did not believe that it was a proper way to go about shipbuilding. We just didn't think it would work.

---

* On 27 October 1965 Rear Admiral William A. Brockett, USN, Chief of the Bureau of Ships, and Rear Admiral Charles A. Curtze, USN, Deputy Chief of BuShips, simultaneously submitted requests for retirement. For details see the Naval Institute's oral history with Admiral Curtze.
† FDL was the designation for a forward-deployed logistic support ship that was considered in the 1960s but not constructed at the time. The idea was to have equipment and supplies in ships positioned at various places in the world to avoid transit time during crisis situations. The concept did come to fruition in the 1980s when the Navy began obtaining a series of maritime pre-positioning ships for operation by the Military Sealift Command.
‡ Total package procurement refers to buying an entire class of ships from one defense contractor. The most notable example is that of the Spruance (DD-963)-class destroyers, 30 of which were built by the Litton/Ingalls yard in Pascagoula, Mississippi.

John T. Mason, Jr.: Why?

Admiral Colwell: We didn't feel that you could have adequate knowledge to let you predict what your total program cost was going to be within very good limits. For example, you can expect that a ship should have a life of certainly 20 years, perhaps 30, and in some cases even more. During that period it will undoubtedly be modified and perhaps even converted not once, but maybe two or three times. Over a life of 20 years you really haven't any very good idea of what the state of the economy is going to be. We had already during this period suffered very substantial inflation, and shipbuilding-costs inflation appeared to be substantially more than in other areas of the economy. We were getting 10% a year at that time.

At any rate, maybe it was just because we had always done it the other way that a lot of us felt the old way was better. Regardless of that, we were directed to proceed.

John T. Mason, Jr.: This total-package concept, then, envisioned the total life of the ship rather than just the construction period?

Admiral Colwell: That's my recollection of it, yes. It has since been abandoned. The total-package concept, of course got an enormous black eye in the C-5A.* Whether it was deserved or not I am not prepared to say.

John T. Mason, Jr.: The C-5A aircraft?

Admiral Colwell: Then we had some very substantial overruns on the LHA, which was a new amphibious type, overruns in money and overruns in time.† Those ships were all a couple of years late. We had some overruns in the destroyer 963 class, which were the Spruances. A good part of this was pure and simple inflation. Everything else in the

---
* The C-5 Galaxy is a jet-powered cargo plane, among the world's largest aircraft. Lockheed-Georgia Company delivered the first operational Galaxy to the 437th Airlift Wing, Charleston Air Force Base, South Carolina, in June 1970.
† LHA is the designation of a type of amphibious assault ship. The first of the type, USS Tarawa (LHA-1), was commissioned 29 May 1976.

economy was costing more, so did ships. This, of course, brought on a great deal of recrimination in the Congress, GAO, and you name it.

John T. Mason, Jr.: Why? Because they had bought this other concept?

Admiral Colwell: They were just mad because of the overruns, and they didn't really want any explanations of how it happened. All they wanted was somebody to whip. This isn't new. It happens all the time.

John T. Mason, Jr.: Oh, yes, it does, but had the Congress bought this concept of McNamara's?

Admiral Colwell: Yes, they had. I don't know whether many of them had the same feelings we had or not. I do recall, going back to the time you mentioned when the Chief of BuShips and his deputy both chose not to continue. The Chief of BuShips, who was Ed Fahy, and I were testifying on the shipbuilding bill.* He always supported me at these hearings, properly. And we were asked questions about what we thought of this concept as far as shipbuilding was concerned.

Well, of course, you are committed—in fact, you are required by law to support the new budget if you testify. If you can't do that, you don't testify. So, as I recall, our answers went generally along the line that the plan as proposed held promise of improved procurement, and it did. Whether it would turn out to actually occur that way remained to be seen. As I recall, our testimony was somewhat along this line.

John T. Mason, Jr.: You really were on the hot seat as far as the Secretary of Defense was concerned, weren't you?

---

* Rear Admiral Edward J. Fahy, USN, served as Commander Naval Ship Systems Command from 1966 to 1969. He succeeded Rear Admiral Brockett.

Admiral Colwell: We had no choice, but I think we weaseled it about as good as we could! In theory, it did have promise. In practice, it didn't work out.

The best thing you can do, if you want to build a ship is to get your experts, presumably the people at BuShips, supported by a number of very good ship-design contract people, get them to estimate how much the ship is going to cost. I don't know any way to get a better idea of what it will actually cost. Then you feed in what you think inflation is going to be over the building period. If anybody knows a better way to get a guess on what it'll cost, I don't know it.

John T. Mason, Jr.: It seems to me only God would know what is in the future!

Admiral Colwell: That's right.

John T. Mason, Jr.: And what might have bearing.

Admiral Colwell: Over the years inflation has consistently—I would say certainly for the last ten years, in the shipbuilding business—been higher than people have anticipated. And, as I said earlier, during the period when I was 03 we were experiencing shipbuilding inflation that was perhaps twice as much as in the rest of the economy. How you can guess this, I'm sure I don't know.

John T. Mason, Jr.: Because of your concern and active interest in the shipbuilding program, did you get involved with some of the shipbuilding yards, and did you get involved with contracts and that kind of thing?

Admiral Colwell: No, I had no involvement with contracts at all, and this is a very good way to keep it. Let the contracting business be done by the people who build ships. The people who tell them what they want built have no business in the contracting business. I had nothing to do with contracting.

Now, I did have some meetings with people in shipyards. These were primarily just get-acquainted meetings. I met the men who run the Bath Iron Works, the men who run the Newport News Shipbuilding Company, now a part of Tenneco, the Pascagoula works of Litton and Company, and so on. I didn't meet all of them, but I met quite a number of them. This was largely just to get acquainted with them, because I did not have anything to do with the contracting.

John T. Mason, Jr.: Did you keep an active hand in the nuclear submarine program, the Polaris and the Poseidon?

Admiral Colwell: Oh, yes, because I was charged with sponsoring the shipbuilding and conversion bill, which included those ships. We had direct concern with those people at all times. And, of course, for another reason I had a direct concern with the progress of shipbuilding and conversions, when were they going to be finished. This led into the readiness side of my charter. It was very important to know and be able to advise the fleet commanders when they could expect to have these new and converted ships reporting to them so that they would know when they would go on the line because they knew how long it would take to shake them down, when could they start deploying them and getting some use out of them, which was very important to them, and it was important to me. We kept very close track of progress.

Another angle with which we were concerned in OP-03 was the modification and modernization of hulls, alterations. For very good and obvious reasons, a ship captain or his type commanders were not authorized to make alterations in hulls, because otherwise you would have nothing but chaos. Alterations must be approved and blueprints drawn and the end accomplished in a particular hull at a given time when the ship can be made available and when you have money to do it.

John T. Mason, Jr.: Does this include all ships in a class or just an individual ship?

Admiral Colwell: It may be an individual ship or it may be an entire class. There are very often a number of variations within a class, so that there are modifications in alterations. You might find a compartment was a different size. But this is something that we had a continuing interest in. We worked directly with OP-04 who is the Deputy for Logistics and, at the time at least when I was there, he was the sponsor of the particular bill before the Congress which handled that kind of money, and that's a different colored money from conversion money, which I handled.

It's one of the most difficult areas to handle, not only before the Congress but throughout the year, because there is never enough money to do all of the repairs and alterations that you want to do. This was particularly true during the Vietnam business, because we just ran the ships to death, and when a ship broke down in the Western Pacific it had to be repaired. You don't have any hidden kitty of money. If you spent $10 million on a ship that had not been planned, somebody else loses, and this is something that OP-04 had to wrestle with every single day. And we worked continually with him because we had an interest in what was going to be done, and there would frequently be good-sized conferences on what the choices ought to be.

John T. Mason, Jr.: What percentage of the ships employed in Vietnam were serviced and repaired in Japanese shipyards?

Admiral Colwell: I couldn't answer that. I would say probably the percentage was small because Yokosuka was a long, long way from the operating area. Mostly the repairs were done in Subic Bay.*

John T. Mason, Jr.: Well, even that was helpful, to you budget wise, was it not?

Admiral Colwell: Oh, yes, indeed.

---

* Subic Bay is a protected anchorage on the island of Luzon in the Philippines. It borders the Bataan province and is about 35 miles north of the entrance to Manila Bay. During the Vietnam War, Subic had a strong role as a support base for the U.S. Navy. Included were a naval air station, piers, ship repair facility, supply depot, and recreational outlets for ships' crews.

John T. Mason, Jr.: And time wise?

Admiral Colwell: Yes. Without Subic it could have been an entirely different kind of a ball game on keeping ships on the line. We built quite a large repair facility both ashore and in tenders.

John T. Mason, Jr.: What did you consider the actual life span of a destroyer? How many years? Even though you put it through a FRAM program.[*]

Admiral Colwell: Certainly not less than 25, during which it would probably get converted and modernized at least twice. The World War II destroyers, most of which have gone now, during the Vietnam War continued to run. They were in pretty bad shape, most of them, from a material point of view. They ran through World War II, they ran through the Korean War, and through Vietnam. In between wars, we had maintained overseas deployment of a substantial size, both Atlantic and Pacific. But the people had managed to hold them together. Now, say those ships were just coming in about 1945 and in 1970 they were 25 years old and still running. So you can certainly expect to get 25 years out of a destroyer.

A nuclear ship you might get more. The engineering plants of nuclear ships are, not surprisingly, built to a little tighter—perhaps not tighter specifications, but a little greater safety factor, and we may get more years out of those.

Eventually you get to the point where it is really not economical to further modernize a hull. You run out of growth space for one thing, with the advent of new weapons. You still have some of the old weapons, so that even though your new ones are more self-contained and they require fewer men, you've still got some of the old ones, so it's very difficult to reduce the crew in old ships, and there's a limit to how far you can go in encroaching on living space. That's a self-defeating process. So you get to a point where, even though it might be possible to put massive material improvements on a hull, it is not

---

[*] FRAM is an acronym for the fleet rehabilitation and modernization program. Under this program many U.S. destroyer-type ships of the 1950s and 1960s were substantially modernized by extensive rebuilding that incorporated later technology than that available at the time of original construction.

an economical thing to do because you don't get enough military improvement to warrant the expense of the materials.

You find the same thing in merchant hulls, like liners, for example. You finally get to the point where it's just not economical to refurbish an ocean liner.

John T. Mason, Jr.: With warships you have the weight factor, too, when you add ordnance?

Admiral Colwell: That's true. Ships, of course, are built with some growth factor in them, both size and tonnage, but eventually you use that up, and there just isn't any way that you can build any more into it. We did with our old battleships, you may recall. They were given blisters, some of them before World War II and some of them during it, in order to give them a greater displacement and let them absorb an additional weight growth.

John T. Mason, Jr.: At the expense of speed, however?

Admiral Colwell: They lost some speed, yes. There's a limit to what you can do. It was an expedient.

John T. Mason, Jr.: By what you said just a few minutes ago about the longer life of nuclear-powered ships, did you imply that even though the expense of building one is greater—the initial expense—that in the long run perhaps you broke even, than the more conventional type?

Admiral Colwell: I wouldn't care to make any guess on what the balance might be. The investment that you have in any nuclear-powered ship is so great that certainly you are forced just by common sense to get all the usage you can out of it. I really wouldn't have any guess on what the balance might be, answering your question.

Big ships like the Long Beach, she's going to outlive her armament, as far as her material condition is concerned, I'm quite sure.* She has Talos, the long-range missile. Those are now approaching the end of life because it is becoming uneconomical to further modify and repair the Talos fire-control system, so her engineering plant will probably outlive her ordnance. But she can be modified and be converted; remove Talos and give her something else.† This then becomes a problem of how much it is going to cost, and is it a good idea? I don't think the Navy has had to face that problem yet, at least face the answer to it. They know they have the problem.

Some of the early nuclear submarines I would think could best be classed now as not quite first line because the early ones are fairly noisy. We've learned a great deal about nuclear submarine silencing, quieting the engineering plant, so that the new ones that we have now are very quiet. They're very hard to detect. They're high speed, of course, and you get propeller noise. There isn't any way to avoid it. You're pouring horsepower into the water, and it makes noise. Aside from the relative noise of the earlier nuclear boats, you run into the space and weight problem on that too. You want to give them a new set of sensors; you want to give them a better sonar, for example. Better sonars are almost by definition bigger and heavier. So you eventually run out of weight and space in such a thing as a nuclear submarine, like anything else. They're still useful. As long as the engineering plant is good, they're very useful, and the normal progression for the submarine is when it falls out of first grade, second grade, and eventually becomes a training boat. But they're still very useful for that purpose.

John T. Mason, Jr.: Then as a last resort a museum piece!

Admiral Colwell: Last resort.

---

* USS Long Beach (CGN-9), the Navy's first nuclear-powered cruiser, was the only ship of her class. She was commissioned 9 September 1961. She had a standard displacement of 15,540 tons, was 721 feet long, 73 feet in the beam, and had a maximum draft of 31 feet. Her top speed was 30-plus knots. She was armed with two twin launchers for Terrier missiles, one Talos missile launcher, and ASROC. She was eventually decommissioned 3 May 1995.
† In 1979, a few years after this interview, the twin Talos launcher in the aft part of the Long Beach was removed and replaced with a launcher for the Terrier/Standard surface-to-air missile.

The overhaul of nuclear-powered ships is a frightfully expensive thing, but there isn't any way to avoid it. It's one of the things that goes along with nuclear power. When you start building nuclear ships you have automatically bought yourself an expensive job of overhaul. The people who design and develop nuclear power plants have done what I consider to be wonders with extending the life of a nuclear charge. The earlier ones, it was just a small number of years before you had to take the ship in for a very expensive refueling and recoring business. Now cores last many years, and this has been just a remarkable evolution in the development of nuclear power plants.

Speaking of nuclear power, I had a large number of contacts with Admiral Rickover. He and I saw eye to eye on a great many things over the years when I was OP-03. We gave mutual support to a number of shipbuilding programs which we were thoroughly convinced were important for the Navy.

John T. Mason, Jr.: You found him not the thorny character that some people do?

Admiral Colwell: Oh, no, I think Admiral Rickover is quite a thorny character, yes indeed. A man of very strong opinions. He has no compunction whatsoever about expressing them. But he and I did see eye to eye on a great many things and we gave mutual support on the ones that we did agree on.

John T. Mason, Jr.: This represented a new attitude, a new era, in the department vis-à-vis Rickover?

Admiral Colwell: No, I don't think so. I think there has been a great deal of misinformation spread around by various writers who like to make sensational statements about the amount of opposition that Admiral Rickover had from various people throughout the Navy. I am quite certain that there was a great deal of opposition early in the game, before people understood him. By the time I got to the position of being a vice admiral, I don't think that I could pinpoint any of this anywhere that I ever ran into. The uses and values of nuclear power, particularly in submarines and aircraft carriers and also in the big escorts like our nuclear frigates, were quite apparent to everybody that I ever talked to. Although a great many people found Admiral Rickover a rather crusty individual to deal with, I don't think I ever ran into anybody-and this is later in my career—who did not freely admit the tremendously valuable contributions of Admiral Rickover to nuclear power and, thereby, to the Navy.

I am not talking now about Admiral Rickover's often-expressed opinions on the subject of education, particularly higher education. I'm not qualified to agree or disagree in this area. I'm talking now about his contribution to the Navy through the nuclear-power program, which has been very, very great.

John T. Mason, Jr.: What about Admiral Rickover in the realm of personnel and his insistence on keeping a hand on the Polaris personnel program?

Admiral Colwell: Well, it was not only Polaris. Anything to do with nuclear power. There certainly was a great deal of dissatisfaction with Admiral Rickover's presumption of full control over nuclear-qualified people. A great many people felt that this was improper, that that sort of control should rest in the Bureau of Personnel, where all other personnel control was. There was a lot of dissatisfaction with this. I would assume that the various Chiefs of Naval Personnel came to a certain amount of agreement with this. They certainly came to live with it because it continued. I don't recall that I ever discussed it with the Chief of Naval Personnel.

John T. Mason, Jr.: Who was that, Admiral Smedberg?

Admiral Colwell: Yes, and then Admiral Semmes, and later on Admiral Duncan.[*] I was quite friendly with all of these, as I was with all the deputies. We all worked together very

---

[*] The following officers held the billet of Chief of Naval Personnel in succession: Vice Admiral William R. Smedberg III, USN, 12 February 1960 to 11 February 1964; Vice Admiral Benedict J. Semmes, Jr., USN, from 1 April 1964 to 31 March 1968; Vice Admiral Charles K. Duncan, USN, 5 April 1968 to 21 August 1970. The oral histories of all three are in the Naval Institute collection.

well, I thought. I thought that the CNO during the time I was there was very well served by what I call his board of directors.

John T. Mason, Jr.: He being McDonald?

Admiral Colwell: McDonald was there when I went there, and then Tom Moorer relieved him.* It was my feeling then and is still my belief that his deputies did work together well and, although they stood out very strongly for their own programs, they were statesmanlike in their final arguments and final decisions for the Navy. Everybody can't have everything he wants.

John T. Mason, Jr.: A model for the Joint Chiefs of Staff to follow!

Admiral Colwell: Compromise is the name of the game. There just isn't any way to get around it.

John T. Mason, Jr.: There was one class of new destroyers that comes to mind, I think they were built probably before your regime in OP-03, the Mitscher class, which didn't turn out so well.† Were there other examples of that in your time?

Admiral Colwell: Yes. There always are. Hindsight in shipbuilding is great—great vision. I don't suppose a new ship has ever come out that you couldn't look at it and say, well, you should have done this or that, some in greater degree than others. There is a new class now, the Spruance class, of 963s, which is just starting to come out, which has drawn a great deal of criticism.

John T. Mason, Jr.: What's their size?

---

* Admiral David L. McDonald, USN, served as Chief of Naval Operations from 1 August 1963 to 1 August 1967. Admiral Thomas H. Moorer, USN, served as CNO from 1 August 1967 to 1 July 1970. The oral histories of both are in the Naval Institute collection.
† USS Mitscher (DL-2) was originally commissioned as an all-gun destroyer leader, or frigate, on 15 May 1953. She was the first of a four-ship class, and all were noted for having engineering problems.

Admiral Colwell: They're big ships. They're about 6,500 tons, I think.

John T. Mason, Jr.: I thought they determined at the time of the Mitscher class that 4,000 was probably a limit?

Admiral Colwell: It depends on what you want to put on it. One of the things we found out about Mitschers was that they didn't have very long legs and ought to have some more oil in them. This went through a very long period of iteration on what the ship ought to have in it, and this automatically determined how big they were. So it was determined that these ships ought to have big, long legs so that they could travel with the carriers, including nuclear-powered carriers. This meant that they were going to be big ships. They're also big enough to have good sea-keeping qualities when a sea is running. The biggest argument about them is, first, they cost too much, and second, that they don't have enough on them in the way of offensive armament.

John T. Mason, Jr.: In that, they differ from the light cruisers?

Admiral Colwell: Yes. I think a lot of the dissatisfaction among people about the offensive armament on these is that they don't have enough guns on them. I'd be very happy to see another gun or two on them also. You can't have it all. Maybe we built too long legs on them. Maybe they should have had another gun and less oil, I don't know. But a long iteration was given these things. It was subjected to determining what the characteristics should be. I didn't determine them, though I finally, among others, recommended them to the CNO, and I have no apologies for it. I think they'll be good ships.

John T. Mason, Jr.: How many are intended?

Admiral Colwell: Thirty of them, and I think the last of the 30 are to be funded next year.[*]

Another class that has come in for a great deal of criticism has been the class of DEs called the 1052s.[†] This was quite a large number of ships built in a number of shipyards, and they came in for a great deal of criticism. First of all, none of the old-timers disliked the fact that they only had a single screw. I like twin screws. I think it's real handy if one engine breaks down to have another one to come home on. But you can't have it all. Within a given price there are limits, and compromises have to be made. A lot of people complained because they weren't fast enough to go with the carriers. They were never designed to go with the carriers. You need escort ships for other purposes also.

There's a new class now, just getting started, called the PF—patrol frigate.[‡] This one is drawing criticism, mainly from old-timers. They don't like the single screw and they don't think it has enough guns on it, they don't think it's big enough, they don't think it's fast enough. It's just a question of what you can build within an amount of money.

It became quite apparent with the end of life of the World War II destroyers, which were very numerous, that when all of those were gone we were going to have to have a substantial number of those new escorts to replace them. Not as many as we had had in World War II. That was out of the question. But a substantial number. Now, it was also quite apparent to anybody with an ounce of common sense that all of these were not going to be $150 million ships with guided missiles. There had to be another way, so again through a process of iteration it was determined that a ship with the characteristics of the present patrol frigate would be adequate for escort duties, not with the carriers, and could be built for roughly $50 million. And on that basis, the characteristics of the patrol frigate were selected. I think it's going to be a very useful ship.

But the people who are running the shipbuilding business are always subject to a great deal of criticism for not doing this and not doing that, and why didn't you do it this way? This is just something that goes with the job. You have to take it and try to explain what you're doing. I always felt that if I could explain it to the satisfaction of the CNO so

---

[*] Eventually the class came to comprise 31 ships. The last one was the USS Hayler (DD-997), commissioned 5 March 1983.
[†] USS Knox (DE-1052) went into commission on 12 April 1969 as the lead ship of a class of 46 single-screw ocean escorts. They were reclassified from destroyer escorts to frigates in 1975.
[‡] The PF-109 class was redesignated as the FFG-7 class before the first ship was completed.

that he would support it to the extent of putting it in the budget, probably I'd done a pretty good job of explaining. The same thing is true today.

John T. Mason, Jr.: I suppose it's inevitable; ship handlers, those whom I've known, are rather positive people.

Admiral Colwell: Oh, yes, they are. If they're not, they're not very good shiphandlers. You have to make up your mind right now what you're going to do and do it. Shiphandling, incidentally, as you well know, is one of the great joys of being a naval officer. Sometimes you think it's the only joy there is!

John T. Mason, Jr.: In a related area, in 1965, I believe, when you came into this new job, the Claude V. Ricketts was in operation as a multi-national-crew ship.* Do you want to talk about that and the success of the experiment, if it was?

Admiral Colwell: Actually, I had practically nothing to do with that because it was a matter that was run by CinCLantFlt in CinCLant, he being not only a U.S. commander but also a NATO commander, and the ship operated extensively in European waters, understandably. As far as I know, it was a substantial success and it worked quite well. I'm not sure that it was a terribly useful thing to do. It may have been more of a stunt, as there were obvious difficulties with it. Food, for one thing. A Frenchman or an Italian is used to having wine with his meals; they like different kinds of food. As far as I know, these problems were all surmounted without too much difficulty, and I think the experiment was a success, but I rather suspect it was eventually determined that it really wasn't terribly useful.

John T. Mason, Jr.: It didn't prove anything.

---

* DDG-5, commissioned originally as the USS Biddle on 5 May 1962, was renamed Claude V. Ricketts on 28 July 1964 to honor the recently deceased Vice Chief of Naval Operations who had advocated the NATO manning program. For pictorial coverage of the multinational experiment, see "The Mixed-Manning Demonstration," U.S. Naval Institute Proceedings, July 1965, pages 87-103. The issue has a painting of the USS Claude V. Ricketts on the cover.

Admiral Colwell: It didn't really prove anything, no.

John T. Mason, Jr.: It hasn't been duplicated?

Admiral Colwell: As far as I know, it has not. Now, as a substitute for that, there has been in operation for some time and, as far as I know, still is, a small mixed squadron, where instead of having the mixture in one hull the mixture is in several hulls in a division or a squadron.* As far as I know, this one is still in operation.

John T. Mason, Jr.: So they can have their own dietary practices!

Admiral Colwell: Yes, and I would think that this would probably be a very useful training device, where you can train rather large numbers of people to operate in multinational formation.

John T. Mason, Jr.: These being multinational ships also, aren't they, owned by their respective countries?

Admiral Colwell: Yes, that's correct. We have, of course, within NATO standard signals, standard operating methods, standard fueling methods, and so on, so that as these ships work together you get a chance to exercise those and people get used to using them, even radio-telephone. There are standard procedures, standard words that are used by all of the NATO navies, and they work, but they have to be exercised; otherwise people forget.

John T. Mason, Jr.: In your capacity as OP-03, did you have active cognizance of the Service Force?

---

* This multinational group of ships is known as the Standing Naval Force Atlantic.

Admiral Colwell: Not really. You see, the term Deputy CNO for Operations is rather a misnomer, because the operations are actually conducted by the fleet commanders, and they are largely ordered by the Joint Chiefs.

John T. Mason, Jr.: This, after the amendment to the act of 1958?[*]

Admiral Colwell: Because CinCPac and CinCLant worked for the Joint Chiefs and nobody else. There are certain minor areas that can be directed by the CNO to CinCPacFlt or CinCIantFlt which don't interfere with Joint Staff directives, and in these the Deputy CNO for Operations comes into play. This doesn't turn out to be a very large part of your job.

One associated important part of 03 is the maintenance of the CNO's plot, which is the chart in which the assigned staff maintains continuous information where all the ships are and what they're doing, what their status is. This is an information service available to all of OpNav and, in particular, to the CNO.

John T. Mason, Jr.: Does he have briefings in the room?

Admiral Colwell: In the adjacent briefing room, yes. There is also adjacent higher classification intelligence room where certain information is available to him.

But the Deputy CNO for Operations doesn't actually operate anything. He is an advisor to the CNO on operations.

John T. Mason, Jr.: In this operational room, is there also a chart of merchant shipping or auxiliary ships? Their whereabouts and their status?

---

[*] The Department of Defense Reorganization Act of 1958 contained a number of provisions, including removal of the service secretaries from the chain of command; removal of the service chiefs' command authority over their forces; establishment of the principle that the Joint Chiefs of Staff could act only under the authority of the Secretary of Defense; and transfer of control of the Joint Staff from the JCS as a whole to the Chairman.

Admiral Colwell: Auxiliary ships, yes, MSTS or ships that are under charter to MSTS, which is most of their operations.

John T. Mason, Jr.: And those are pinpointed also?

Admiral Colwell: Yes, they maintain all that. It's very difficult to maintain any kind of a chart on merchant shipping, because there isn't any way you can find out where they are. The chart room has access to Lloyds reports and certain other merchant ship reports, but they are very incomplete.

John T. Mason, Jr.: Don't our naval attachés report?

Admiral Colwell: You can get some information on ships sailing from foreign ports, but it's very incomplete. There isn't any system to supply it. This has been a matter for discussion certain amount of concern and puzzlement for many, many, many years, and nobody has been able to figure out a way to do it, because you can't force these people to make reports. There's no way of forcing them.

John T. Mason, Jr.: It's private business!

Admiral Colwell: They don't hold to schedules. A ship captain who runs into bad weather does what he thinks best. Navy ships do the same thing, although we have to report if we don't hold to a schedule. Merchant ships don't, and there's no way to require them to.

John T. Mason, Jr.: Did you have under your aegis as OP-03 the air-sea rescue service for the astronauts in the Gemini Program in your day?[*]

---

[*] Gemini was a National Aeronautics and Space Administration (NASA) program in the mid-1960s in which a capsule manned by two astronauts went into space for several days at a time. It was a follow-on to the Mercury program and precursor to Apollo, the one that went to the moon in the late 1970s.

Admiral Colwell: Insofar as responsibility for rescue, yes. The actual execution of it, of course, came under the respective fleet commanders in the Pacific or the Atlantic, and he had his own rescue organization. We did deal directly on this. It became a responsibility of my office to detail the type of ship that would be used. At first, we never used anything except a full-blown aircraft carrier which could operate both helicopters and fixed-wing aircraft. Later on, we were able to convince people that it was entirely possible to do this job with a ship that had only helicopters, and that's the way it's done today. We were directly involved in this sort of thing, yes.

John T. Mason, Jr.: In consultation with NASA?

Admiral Colwell: Yes, but the detailed work on it was all done by the key people who were going to have to execute it.

John T. Mason, Jr.: Since we've been talking about shipping and such, what was your liaison and what was your active relationship with the Maritime Administration?

Admiral Colwell: I had none.

John T. Mason, Jr.: Was there any?

Admiral Colwell: MSTS all the time.

John T. Mason, Jr.: But other than that?

Admiral Colwell: Not to my knowledge. There may have been. I don't know.

John T. Mason, Jr.: What was the view of the Navy toward the merchant shipping industry?

Admiral Colwell: We supported them at every turn as best we could. This was mainly through oral support, but a healthy merchant marine—it was quite apparent to all of us who gave it any thought that a healthy merchant marine was absolutely essential to the country and, of course, to the Navy. If you are going to have any kind of an overseas operation, military operation, you must have a lot of merchant marine support. There isn't any way to get around it. And, on the other side of the coin, a healthy economy in the United States certainly depends on a healthy merchant marine, and in times of trouble totally dependent. You cannot trust merchant assistance that you cannot control, from the governmental point of view.

John T. Mason, Jr.: One of the primary duties of the U.S. Navy, as it was seen when the Navy was first established, was to protect merchant shipping. Has this been relegated to the background, or is it still paramount?

Admiral Colwell: I think it's still equally important. It's sometimes given other terminology, because you can always find an argument about protecting merchant shipping. It usually gets shunted off into a sort of nonsensical discussion about whether they ought to run alone or whether they ought to be convoyed. The answer to that it turns out to be whichever seems to be doing the job best after you get into trouble.

"Control of the sea lanes" is a rather popular term now, and this all means the same thing. If you control the sea-lanes you make the ocean safe for our merchant ships to travel, and whether you do that by going out and killing off submarines or whether you protect them by convoy, how you do it is probably a combination of things, it all means the same thing. One way or another you get to bring home the bacon.

John T. Mason, Jr.: There are other areas in which OP-03 must have been interested and active. I know that in 1966 we sent units of the Mediterranean fleet into the Black Sea for training purposes and for other reasons. Tell me about this.

Admiral Colwell: These were generally planned by other than OP-03 people. Of course, we had a direct interest in it and worked with the planning unit. That was designed to maintain an occasional presence in the Black Sea, simply to ensure that nobody on the other side got the idea that we were no longer interested or that we had abandoned this right.

John T. Mason, Jr.: That the rights weren't atrophied!

Admiral Colwell: That's correct. We had some arguments with the other side now and then about the armament that was on these ships. There are certain rules in I think it's the Montreux Convention about passage in and out of the Black Sea.* We always stuck to our guns on it and didn't have any difficulty other than a certain amount of argument. These were actually conducted, of course, by units of the Sixth Fleet.

John T. Mason, Jr.: And under the direction of the Joint Chiefs?

Admiral Colwell: Yes.

John T. Mason, Jr.: And with the cooperation of the State Department?

Admiral Colwell: Oh, yes, everybody was in on the act.

John T. Mason, Jr.: Did they serve the purpose intended?

Admiral Colwell: As far as we know, yes. I don't know whether we're continuing to do that or not. I suppose we are but it draws so little attention you never even read about it.

---

* Signed at Montreux, Switzerland, on 20 July 1936, the multinational Montreux Convention restored to Turkey control over the Turkish straits, the Dardanelles and the Bosporus. Control had been taken away by the Lausanne Conference of 1922-23. The 1936 convention also placed limits on the armament of warships passing through the straits while passing between the Mediterranean and the Black Sea.

The Russians use the Bosporus quite freely, but as far as I know they observe the convention.

John T. Mason, Jr.: What about our practice of maintaining a ship or two in the Persian Gulf?

Admiral Colwell: We still do that.

John T. Mason, Jr.: What value is that?

Admiral Colwell: Oh, you show the flag just to remind people that we have an interest in it. That may have been withdrawn now.[*] I guess probably it has because of current troubles with the Arabs, but before that we maintained a ship or two there in order to just remind people that we had an interest in area, a very strong commercial interest, and to maintain a physical means of keeping ships there if we wanted to, dock space, fueling arrangements, some living arrangements for the members of the staff, and so on. That may have been withdrawn now; I'm not sure about that.

John T. Mason, Jr.: This whole area of showing the flag for one reason or another, political or otherwise, was this a part of Operations and Readiness?

Admiral Colwell: It's part of fleet operations so that we had a concern with it insofar as Washington was concerned. Another element of it would be the Unitas cruises around South America, which were cooperative antisubmarine operations with the navies of South America

John T. Mason, Jr.: That was somewhat educational, too, wasn't it?

---

[*] For many years the U.S. Navy maintained a small Middle East Force in the Persian Gulf as a show-the-flag presence. In the years since this interview, the size of the presence has varied, growing most notably during the tanker wars of the late 1980s and the Gulf War of 1991. The U.S. Fifth Fleet now has its headquarters at Bahrain in the Persian Gulf.

Admiral Colwell: Oh, yes. Very few of those navies have any means of getting live training on submarine warfare or any means of running combined operations with surface ships, submarines and aircraft, so this was a very important training exercise for those navies.

Another thing that was done several years ago was a series of cruises to a great many African countries. This was largely "show the flag," to introduce our people to those countries and, conversely, introduce those people to some of our people. They took along a Navy band and gave band concerts. They did a lot of sort of off-the-cuff helping jobs for the local communities where they stopped. I think they were very useful. They were very well received.

John T. Mason, Jr.: Was there any policy emanating from OP-03 as to the kind of conduct that ship personnel should follow?

Admiral Colwell: Not from OP-03. There was a great deal of input from the intelligence side about how people should behave and what they should do and where they should go, and what they should not do. Behavior of personnel in foreign ports was very largely a matter for personnel and for the JAG people, the law people.

John T. Mason, Jr.: I have run into accounts of individual skippers being concerned and conducting an educational program on board before they arrived at a port, but I wondered if there was an overall plan?

Admiral Colwell: Oh, yes, operated by the fleet commanders with certain broad direction from Washington. But those programs were operated by the fleet commanders. This goes back a long time. I guess almost as soon as the Sixth Fleet was started and probably long before that there was pre-arrival instruction on how to behave in foreign ports, frequently not adhered to very tightly. Those things are largely run by the afloat commands. The

Sixth Fleet Commander had his own rules, and they were very stringent. He, of course, was the man on the spot and the one who had to suffer if anything went wrong.

This sort of pre-arrival instruction has been going on for many years.

John T. Mason, Jr.: It's part and parcel of showing the flag and doing it properly, isn't it?

Admiral Colwell: Oh, yes, that's right.

John T. Mason, Jr.: In this area of personnel what were your obligations and interests and responsibilities—in the general area of naval personnel?

Admiral Colwell: It was largely a matter of cooperation with the Bureau of Personnel. We were, of course, intensely concerned with the provision or lack thereof of people in the ratings that were short, particularly in the more complex ones such as the electronics technicians, and this was a chronic shortage. We never had enough and particularly never had enough of the more senior ratings, ones who really knew what they were doing. This is something that's been going on for years and years and still exists. We were intensely concerned with this because of our readiness. It would rear its ugly head any time you wanted to deploy a ship or a division of destroyers or a group. It was just a continuing problem.

BuPers had the primary responsibility for providing some kind of a solution to the problem, but we in 03 and, in fact, throughout ops had just a continuing concern with this. How are we going to solve the immediate problem, and how are we going to do better in the long run? It's the kind of thing that doesn't have very many solutions. It was this sort of a problem and the attempt to find a solution for it that resulted in what they call propay—you get extra pay in certain grades. It resulted in the variable reenlistment bonus, where people with particular skills can draw several thousand dollars as a reenlistment bonus.

All sorts of things have been tried. Sea pay is another solution to the problem. All sorts of things have been tried with varying degrees of success. The loss of these skilled people was, of course, aggravated by the general discontent throughout the country with the Vietnamese War, by the improved economy in the country where these people with particular skills could leave the Navy and go out and get better paying jobs as electronic technicians, for example.

Some of our ships, through necessity, were being deployed watch and watch. Actually, it wasn't even that good. They might be out for eight months back and forth and out for another eight. Well, it's obvious that people can get real tired of this in a very short time, and there was quite understandable pressure from the family back home to get out of this silly rat race and do something else. As a consequence we suffered for years, actually still are suffering, from the loss of these highly skilled people who were essential to our continued useful operation.

John T. Mason, Jr.: Did your active interest, under the umbrella of readiness, extend to the Reserves and Reserve training?

Admiral Colwell: Yes. Not so much their actual training as the provision of training ships. I don't recall that I had anything to do with the provision of training centers ashore, reserve training buildings and centers, except as the requests for building funds would come up annually in our round-table discussions of what ought to be built with the public works bill. I didn't have anything to do with that directly.

We did have always to do with the provision of reserve training ships and with their overhaul. The actual operations, of course, were conducted by the fleet commanders, just like any other operations. But we kept an eye on the ships. That's sort of the low man on the totem pole. As ships begin to get old, they finally fall into the reserve training category and eventually fall out. So every year we would make some adjustments in the assigning of training ships. These had to be very carefully coordinated with the congressmen from the districts involved. They always maintained a very high interest in these matters. I think we did move one once without telling the congressman, but we didn't do that anymore.

John T. Mason, Jr.: In 1965 it was apparent that the Soviets were much more active in terms of their submarines. They were operating freely in the Mediterranean, the Philippine Sea, and other places. Then in 1966 intelligence out of London stated that the Russians had at least 40 submarines, nuclear and otherwise, with missiles. This must have been collectively a matter of real concern to you in Operations and Readiness?

Admiral Colwell: Yes, it was. We—by that I mean all of OpNav, the intelligence community, and we in operations, and certainly the people in the deputy positions—kept as close a watch on this as we could with the facilities that were available to us. The fleet commanders were, of course, immediately concerned and had operation of the facilities and the ships and the aircraft which were used in attempting to keep track of the locations and movements of all these ships.

I don't recall that there was ever any panic on the subject, but it was a matter for concern. We wanted to know where they were, and if there seemed to be some rather unusual concentrations, then there was always speculation as to why. I think our concern was certainly properly in order, but I don't think that anybody ever got overly concerned. It never came to that point.

John T. Mason, Jr.: At that time was the Russian development in the area of naval deployment considered a kind of a result of the missile crisis? Was that looked upon as a watershed period in this area?

Admiral Colwell: I think there may have been a connection with it in that it brought home very strongly to the Russians—I'm inventing this now—it could have brought home very strongly to the Russians the realization of what sea power really meant. They could have taken at that time a decision that they were, by golly, from then on going to operate their ships in all corners of the world and find out where they could operate best and how they could operate best. So that I think these rather massive deployments of theirs, in hindsight, were probably greatly stepped-up training and they did such things routinely, as anchor in the open ocean. Down near the Canaries I believe they had found a shallow spot where they would send a tanker and a repair ship, a submarine depot ship. They would anchor there, and they would act as a mother group for maybe three or four submarines. The submarines would come in and fuel and actually tie up alongside the depot ship and presumably make repairs there in the open ocean.

They did this routinely in the Mediterranean. They had several anchorages that they used routinely. They found shallow spots and there they anchored. It depended to some extent on the weather, of course, but it was sort of a new idea. They developed it. Then they started sending numbers of ships into the Indian Ocean. These were, I would guess, double-barreled cruises. One was simply training, and the other was to introduce the nations around the Indian to the fact that the Russians had ships that operated there and intended to operate there, and don't you forget it. Showing the flag!

John T. Mason, Jr.: Were these Russian tactics reflected in any way in our shipbuilding program?

Admiral Colwell: Yes, and a lot of people think rather belatedly and that's probably true. We had an increased concern for our imperfect defense against cruise missiles, for example. The Russians carry a lot of these, both in submarines and in surface ships, cruisers and destroyers, and, of course, everybody knows about their PT boats, Komars and Osas, I think, are the two classes. They can launch a cruise missile that has a range of several miles. They're very tough targets, they're hard to hit—in fact, the missiles that sank the Israeli destroyer, the Eilat—very tough targets.[*]

Concern over defense against this type of attack was increased, and we began, well, I certainly wouldn't call it a crash development, but a high-speed development of short-range defenses.

John T. Mason, Jr.: In reaction!

---

[*] On 21 October 1967, while near the entrance to the Suez Canal, the Israeli destroyer Elath, also known as Eilat, was sunk by Styx surface-to-surface missiles fired from an Egyptian patrol boat inside the harbor at Port Said, Egypt. The attack killed 59 of the 250 crew members on board the Elath.

Admiral Colwell: Reaction, right. There was almost panic in some sectors, people who were not really very familiar with how you operate ships at sea.

John T. Mason, Jr.: In the political sector?

Admiral Colwell: No, this was down in OSD. I heard the statement made "They're going to drive us off the surface of the ocean," to which I replied, "Nonsense." These were worries and almost panic by people who, as I said, were not familiar with the way you operate groups of ships. Some of these people had invented a scenario in which we were going to be boxed in in the Mediterranean where a bunch of Komar boats operating from 600 miles away. Nonsense. In the first place, if you were faced with a threat of that sort you don't send your ships in where they're going to be sitting ducks. In the second place, you operate a balanced force, you use your aircraft and other ships. And in the third place, people were assuming that we were automatically going to be assaulted by surprise. If this should happen, anybody is going to get hit. If the assault is going to be a surprise you're going to get hit. There isn't much you can do about it, because the enemy is authorized to be out there practically as close as he chooses to get, and if he wants to haul off and let you have a haymaker in the middle of the night, there isn't anything you can do to stop him.

Well, at any rate, there was a great deal of by-play about this, and we went about our business of trying to supply defensive armament to our ships. As I said, I think that this was a belated effort, but I must accept certainly some of the responsibility. We're still working on it. The Navy is now engaged in the development and bringing into production of a cruise missile of our own, which will give us a weapon with substantially greater range than anything we've had before, except for aircraft.* This will be a useful thing to have, but it is not always necessary to have exactly the same suit of weapons the enemy has. It depends on your method of operation and where you would propose to operate. Our fleet, I have always said, was predicated on the idea that we were going to operate balanced forces

---

* Harpoon is an antiship missile with a range of approximately 75-80 nautical miles. It can be fired from surface ships, submarines, and aircraft. It reached initial operational capability for shipboard use in 1977 and for aircraft in 1979. The first combat use of Harpoon was against Libyan missile craft in the Gulf of Sidra in 1986.

if we had aircraft carriers with very-high-performance aircraft embarked which gave us long-range striking, and, above all, we had built a blue-water navy. We did not propose to get engaged in battles with superior groups of small ships in little, confined spaces such as some bay in the Mediterranean. Anybody that gets boxed into that except by sheer accident deserves to be relieved the next morning.

These things are not black and white. There are compromises and discussions to be dealt with.

John T. Mason, Jr.: Did that involve you in that continuing controversy over the tremendously big nuclear carriers that we construct versus smaller—?

Admiral Colwell: This was always one of the arguments, about going out there as a great big sitting duck and highly vulnerable, it's never going to get its aircraft off, it'll never be able to do anything. This was a continuing argument. There were always a lot of people who never did like aircraft carriers, principally because they don't understand them very well. But they don't understand fleet operations. They see an aircraft carrier sitting in the harbor at Nice, for example. Someone can come up and knock that off any time he wants. Sure he can; what's to stop him? But you didn't have to wait till they got Komar boats to do it; you could do it easier with a submarine. If anybody wants to make a sneak attack, they can make it any day of the week. There isn't any way to stop it. We could do the same thing to them while they're at anchor, but I don't think we're going to.

John T. Mason, Jr.: The Navy set up a new office in 1966. Did you have a hand in that, the oceanographer?

Admiral Colwell: Not very much of one, no. Of course, I was given a shot at the charter for the oceanographer and, as I remember, there were some suggested changes, which were primarily matters of clarification about who did what. We had a continuing business back and forth with the oceanographer because he was interested in operations at sea and so were we.

Then we had another interest with the oceanographer and that was in the shipbuilding business, the provision of ships for him to operate.

John T. Mason, Jr.: Specially equipped ships!

Admiral Colwell: For the oceanography business, that's right, some of which were operated by civilian institutions such as Woods Hole or Scripps.

John T. Mason, Jr.: Also in that same year the Secretary of the Navy, Nitze, announced that the whole Navy structure, the department, was to be reorganized and revitalized, functional commands, and so forth.[*]

Admiral Colwell: You're referring now to the establishment of the Chief of Naval Material?[†]

John T. Mason, Jr.: Yes.

Admiral Colwell: And the realignment of the entire material side of the Navy?

John T. Mason, Jr.: Yes.

Admiral Colwell: That was an unusual performance in that none of the deputies were drawn into this in any way, and in fact they were excluded from it. They didn't even know anything about it until it was an accomplished fact.

John T. Mason, Jr.: The reasoning back of that being what?

---

[*] Paul H. Nitze served as Secretary of the Navy from 29 November 1963 to 30 June 1967.
[†] A reorganization effective 1 May 1966 created a new Naval Material Command. The reorganization abolished the Bureau of Naval Weapons and assigned its elements to three new commands: Naval Air Systems Command, Naval Ordnance Systems Command, and Naval Electronic Systems Command. The Bureau of Ships became the Naval Ship Systems Command. The Bureau of Supplies and Accounts became the Naval Supply Systems Command.

Admiral Colwell: I guess they figured we'd all fight it, and they didn't want to argue with us. I don't know that we would all have fought it at all. I don't think we would. I think it was quite apparent that the material side of the Navy was deficient in its method of operation, and there was a lack of directive force, so that we on the OpNav side had to deal with a number of people.

Take shipbuilding, for instance. We dealt with BuShips for the ship design, for sonar, for search radar, we dealt with BuOrd for weapons, for fire-control radar. All these things had to come together somewhere, and there had been in the past some rather severe cases of square pegs in round holes because people had not gotten together and established the necessary power supplies or some such. I'm inventing reasons. There did appear to be a need for a better directive force on the material side.

At any rate, this was presented as an accomplished fact. We had a new Chief of Naval Material, who immediately began setting up his directing staff. I think the unfortunate part of this was that a large number of the best and most effective people in the bureau were extracted from the bureau and placed on the chief's staff so that they became the bosses instead of the doers.

John T. Mason, Jr.: Promotion!

Admiral Colwell: It was promotion, that's right. This resulted in what I considered to be a very serious weakening of the ability of the material bureaus to function as they should. They lost a great deal of their capability for design, and this had been strong. There were excellent ordnance designers in the old BuOrd. I wouldn't say that this particular move was totally responsible for the loss of design power, but it magnified it. There was something of the same thing with BuShips.

This change that we're speaking of performed one function which I think was highly important and highly significant. Before the establishment of the Chief of Naval Material, the chiefs of bureaus had reported to the Secretary and not to the CNO. Actually, this wasn't like falling off a cliff. The people in OpNav could direct the bureaus to do things, and they did, and the bureaus did them, but they didn't have to. They could come back and argue about it. Under the new arrangement, the Chief of Naval Material reported to the CNO. He still had access to the Secretary, naturally. He should. But he reported to the CNO so that OpNav could direct what they wanted done in the material bureaus. This was a significant and important improvement.*

It didn't have too great an effect on OP-03, for example. At least, if it did it wasn't apparent to me, but I'd never had any real trouble with these people anyhow. But it did establish a line of command which had not existed before. It cleaned it up.

John T. Mason, Jr.: But would you say that it perhaps would have been a smoother transition if the chiefs had been notified in advance and consulted?

Admiral Colwell: Well, there was a little unhappiness about it. I think most of us felt that we had been excluded from this as though we were small children and they didn't want our input and didn't want us arguing about it. We felt it wasn't the proper way to treat deputies!

John T. Mason, Jr.: It's often done that way anyway, isn't it?

Admiral Colwell: That's the only thing I ever heard of. But they may have done this recognizing that the more people you had in the act the longer it was going to take to do it. You get action by committee, and you automatically slow down. I think we were just a little bit put out because we thought that we were in positions of importance and we should have been notified of what was going on. I think that was the main feeling.

John T. Mason, Jr.: Admiral, were naval salvage operations in your purview?

Admiral Colwell: To the same extent that any other operation at sea was. The Chief of Salvage was physically located in BuShips, now the Naval Ship Systems Command. This

---

* Ironically, the change was reversed nearly 20 years later. In 1985, Secretary of the Navy John Lehman disestablished the Naval Material Command and redistributed functions among the various systems commands. For a summary of the reorganization, see Norman Polmar, "The U.S. Navy: Command Changes," U.S. Naval Institute Proceedings, December 1985, pages 156-157.

was so that he could develop methods and materials and put an organization together. When we had a salvage job, then this became a sort of joint operation between the fleet commander, his designated representative in the area, and the Chief of Salvage, who would either go and take charge of the technical side of any job or send one of his people. So that you had an operational commander on the scene and a technical commander. He was more than an advisor, he was in charge and the technical commander at the scene.

I didn't have anything directly to do with it any more than I had with any other operations at sea.

John T. Mason, Jr.: I was wondering when a salvage operation involved not only our own naval ships but also got involved with a foreign country, did you get concerned? I'm thinking specifically of the loss of that nuclear weapon off Spain.*

Admiral Colwell: That was quite a fancy operation. It went on for a long time. We sent a flag officer over there with no other duties than to conduct this salvage operation and do whatever had to be done. He had pretty wide authority. The operation included some operations ashore, and this of course involved the embassy.

John T. Mason, Jr.: It was a sensitive situation, wasn't it?

Admiral Colwell: Yes, and of course many of the operations on Spanish soil had to be arranged by the embassy people. Our Navy man over there could go and deal with individuals, of course, but not without the full consent of the embassy because they were quite familiar with the local laws and the local customs, how feelings were running, how the government felt. So it was sensitive, yes. I thought that our man really did a splendid job.

---

*On 17 January 1966 two U.S. Air Force planes collided. One of them, a B-52 bomber crashed, dislodging four hydrogen bombs. Three were recovered quickly; the fourth had fallen into the sea near Palomares, Spain. That bomb was located by the U.S. Navy's deep-diving research vessel Alvin on 17 March. Once lines were attached to the bomb, it was brought to the surface on 7 April by the submarine rescue ship Petrel (ASR-14). The Hoist took part in the recovery operation.

We were fortunate in having some new devices that could operate at depth. Some were manned and some were unmanned. We had a chance to put these to work, and they were effective. We found it. So the whole thing was eventually cleaned up. It was difficult, a long-drawn-out operation and, to my mind, it was very well done. They had to find it and it was in rather a large area that had to be searched.

John T. Mason, Jr.: It was off Barcelona somewhere, wasn't it?

Admiral Colwell: I've forgotten just exactly where it was. It was at depth and we were fortunate in having these new devices so that we could use them.

Later on we had an even more difficult search problem when we lost the Scorpion.*

John T. Mason, Jr.: Yes.

Admiral Colwell: This was a very long, drawn-out search problem in very deep water, about 12,000 feet. We knew only very roughly where to start to look. We sent out search forces. We sent messages to various foreign countries asking them to check with their merchant fleets and see if anyone had any information of any kind, whether they'd seen anything or heard anything. We eventually were able to work the search area down to some reasonable size, and we sent the Trieste down, which, of course, is capable of going down to 35,000 feet. She had been there out in the Marianas Trench.

They eventually found the ship and took a whole series of very good photographs of parts of the ship on the bottom at 12,000 feet. The photographs were sufficiently good and sufficiently detailed to enable the investigative body to generate some theories on what might have happened. It was impossible to be conclusive.

John T. Mason, Jr.: It was an interior matter, wasn't it?

---

* The submarine Scorpion (SSN-589) was lost with all hands while en route from the Mediterranean to Norfolk. She was last heard from on 21 May 1968. On 27 May she was reported overdue and on 5 June presumed lost with her entire crew of 99 officers and men. The wreckage was located on 30 October of that year. No definitive conclusion has been reached as to cause.

Admiral Colwell: Hard to tell. There was some theory that one of their own torpedoes had gotten loose. I think that theory developed simply because nobody could think of anything else. I couldn't find anything to really support it. The ship had obviously been on a nose dive, of course, after it sank. It had long since passed crush depth. It had hit nose down at an angle, and the picture shows where it had gouged a furrow into the floor of the ocean, and when it hit nose down the engineering department, the shaft and all that had gone to the forward part of the boat. But that had happened on impact. The ship had long since been lost and all the people were before that. But we didn't find out what happened to her and never will.

It was during this same period that we were continuing with the development of a manned and propelled rescue unit which can best be described as a much overgrown torpedo. This rescue vessel can be ferried to the area of the downed submarine which was on the bottom but not lost, not crushed, and you could mate it with a hatch designed to fit it and extract the people alive.

John T. Mason, Jr.: The same sort of technique they use for the astronauts now and Skylabs?

Admiral Colwell: Yes, sort of like that. We'd had one, of course, for many years, called a McCann Chamber which we lowered from a surface ship on the keel and mated with the submarine. This had been used many, many times in submarine operations, but it was limited to relatively simple depths, only 600 or 800 feet.

So we set about developing a rescue vessel, self-propelled and manned. It would do a certain amount of searching to find the downed submarine, and it would operate at as much depth as would be required to rescue people from any ship that was on the bottom and undamaged, that is, not crushed. That has since been developed but I have no information on the success of its operations. There has not been a requirement to use it on a sunken ship, fortunately.

J.B. Colwell, Interview #8 (2/5/74) - 287

John T. Mason, Jr.: Since you were Fleet Readiness, what relationship did you have with the various and sundry fleet exercises that were conducted in both oceans?

Admiral Colwell: Not very much in the way of a direct connection. These were things that were planned by the fleet commanders and scheduled by the fleet commanders and operated by the fleet commanders. We, of course, were interested in their progress, and we were interested in what the fleet commanders were planning, what they expected to prove, and what did they expect to exercise in the particular type of operation. But these were primarily the province of the fleet commanders who were directly charged with the training.

John T. Mason, Jr.: What about the area of R&D?

Admiral Colwell: Like practically everything else that went on in the Pentagon we had continuous dealings with the R and D people on what they had in mind, what they thought was coming along. As a deputy, I was one of the rest of the board of directors involved in the final choices of the R&D budget.

John T. Mason, Jr.: You had a very real voice?

Admiral Colwell: Oh, yes, a very real voice. You see, what I call the board of directors was the CNO's advisory board, and this involved the deputies and several other men in charge of the most important offices, like the budget and program planning, and so on. We sat frequently in discussions on the things that were of concern to the CNO and his staff and the Vice Chief were there and we would discuss these things. Everyone had his opportunity to say his piece.

All of the budget submissions from the various sections came under scrutiny by the CNO Advisory Board called the CAB, all of these came under scrutiny. Therefore, everybody had an input to the R&D budget. In addition to that, there were frequent meetings all year long over R&D development, and if the deputy for R&D thought that he had something of immediate interest to me, why, he called me on the phone and said, "We've got something. Would you like to see a little presentation of it?" Well, of course, I would. There was a tremendous amount of this interplay in all parts of OpNav.

Tom Connolly was the deputy for Air when I was there, and he and I had a great deal to do with each other in the development of aircraft and the impact on aircraft carriers, both existing and projected.* Every time you develop a new type of aircraft and put it into the fleet, it has an immediate material effect on every carrier from which it's going to operate. You may have new test equipment. As an extreme, you might have catapult modifications, you might have arresting gear modifications. That's rather an extreme notion, but you might. So Tom and I had a great deal to do with each other and always got along very well.

I had almost daily dealings with OP-04, the logistics, on the subject of alterations and repairs. He was faced with a money problem practically daily, and he would want advice and suggestions on how to juggle his money in order to do what had to be done and who was going to get hurt.

There was never any question of somebody not talking to another deputy. That had happened in years past. It had, they refused to talk to each other. Ridiculous, childish! We had, I thought, excellent relations.

John T. Mason, Jr.: You say you really liked this job?

Admiral Colwell: Yes. I always thought it was just about the best job in the Pentagon and I enjoyed it thoroughly. I remember telling the CNO one time how much I enjoyed it and how important I thought it was, and I told him that any time I got tired of coming to work I'd let him know, and then it would be time for me to leave. After I'd been there, oh, I suppose three and a half years I talked to the CNO one day and pointed out that I'd been there quite a long time and I was unfortunately approaching the end of my career, 62 not being too far off. I told him that I recognized that he might feel that it was getting to be

---

* Vice Admiral Thomas F. Connolly, USN, served as Deputy Chief of Naval Operations (Air) from 1 November 1966 to 31 August 1971. Admiral Connolly's oral history is in the Naval Institute collection.

about time to get a younger officer and give him this type of very valuable experience as a growth factor.

He thanked me for the idea. So some months later I decided that maybe I was getting kind of tired. Maybe it wasn't as much fun to come to work any more as it used to be. So I suggested to the CNO, as I remember, that maybe I was ready to request retirement. And when I suggested that maybe I was ready to retire, this would have been just over two years before I would have to retire at the age of 62.

No other jobs were offered to me at that time. In fact, I guess maybe there weren't any available, so there was no objection to my requesting retirement and I just went ahead and did retire.

John T. Mason, Jr.: At the age of 60?

Admiral Colwell: Just before I was 60.

John T. Mason, Jr.: You retired on the first of August 1969.

Admiral Colwell: First of August, and I would have been 60 in November. I suppose if some other job had been available and had been offered to me that I would have stayed on. It would have been a change of scene, but I had had about enough of Pentagonia, and I certainly had had all I wanted of congressional hearings. Just for fun, I had my aide run a check on previous incumbents at OP-03, and I discovered that I had been there longer than any previous one by a rather considerable margin—something just over four years—and I figured that was long enough.

Just as a little sidelight on retirement, I had at least one person tell me, "Oh, you're going to have a terrific readjustment after all these years in the Navy. You'll retire and there'll be a long period of readjustment." To which I could only say, "Hogwash!" I've never looked back. End of story.

John T. Mason, Jr.: Well, I certainly thank you for this series. It was a tremendous one. Very worthwhile.

Index to the Oral History of
Vice Admiral John Barr Colwell,
U.S. Navy (Retired)

Aaron Ward, USS (DD-132)
At one point in the 1930s had a very limited group of officers to run the ship during a summer cruise, 12; fleet operations, 14-15; crew size was limited by the Depression, 15

Aaron Ward, USS (DD-483)
Destroyer that was sunk in April 1943 by Japanese aircraft while operating near Guadalcanal, 51

Air Force, U.S.
Opposition in the late 1950s to the Navy's Polaris ballistic missile development program, 153-154; in the early 1960s the Navy was cognizant of Air Force strategic assets when it did Navy planning, 208-209; in the mid-1960s provided excellent service for the air evacuation of men wounded in Vietnam, 225; recovery of a U.S. Air Force nuclear bomb lost at sea off Spain in 1966, 284-285

Ammunition
During World War II was stored at various island bases for use by the South Pacific Force, 52-57; bomb explosion at Noumea, Caledonia, 54; ammunition dump explosion at Guadalcanal, 54; belting of antiaircraft ammunition at Guadalcanal, 55; the heavy cruiser Newport News (CA-148) had a premature detonation of a projectile while firing in 1972, during the Vietnam War, 84

Amphibious Force Pacific Fleet
In the mid-1960s this type command had both operational and administrative duties, 217-218; the job involved social contact with the civilian communities of San Diego and Coronado, California, 219-220; in 1964 began establishing bases in South Vietnam to facilitate fighting the war in that nation, 220; training of amphibious forces in the Eastern Pacific to prepare them for Vietnam deployments, 221-222, 228-229; shipboard medical care provided for those wounded in Vietnam, 223-225; development of riverine warfare craft and doctrine for Vietnam, 226; role of underwater demolition teams in Vietnam, 231-232; support of Seventh Fleet operations during the Vietnam War, 233-234

Amphibious Group Four
Makeup and missions of the command in the early 1960s, 191-192; training exercises, 192-195

Amphibious Warfare
Training exercises in the Atlantic in the early 1960s involving the men and ships of Amphibious Group Four, 192-195; training of amphibious forces in the Eastern

Pacific in the mid-1960s to prepare them for Vietnam deployments, 221-222, 228-229; development of riverine warfare craft and doctrine for Vietnam, 226; potential of surface effect ships in amphibious warfare, 229-230, 248-249; role of underwater demolition teams in Vietnam, 231-232

Antiair Warfare
Installation of light antiaircraft guns on U.S. warships early in World War II, 41-42; belting of antiaircraft ammunition at Guadalcanal in World War II, 55; training for antiaircraft gunners at Noumea, New Caledonia, in World War II, 57; during the Battle of the Philippine Sea in June 1944 U.S. ships fired at a Japanese airplane that made a long approach on an American aircraft carrier, 75; in 1958 the light cruiser Galveston (CLG-3) was commissioned as the Navy's first warship armed with Talos surface-to-air missiles, 163-166, 169-172

Argonne, USS (AG-31)
Auxiliary that served for a time in 1942 as flagship for Commander South Pacific Force, 47

Armor
Testing of armor plate and projectiles in the late 1930s at the Naval Proving Ground, Dahlgren, Virginia, 21, 23-26; armor testing in the mid-1940s at Dahlgren, 81-82

Army, U.S.
Consideration in the mid-1950s of the Army's Jupiter missile for use in the Navy's fleet ballistic missile program, 132-134

Atlantic Missile Range
Testing in the late 1950s of Talos surface-to-air missiles, 169-172

Atomic Bombs
Late in World War II the Naval Proving Ground did experimental work on fuzes for the first atomic bombs, 81

Australia
During World War II Colwell went to Sydney for rest and recreation while on leave, 48-50; contribution to the Allied war effort in the South Pacific in World War II, 65-66

Ballistic Missile Committee
Role of this joint Army-Navy committee in the late 1950s as Polaris was being developed, 159-160

Black Sea
In the late 1960s the U.S. Navy sent ships from the Mediterranean into the Black Sea to demonstrate freedom of the seas, 272-273

Bombing
Testing of bombs and bombsights in the late 1930s by the Naval Proving Ground at Dahlgren, Virginia, 22, 26-27; bomb explosion during World War II at Noumea, New Caledonia, 52-54; late in World War II the Naval Proving Ground did experimental work on fuzes for the first atomic bombs, 81; Rolling Thunder bombing campaign in the mid-1960s in Vietnam, 238

Bougainville, Solomon Islands
In World War II an Allied coast watcher barely escaped capture by the Japanese, 60

Brazil
President Harry S. Truman used the battleship Missouri (BB-63) as a base during his 1947 visit to Rio de Janeiro, 92-94

Budgetary Considerations
When the Special Projects Office was established in late 1955 to develop the Polaris fleet ballistic missile, the initial funding came out of the hide of the rest of the Navy, and then the program got its own money, 127-129, 136; infighting among the military services in the late 1950s over strategic weapon systems, 152-153; role of OP-90 in the late 1950s and early 1960s in the Navy budgeting process, 173-176, 178-189; establishment in the early 1960s of the Office of Program Planning, 187; one of the chief concerns of OP-03 in the OpNav staff in the 1960s was the Navy's annual shipbuilding program, 244-256, 264-266

Bureau of Naval Personnel, Washington, D.C.
Coordination in the late 1960s with OP-03 in ensuring adequate manning of billets, 275-276

Bureau of Ordnance, Washington, D.C.
In the 1930s and 1940s the bureau determined the projects to be undertaken by the Naval Proving Ground at Dahlgren, Virginia, 24, 83; role in the late 1950s in connection with administering the Polaris development program, 145-146; in 1966 the Naval Material Command was established, including the Naval Ordnance Systems Command, 282

Bureau of Ships, Washington, D.C.
In the mid-1960s both the bureau chief and his deputy retired to protest ship-procurement practices, 251-252; role of the bureau chief in testifying before Congress on shipbuilding programs, 254-255; in 1966 the Naval Material Command was established, including the Naval Ship Systems Command, 282

Burke, Admiral Arleigh A., USN (USNA, 1923)
In 1943-44 commanded Destroyer Squadron 23 during operations in the Pacific, 67-73; as Chief of Naval Operations in the 1950s was sometimes difficult to understand because of the way he spoke, 70; personal qualities, 70-71; as CNO gave

great support to the development of the Polaris fleet ballistic missile program, 129; planned a cut-off date for Polaris if it didn't work, 144-145

California, USS (BB-44)
In the early 1930 was flagship for Commander Battle Force, 10-11

Carney, Rear Admiral Robert B., USN (USNA, 1916)
During World War II served as chief of staff to Admiral William Halsey, Commander South Pacific Force, 47-48, 51, 59, 61, 67

China, People's Republic
Support for North Vietnam in the 1960s, during the Vietnam War, 240

Civil Service Commission, Washington, D.C.
Role in the late 1950s in connection with providing civilian workers for the Polaris development program, 145-146

Classified Information
At the outset of World War II the U.S. Navy made knowledge of radar a tightly held secret, 40

Claude V. Ricketts, USS (DDG-5)
In the mid-1960s this guided missile destroyer was operated for a time by a multinational NATO crew as an experiment, 266-267

Coast Watchers
Provided valuable information while operating in the South Pacific during World War II, 59-61

Colwell, Vice Admiral John B., USN (Ret.) (USNA, 1931)
Parents of, 1-2; education of, 1-2, 4, 8; siblings, 2; from 1927 to 1931 was a midshipman at the Naval Academy, 2-7; in the early 1930s went through preliminary flight training, 8-9; served 1931-33 in the battleship Maryland (BB-46), 9-10, 12; served in 1933-34 on the staff of Commander Battle Force in the battleship California (BB-44), 10-11; spent a few months in 1934 in the destroyer Rathburne (DD-113), 11-12; served 1934-37 in the destroyer Aaron Ward (DD-132), 12, 14-15; from 1937 to 1939 studied ordnance engineering at the Naval Postgraduate School, 13, 18-31; served 1939-42 in the crew of the battleship Idaho (BB-42), 16, 31-45; wife of, 31-32; children of, 32; duty from 1942 to 1944 on the staff of Admiral William Halsey, Commander South Pacific Force, 46-66; commanded the destroyer Converse (DD-509) from January to September of 1944, 67-79; service from 1944 to 1947 at the Naval Proving Ground, 80-91; in 1947-48 was executive officer and acting commanding officer of the battleship Missouri (BB-63), 91-99; from 1948 to 1951 served on the staff of Commander in Chief Pacific Fleet, 99-105; was in the Bureau of Ordnance, 1951-53, 105-106; in 1953-54 served as aide and administrative assistant to the Deputy Secretary of Defense, Roger M. Kyes, 106-118; in 1954-55

commanded the fleet oiler Elokomin (AO-55), 119-125; work from 1955 to 1958 on the Polaris fleet ballistic missile program, 126-162; in 1958 was PCO and first commanding officer of the guided missile cruiser Galveston (CLG-3), 147, 162-173; selection in July 1958 for rear admiral, 169; service in 1958-59 and 1960-61 in OpNav's budget shop, 173-176, 178-190; in 1959-60 was advisor to the Director of Defense Research and Engineering, 176-178; in 1961-62 commanded Amphibious Group Four in the Atlantic, 191-196; in 1962-63 was director of the Navy's Long-Range Objectives Group, 196-216; in 1964-65 commanded Amphibious Force Pacific Fleet, 217-237; final tour of duty was from 1965 to 1969 as Deputy Chief of Naval Operations (Fleet Operations and Readiness), 243-289; retirement from active duty in 1969, 289

Commercial Ships
In its long-range planning in the early 1960s the Navy was cognizant of the roles and needs of commercial ships, 209-210; role of Soviet merchant ships in supporting the Soviet Navy, 210-211; Navy support in the late 1960s for the U.S. merchant fleet, 271

Communications
For Polaris ballistic missile submarines when they went into service in the early 1960s, 155-156

Congress
Role in the late 1950s and early 1960s in the Navy budgeting process, 176, 179-180, 183-185, 190; in the mid-1960s OP-03 submitted to Congress a letter on the projected shipbuilding program, 200; in the 1960s Colwell testified before Congress on the annual shipbuilding program, 244-245; testimony in the 1950s concerning the Polaris program, 245-246; unhappy in the 1960s with cost overruns on Defense Department procurement projects, 253-254

Converse, USS (DD-509)
Operated in early 1944 as part of Captain Arleigh Burke's Destroyer Squadron 23, 67-73; was later part of the fast carrier task force antiaircraft support, 73-76; had capable radar equipment during World War II, 75-76; after hard operations in the war zone, the ship went to Pearl Harbor and then to San Francisco for overhaul, 76-78; in Hawaii Colwell made his crew shave off their beards for liberty, 77-78; the ship had an excellent group of officers, 78-79

DC-3 Skytrain
Transport aircraft that arrived at Guadalcanal in April 1943 during a Japanese air attack, 50-51

Dahlgren, Virginia
See: Naval Proving Ground, Dahlgren, Virginia

Defense Department
Organization of in the mid-1950s, 112

See also: McNamara, Robert S.

Dennison, Captain Robert L., USN (USNA, 1923)
In 1947-48 commanded the battleship Missouri (BB-63), 91-92; description of personality, 91-92; in early 1948 left the ship quickly to become President Harry S. Truman's naval aide, 96-97; in 1949, as presidential naval aide, called Colwell to let him know he had been selected early for captain, 101

Destroyer Squadron 23
Operations in the Solomons during World War II, 67-74; DesRon 23 was known as the "Little Beavers" because of a cartoon strip character by that name, 71-73; after leaving the Solomons the squadron served as part of the escort for the fast carrier task force, 74

Education
Schooling that Colwell received in the 1910s and 1920s in Nebraska, 1-2, 8; at the Naval Academy during the 1927-31 period, 4; course of study in the late 1930s for officers who came to the Naval Postgraduate School from sea duty, 18-25

Eller, Commander Ernest M., USN (USNA, 1925)
In December 1942, as Pacific Fleet gunnery officer, visited Guadalcanal, 54-55

Elokomin, USS (AO-55)
In the mid-1950s operated in the Atlantic and Mediterranean, 119-124

Erskine, General Graves B., USMC (Ret.)
From 1953 to 1961 concentrated on intelligence matters while serving as Assistant to the Secretary of Defense, 109, 112, 117

Espiritu Santo
Seabees built an ammunition depot there in World War II, 51; native youngsters were impressed by things from America, 62

Fechteler, Vice Admiral William M., USN (USNA, 1916)
In early 1948 summoned Captain Robert L. Dennison from command of the battleship Missouri (BB-63) to become President Harry S. Truman's naval aide, 96-97

Fleet Operations and Readiness
See: OP-03 (Fleet Operations and Readiness)

Galveston, USS (CL-93/CLG-3)
Light cruiser that was mothballed while under construction in the 1940s and later completed in 1958 as a guided missile ship, 162-166; radar equipment, 164, 170-171; problems with the racks designed for missile stowage, 165-166; selection and

training of the crew, 167-169; exceeded design speed on sea trials, 168; missile firing tests, 169-172

General Accounting Office
Role in the late 1950s and early 1960s on behalf of Congress in investigating various aspects of government operations, 182-184

George Washington (SSBN-598)-Class Submarines
Design and construction of this class of submarine in the late 1950s to carry Polaris ballistic missiles, 140-141; decisions on number of submarines and number of missiles per submarine, 151-152; the decision to have two crews per submarine, 153-154; concerns about prolonged periods underwater for the crews, 154-155; communications and navigation, 155-156

Germany
In the summer of 1930, the early days of the Hitler Youth Movement, U.S. Naval Academy midshipmen visited Kiel, 5; in 1953 was visited by a U.S. Defense Department group that included Deputy Secretary of Defense Roger Kyes, 109-111

Greenland
In 1953 was visited by a U.S. Defense Department group that included Deputy Secretary of Defense Roger Kyes, 109-110

Guadalcanal, Solomon Islands
A DC-3 Skytrain Transport aircraft that arrived at Guadalcanal in April 1943 during a Japanese air attack, 50-51; availability of ammunition, 52, 55; site of an ammunition dump explosion in World War II, 54; in December 1942 conditions on the island were miserable for American forces, 54-56; gradual improvement of the island, 56; coast watchers provided valuable information, 59-61; conditions for the local populace in wartime, 62-63

Guam, Mariana Islands
In 1944 was attacked by the destroyer Converse (DD-509) and other ships of Destroyer Squadron 23, 74

Gunnery-Naval
As operated in the 1930s by various Navy ships, 12-13; testing of armor plate, projectiles, and machine guns in the late 1930s at the Naval Proving Ground, Dahlgren, Virginia, 21, 23-28; radar spotting of projectiles, 27-28; testing during World War II of proximity fuzes, 28; testing in the 1940s of the rapid-fire 8-inch gun, 29-30, 86-87; late 1930s work of the naval powder factory at Indian Head, Maryland, 30-31; installation of light antiaircraft guns on U.S. warships early in World War II, 41-42; in early 1944 ships of Destroyer Squadron 23 bombarded Kavieng, New Ireland, 68; during the Battle of the Philippine Sea in June 1944 U.S. ships fired at a Japanese airplane that made a long approach on an American aircraft carrier, 75; testing late in World War II of various guns by Dahlgren, 82; the heavy

cruiser Newport News (CA-148) had a premature detonation of a projectile while firing in 1972, during the Vietnam War, 85; long-standing controversy over the use of Vieques Island for gunnery training by the U.S. Navy, 172-173

Halsey, Admiral William F., Jr., USN (USNA, 1904)
Actions while serving from 1942 to 1944 as Commander South Pacific Force, 46, 58

Hong Kong, British Crown Colony
In the mid-1960s visits by U.S. warships were strictly limited because of U.S. participation in the Vietnam War, 222-223

Honsik, Captain Cyril J., MC, USN
As medical officer on the staff of Commander Amphibious Force Pacific Fleet in the mid-1960s, had a substantial role in providing for medical care of men wounded in Vietnam, 223-225

Iceland
In 1941 the battleship Idaho (BB-42) escorted troops from the United States to Iceland and then used Iceland as a base of operations, 34-38; Icelanders were not friendly to the American visitors, 35-36

Idaho, USS (BB-42)
In 1939, as a result of the war then in progress in Europe, the ship began receiving a large number of recruits for the crew, 16; service in 1939-41 in the Pacific, 32; transfer to the Atlantic in June 1941 and subsequent operations there, including Neutrality Patrol and escort of troops to Iceland, 33-38; subject to heavy winds while operating out of Iceland, 38; in December 1941 steamed to Norfolk to have radar and antiaircraft guns installed, 41-43; operation early in 1942 of the new radar system, 42-43; operations in 1942 in the Pacific Fleet, 43-45

Intelligence
In the 1950s various agencies within the U.S. Government were involved in intelligence collection and assessment, 117-118

Joint Chiefs of Staff
In the mid-1960s the members of the JCS protested the conduct of the Vietnam War but their advice was not taken, 239, 240-241

Jupiter Missile
Army missile that was considered briefly for the Navy's submarine-launched ballistic missile program but was not adopted, 132-134

Kavieng, New Ireland
In early 1944 was bombarded by ships of Destroyer Squadron 23, 68-70

Knox (DE-1052)-class Destroyer Escorts
This class of ships, which entered the fleet in the late 1960s and early 1970s, has drawn criticism for a variety of reasons, 265

Korean War
The beginning of the war in 1950 brought increased demands for personnel and ammunition in the Western Pacific area, 100-101; the U.S. stockpile of mines was not robust at the outset of the war, 102-103; the U.S. Navy was also short in minesweeping capability at the time, 103

Kyes, Roger M.
Hard-driving businessman who, in 1953-54, served as Deputy Secretary of Defense under Secretary Charles Wilson, 106-118; made a trip to Europe to discuss defense matters with allies, 109-111

Leave and Liberty
During World War II Colwell got some leave while on the staff of Commander South Pacific Force and went to Sydney, Australia, 48-50; when the destroyer Converse (DD-509) stopped at Pearl Harbor in 1944, Colwell made his crew shave off their beards before they could go ashore, 77-78; crew members from the battleship Missouri (BB-63) had an enjoyable time during their 1947 visit to Rio de Janeiro, Brazil, 93; in the mid-1960s, for political reasons, the Western Pacific liberty ports available for visits by U.S. warships were limited, 222-223; Navy men developed morale problems during the Vietnam War because of limited opportunities for rest and recreation, 234-235

Long Beach, USS (CGN-9)
Potential updating of the missile system in this Talos-armed cruiser, 260

Long-Range Objectives Group
See: OP-93 (Long-Range Objectives Group, OpNav)

MacArthur, General Douglas, USA (USMA, 1903)
Coordination during World War II with Admiral William Halsey, Commander South Pacific Force, 64-65

Madrid, Spain
In 1953 a U.S. group led by Deputy Secretary of Defense Roger Kyes visited Madrid, 111

Manpower
During the Depression in the 1930s Navy ships were undermanned because of funding limitations, 15-16; imbalance of personnel in the crew of the battleship Missouri (BB-63) in 1948 because of post-World War II demobilization, 97-98

Mariana Islands
In June 1944 the ships of Destroyer Squadron 23 were used in support of the forces that attacked these Japanese-held islands, 74-75

Marine Corps, U.S.
In the mid-1960s Marines deployed to South Vietnam to take part in the war then in progress in that country, 221, 227-228; shipboard medical care provided in the mid-1960s for those wounded in Vietnam, 223-225

Maryland, USS (BB-46)
Roles of the ship's junior officers in the early 1930s, 9-10, 12

McNamara, Robert S.
The budgeting process during his tenure as Secretary of Defense in the 1960s included the new concept of total package procurement, 175-176, 189-190, 252-254; Colwell assesses McNamara as a disaster, 238; involvement in the 1960s in directing the Vietnam War, 240-241

McNeil, Wilfred J.
Served during the 1950s as Comptroller for the Defense Department, 112

Medical Problems
During World War II, mosquito-borne malaria was a problem in the South Pacific Theater, 55-56; shipboard medical care provided in the mid-1960s for those wounded in Vietnam, 223-225

Military Sea Transportation Service
In the 1960s OP-03 had a role in deciding what types of ships to acquire for MSTS, but then MSTS started working out its own arrangements, 250-251

Mine Warfare
The U.S. stockpile of mines was not robust in 1950, at the outset of the Korean War, 102-103; the U.S. Navy was also short in minesweeping capability at the time, 103; in the early 1960s the Navy's long-range planning view was that mine warfare assets had a low priority because of the belief that they could be procured on short notice when needed, 212-213

Missiles
In late 1955 Rear Admiral William Raborn was chosen to head the Special Projects Office for the development of the Polaris fleet ballistic missile, 126-129; early consideration of the Army's Jupiter missile, 132-134; move toward the solid-fueled Polaris, 133-134; the Polaris development program was greatly speeded up while it was in progress, 139-140; initial failures in flight tests of the missile, 144; decisions on number of Polaris submarines and number of missiles per submarine, 151-152; improvement of the Polaris missiles' range, 156-157; role in the late 1950s of the joint Ballistic Missile Committee, 159-160; in 1958 the light cruiser Galveston

(CLG-3) was commissioned as the Navy's first warship armed with Talos surface-to-air missiles, 163-166, 169-172; potential updating of the missile system in the Talos-armed cruiser Long Beach (CGN-9), 260; after the sinking of the Israeli destroyer Eilat by surface-to-surface missiles in October 1967, the U.S. Navy became quite concerned about its missile defenses, 278-279; development of U.S. cruise missiles, 279-280

Mississippi, USS (BB-41)
While operating out of Iceland in 1941 this battleship lost airplanes and a catapult as a result of heavy winds, 38

Missouri, USS (BB-63)
President Harry S. Truman used the ship as a base during his 1947 visit to Rio de Janeiro, Brazil, and a subsequent trip back to the United States, 92-96; in early 1948 Captain Robert L. Dennison was relieved of command to become naval aide to the President, and Colwell took temporary command, 96-97; imbalance of personnel in the crew because of post-World War II demobilization, 97-98; in 1948 made a midshipman training cruise to the Mediterranean, 98-99

Mitscher (DL-2)-class Destroyers
These destroyers, which entered the active fleet in the 1950s, had numerous drawbacks, 263-264

Mobile Construction Battalions
See: Seabees

Mothball Fleet
Value of mothballed ships as part of the Navy's long-range planning during the early 1960s, 215-216

Moulton, Lieutenant Horace Douglass, USNR (USNA, 1931)
While serving as flag secretary to Admiral William Halsey in late 1942, arranged for Colwell to join the staff of Commander South Pacific Force, 46-47

Naval Academy, Annapolis, Maryland
Disciplined routine in 1927-31 for midshipmen, 2-4; sports, 4; academics, 4; summer cruises, 5-6; extracurricular activities, 6-7; the battleship Missouri (BB-63) was used in 1948 for a summer training cruise to the Mediterranean, 98-99

Naval Material Command, Washington, D.C.
Established in May 1966 by the consolidation of the old material bureaus, 281-283

Naval Postgraduate School, Annapolis, Maryland
Course of study in the late 1930s for officers who came in from sea duty, 18-21; the classroom work at Annapolis was followed by a Cook's tour of ordnance facilities, 21-28

Naval Powder Factory, Indian Head, Maryland
Visited in 1939 by naval officers as part of their Cook's tour following postgraduate work in ordnance engineering, 30-31

Naval Proving Ground, Dahlgren, Virginia
Colwell was introduced to this command and its ordnance testing in 1939 during a Cook's tour following his postgraduate education, 13, 21-28; commercial companies tested their products at Dahlgren, 26; testing in the 1940s of the rapid-fire 8-inch gun, 29-30, 86-87; mid-1940s experimental work, 80-87; late in World War II the proving ground did experimental work on fuzes for the first atomic bombs, 81; the scientists at the proving ground were great teachers, 90-91

Naval Reserve
Concern by OP-03 in the late 1960s in providing training ships for the reservists, 276

Navigation
For Polaris ballistic missile submarines when they went into service in the early 1960s, 155-156

Neutrality Patrol
In 1940-41 U.S. warships, including the battleship Idaho (BB-42), operated in the Atlantic when Germany was at war, 33-38

New Caledonia
During World War II, Noumea served as headquarters for Admiral William F. Halsey, Commander South Pacific Force, 46-48, 64-65; Seabees constructed an ammunition dump at Noumea, 51-52; bomb explosion at Noumea during World War II, 54; antiaircraft training at Noumea, 57; climate, 58; employment of the local populace during wartime, 63; Seabee construction of steel pontoons, 63

Newport News, USS (CA-148)
Testing in the 1940s of the rapid-fire 8-inch gun that would be used in the heavy cruiser, 29-30, 86-87; the ship suffered a premature projectile explosion in 1972 while operating off Vietnam, 84, 86-87

News Media
During World War II Colwell and other officers from Destroyer Squadron 23 were interviewed by reporters, 71; the battleship Missouri (BB-63) had a large number of reporters on board during a 1947 trip to Brazil and back, 95; interest expressed in the early 1960s in the Defense Department budgetary process, 189

New Zealand
Contribution to the Allied war effort in the South Pacific in World War II, 65-66

Norfolk Navy Yard, Portsmouth, Virginia
In late 1941 installed radar and antiaircraft guns on the battleship Idaho (BB-42), 41-42

North Atlantic Treaty Organization
In the mid-1960s the guided missile destroyer Claude V. Ricketts (DDG-5) was operated for a time by a multinational crew as an experiment, 266-267; subsequently the Standing Naval Force Atlantic was created with ships of various countries, 267

Noumea, New Caledonia
During World War II served as headquarters for Admiral William F. Halsey, Commander South Pacific Force, 47-49, 64-65; Seabees constructed an ammunition dump, 52-53; site of a bomb explosion during World War II, 53; antiaircraft training, 57; climate, 58; Seabee construction of steel pontoons, 63

Nuclear Propulsion
Emphasis in the early 1960s on nuclear power plants in planning for the fleet of the future, 202-204; comparison of nuclear-powered and conventionally powered warships, 258-262, 280

Nuclear Weapons
Late in World War II the Naval Proving Ground did experimental work on fuzes for the first atomic bombs, 82; discussions in the late 1950s on how many Polaris ballistic missile submarines to build and how many missiles to put in each submarine, 151-152; in the early 1960s the Navy was cognizant of Air Force strategic assets when it did its own planning, 208-209; recovery of a U.S. Air Force nuclear bomb lost at sea off Spain in 1966, 284-285

Oil Fuel
In the mid-1950s the fleet oiler Elokomin (AO-55) provided services in the Atlantic and Mediterranean, 119-124

OP-03 (Fleet Operations and Readiness)
In the middle and late 1960s OP-03 was involved in a great deal that went on in the Navy, 243; one of the chief concerns of the office in the 1960s was the Navy's annual shipbuilding program, 244-256, 264-266; role in monitoring the alteration and modernization of ships, 256-260; maintained and ran the CNO's plot, 268-269; worked with the fleet commanders on the recovery at sea of NASA space capsules, 270; cognizance of show-the-flag cruises to various areas, 273-274; coordination in the late 1960s with the Bureau of Naval Personnel in ensuring adequate manning of billets, 275-276; provision for Naval Reserve training ships, 276; increased deployments from the mid-1960s onward of Soviet warships were a concern to the U.S. Navy, 275-278; provision of ships for oceanography, 280-281

OP-04 (Logistics)
During the Vietnam War, this office in the OpNav staff was concerned with the repair of warships, 257

OP-51
    In the late 1950s this office in the OpNav staff provided support for the Polaris ballistic missile development program, 159-161

OP-90 (Program Planning, OpNav)
    Role of the office in the late 1950s and early 1960s in the Navy budgeting process, 173-176, 178-190

OP-93 (Long-Range Objectives Group, OpNav)
    In the early 1960s had the job of predicting the future shape, composition, and missions of the U.S. fleet, 196-216

Operational Test and Evaluation Force
    Comparison of its role with that of the former Naval Proving Ground at Dahlgren, Virginia, 23-24, 84-85, 88

Pacific Fleet
    List of the commanders in chief and some of the staff officers in the late 1940s and early 1950s, 99-100; step-up in activities in 1950 with the advent of the Korean War, 100-101

Pay and Allowances
    Because of the Depression in progress in the early 1930s, Navy men suffered a cut in pay, 17; concern in the 1960s with providing special pay to enlisted personnel with specialized skills, 275-276

Pearl Harbor, Hawaii
    Salvage and cleanup following the December 1941 Japanese air attack, 44-45 when the destroyer Converse (DD-509) stopped at Pearl Harbor in 1944, Colwell made his crew shave off their beards before they could go ashore, 77

Peet, Lieutenant Raymond E., USN (Ret.) (USNA, 1943)
    In 1944 did an excellent job as gunnery officer and executive officer of the destroyer Converse (DD-509), 78-79

Pehrson, Gordon O.
    Civil servant who in the late 1950s developed the PERT system to monitor the progress in the development of the Polaris fleet ballistic missile and the associated submarine, 141-143

PERT
    See: Program Evaluation Review Technique

Philippine Sea, Battle of
During the Battle of the Philippine Sea in June 1944 U.S. destroyers provided antiair protection for American aircraft carriers, 74-75

Planning
Early 1960s role of the OpNav Long-Range Objectives Group in predicting the future shape, composition, and missions of the U.S. fleet, 196-216

Polaris Program
Got started in late 1955 when Rear Admiral William Raborn was chosen to head the Special Projects Office, 126-129; initial funding was at the expense of the rest of the Navy, and then the program got its own money, 127-129, 136, 185-186; Special Projects was able to put together a small group of capable officers from throughout the Navy to work in the program, 130-131, 135-136; early consideration of the Army's Jupiter missile, 132-134; move toward the solid-fueled Polaris, 133-134; work with private defense contractors, 137-138, 149-150; training program for people who would use the hardware, 138-139; the development program was greatly speeded up while it was in progress, 139-140, 161-162; design and construction of the submarine to carry the missiles, 140-141; Gordon Pehrson established the PERT system to monitor the progress of the program, 141-143; establishment of a possible cut-off date to end the program if it wasn't working, 144-145; naval officers attached to the program had to have longer tours of duty than normal, 146-147; Raborn did a great job of building support in Congress and industry for the program, 148-149, 245-246; quality control issues, 149; decisions on number of submarines and number of missiles per submarine, 151-152; security of information about the program, 153; decision to have two crews per submarine, 153-154; submarine communication and navigation, 155-156; improvement of the missiles' range, 156-157; role of the joint Ballistic Missile Committee, 159-160

Program Evaluation Review Technique (PERT)
System developed in the late 1950s by civil servant Gordon Pehrson to monitor the progress in the development of the Polaris fleet ballistic missile and the associated submarine, 141-143

Promotion of Officers
In 1949 Colwell was one of the few in his class selected early for captain, 102-103; in the late 1950s the general rule was that a surface warfare officer had to have a major command to be eligible for selection to flag rank, 147-148

Propulsion Plants
When the new guided missile cruiser Galveston (CLG-3) went on sea trials in 1958 she exceeded her design speed of 33 knots, 168; emphasis in the early 1960s on nuclear power plants in planning for the fleet of the future, 202-204; comparison of nuclear-powered and conventionally powered warships, 258-262, 280

Proximity Fuze
    Testing of with antiaircraft shells during World War II at the Naval Proving Ground at Dahlgren, Virginia, 28

Public Relations
    In the mid and late 1950s Rear Admiral William Raborn and Colwell made public speeches in support of the Polaris fleet ballistic missile program, 136-137

Puerto Rico
    In the late 1950s the guided missile cruiser Galveston (CLG-3) operated out of Roosevelt Roads while conducting early tests with the Talos missile, 171-172

Raborn, Rear Admiral William F., Jr., USN (USNA, 1928)
    In late 1955 became head of the Special Projects Office that developed the Polaris fleet ballistic missile program, 126-128, 131-132; initial Polaris funding was at the expense of the rest of the Navy, and then the program got its own money, 127-129, 136, 185-186; succeeded in getting the program moved to a different track from the plan to use the Army's liquid-fueled Jupiter missile, 134-135; operated with an open-door policy, 135-136; made public speeches in support of the program, 136-137; monitoring of program progress through the PERT system and frequent meetings, 142; involvement with the Civil Service Commission to get personnel for Polaris, 146; agreed to let Colwell leave Special Projects in 1958 to take command of a cruiser, 147-148; did a great job of building support in Congress and industry for the program, 148-149, 160, 245-246; had free access to CNO, 159

Radar
    In the late 1930s the Naval Proving Ground at Dahlgren, Virginia, used radar to spot the splashes of gun projectiles, 26-27; in late 1941 was installed in the battleship Idaho (BB-42) at Norfolk, 39-40; before and during World War II a number of nations were doing simultaneous development of radar, 41; operation early in 1942 of the Idaho's new radar, 43; on board the destroyer Converse (DD-509) during World War II, 75-76; problems with the radar installed in the guided missile cruiser Galveston (CLG-3), which was commissioned in 1958, 164, 170-171

Radio
    Communication for Polaris ballistic missile submarines when they went into service in the early 1960s, 155-156

Reeves, Admiral Joseph M., USN (USNA, 1894)
    In 1933-34 commanded the Battle Force from the flagship California (BB-44), 10-11

Replenishment at Sea
    In the mid-1950s the fleet oiler Elokomin (AO-55) provided services in the Atlantic and Mediterranean, 119-124

Research and Development
In the late 1960s R&D was a major item of interest within the CNO's Advisory Board, 287-288

Reserve Fleet
Value of mothballed ships as part of the Navy's long-range planning during the early 1960s, 215-216

Rickover, Vice Admiral Hyman G., USN (Ret.) (USNA, 1922)
In the 1960s had a mutually supportive relationship with Colwell when they agreed on issues, 261-262

Rio de Janeiro, Brazil
President Harry S. Truman used the battleship Missouri (BB-63) as a base during his 1947 visit to Rio, 92-94

Roosevelt Roads, Puerto Rico
In the late 1950s the guided missile cruiser Galveston (CLG-3) operated out of Roosevelt Roads while conducting early tests with the Talos missile, 171-172

Rockets
Late in World War II the Naval Proving Ground successfully tested rockets, which were then used to arm converted landing ships, which became known as LSMRs, 86

Roeder, Vice Admiral Bernard F. Jr., USN (USNA, 1931)
In the mid-1960s commanded Amphibious Force Pacific Fleet and the First Fleet, both based in San Diego, 236

Salvage
Recovery of a U.S. Air Force nuclear bomb lost at sea off Spain in 1966, 284-285; search for the wreckage of the submarine Scorpion (SSN-589), which was lost in 1968, 285-286

San Diego, California
In the mid-1960s, as in other eras, the Navy and Marine Corps were quite prominent in the area and made a substantial contribution to the local economy, 219-220

Scorpion, USS (SSN-589)
Search for the wreckage of this submarine Scorpion, which was lost in 1968 in the Atlantic, 285-286

Scott, Captain David D., USN (USNA, 1932)
In late 1958 became commanding officer of the recently commissioned guided missile cruiser Galveston (CLG-3), 170

Seabees
During World War II built ammunition storage facilities at various Pacific bases, 51; constructed steel pontoons at Noumea, New Caledonia, 63

Security
At the outset of World War II the U.S. Navy made knowledge of radar a tightly held secret, 40; maintain secrecy in the late 1950s about the capabilities of the Polaris ballistic missile system, 153

Semmes, Vice Admiral Benedict, J., Jr., USN (USNA, 1934)
In 1965, as Chief of Naval Personnel, told Colwell that he would be coming to Washington to serve as OP-03, 221-222

Service Force Pacific Fleet
Provided fleet logistics needs during the Korean War, 104

Seventh Fleet, U.S.
Support of in the mid-1960s by the Amphibious Force Pacific Fleet, 233-235; held training exercises in the mid-1960s for various components of the fleet, 236

Shipbuilding
One of the chief concerns of OP-03 in the OpNav staff in the 1960s was the Navy's annual shipbuilding program, 244-256, 264-266

Shore Bombardment
In early 1944 ships of Destroyer Squadron 23 bombarded Kavieng, New Ireland, 68-70

Sixth Fleet, U.S.
In the mid-1950s the fleet oiler Elokomin (AO-55) provided services to ships in the Mediterranean, 119-124; concern from the 1940s onward about the behavior of Sixth Fleet personnel when they were ashore, 274-275

Smith, Captain Levering, USN (USNA, 1932)
As technical director for Special Projects Office in the late 1950s, did a superb job in the development of the Polaris fleet ballistic missile, 144-145, 150; had a long tenure with Special Projects, 157-158

South Pacific Force, U.S.
During World War II, Noumea, New Caledonia, served as headquarters for Admiral William F. Halsey, Commander South Pacific Force, 46-48, 58-59, 64-65; ammunition storage facilities at various bases, 51-56; role of coast watchers, 59-61; coordination with General Douglas MacArthur's Southwest Pacific Force, 64-65; contribution from New Zealand forces, 65-66

Soviet Navy
Role of Soviet merchant ships in the early 1960s in supporting the Soviet Navy, 210-211; increased deployments from the mid-1960s onward of Soviet warships were a concern to the U.S. Navy, 275-278

Spain
In 1953 a U.S. group led by Deputy Secretary of Defense Roger Kyes visited Madrid, 112; recovery of a U.S. Air Force nuclear bomb lost at sea off Spain in 1966, 284-285

Special Projects Office
Was established in late 1955 under Rear Admiral William Raborn to develop the fleet ballistic missile program, 126-129; initial funding was at the expense of the rest of the Navy, and then the program got its own money, 127-129, 136, 185-186; Special Projects was able to put together a small group of capable officers from throughout the Navy to work in the program, 130-131, 135-136; early consideration of the Army's Jupiter missile, 132-134; move toward the solid-fueled Polaris, 133-134; work with private defense contractors, 137-138, 149-150; training program for people who would use the hardware, 138-139; the Polaris development program was greatly speeded up while it was in progress, 139-140, 161-162; design and construction of the submarine to carry the missiles, 140-141; Gordon Pehrson established the PERT system to monitor the progress of the program, 141-143; establishment of a possible cut-off date to end the Polaris program if it wasn't working, 144-145; naval officers attached to the program had to have longer tours of duty than normal, 146-147; Raborn did a great job of building support in Congress and industry for the program, 148-149; quality control issues, 149; decisions on number of submarines and number of missiles per submarine, 151-152; security of information about the program, 153; the decision to have two crews per submarine, 153-154; relationship with the joint Ballistic Missile Committee, 159-160

Spruance (DD-963)-class Destroyers
Conceived in the 1960s as part of Secretary of Defense Robert McNamara's total package procurement program, 252-253, 263-265

Strategy
In the 1960s the United States employed a limited-war strategy in fighting in Vietnam, 238-240

Surface Effect Ships
In the mid-1960s the Navy explored the potential for using surface effect ships in amphibious warfare, 229-230, 248-249

Sydney, Australia
During World War II Colwell went to Sydney for rest and recreation while on leave, 48-50

Talos Missile
    In 1958 the light cruiser Galveston (CLG-3) was commissioned as the Navy's first warship armed with Talos surface-to-air missiles, 163-166, 169-172; potential updating of the missile system in the Talos-armed cruiser Long Beach (CGN-9), 260

Taylor, General Maxwell D., USA (Ret.) (USMA, 1922)
    In the 1960s, as Chairman of the Joint Chiefs and as ambassador to South Vietnam, was overly optimistic about the Vietnam War, 241

Thach, Captain James H., Jr., USN (1923)
    In 1948-49 commanded the battleship Missouri (BB-63), 92, 97-98

Tirpitz (German Battleship)
    In the early part of World War II she tied down U.S. battleships by her presence in Norway, 33, 36

Total Package Procurement
    Life-cycle budgeting program devised in the 1960s by Secretary of Defense Robert McNamara, 175-176, 189-190, 252-254

Training
    Summer cruises in the 1927-31 period by Naval Academy midshipmen, 5-6; fleet operations out of Pearl Harbor in the period shortly before World War II, 32; learning early in 1942 about the operation of the new radar on board the battleship Idaho (BB-42), 42-43; training for antiaircraft gunners at Noumea, New Caledonia, in World War II, 57; the battleship Missouri (BB-63) was used in 1948 for a Naval Academy summer training cruise to the Mediterranean, 98-99; training program in the late 1950s for people who would use the hardware in the Polaris fleet ballistic missile system, 138-139; in the late 1950s for the crew of the new guided missile cruiser Galveston (CLG-3), 167; exercises in the early 1960s involving Amphibious Group Four, 192-193; training of amphibious forces in the Eastern Pacific in the mid-1960s to prepare them for Vietnam deployments, 221-222, 228-229; rigorous training in the mid-1960s for underwater demolition teams, 231-233; Seventh Fleet training exercises in the mid-1960s, 236

Truk
    In early 1944 ships of Destroyer Squadron 23 operated in the vicinity and sank a Japanese ship after U.S. naval forces staged an air attack, 68-69

Truman, President Harry S.
    Used the battleship Missouri (BB-63) as flagship during a 1947 visit to Rio de Janeiro, Brazil, and subsequent trip back to the United States, 92-97

Underwater Demolition Teams
    Role of UDTs were varied in the mid-1960s during the Vietnam War, 231-233

Vieques Island
Long-standing controversy over the use of this island for gunnery training by the U.S. Navy, 172-173

Vietnam War
The heavy cruiser Newport News (CA-148) had a premature detonation of a projectile while firing in 1972 off Vietnam, 84, 86-87; in 1964 the Amphibious Force Pacific Fleet began establishing bases in South Vietnam to facilitate fighting the war in that nation, 220; training of amphibious forces in the Eastern Pacific to prepare them for Vietnam deployments, 221-222, 228-229; in the mid-1960s, for political reasons, the Western Pacific liberty ports available for visits by U.S. warships were limited, 222-223; shipboard medical care provided for those wounded in Vietnam, 223-225; development of riverine warfare craft and doctrine for Vietnam, 226, 249; threats to U.S. forces by the Viet Cong, 226-227; in the mid-1960s the Navy explored the potential for using surface effect ships in amphibious warfare, 229-230, 248-249; role of underwater demolition teams in Vietnam, 231-233; Navy men developed morale problems because of limited opportunities for rest and recreation, 234-235; in 1965 the commitment to the Vietnam War was not being questioned, but people soon believed that the U.S. forces were not permitted to carry the fight to the enemy, 237-240; Red Chinese involvement, 240; impact on Navy shipbuilding plans, 247-248; role of sampans, 249

Weather
In late 1941 the U.S. warships operating out of Iceland had to endure heavy winds, 38

Wilson, Charles E.
In 1953 became Secretary of Defense and brought with him as deputy Roger Kyes, who had been with him at General Motors, 106-107, 113; involvement in the Polaris fleet ballistic missile program, 132

www.ingramcontent.com/pod-product-compliance
Lightning Source LLC
Chambersburg PA
CBHW080617170426
43209CB00007B/1453